SPORT IN KOREA

RESEARCH IN THE SOCIOLOGY OF SPORT

Series Editor: Kevin Young

Recent Volumes:

Volume 1:	Theory, Sport and Society – Edited by Joseph Maguire and Kevin Young, 2001
Volume 2:	Sporting Bodies, Damaged Selves: Sociological Studies of Sports-Related Injury – Edited by Kevin Young, 2004
Volume 3:	The Global Olympics: Historical and Sociological Studies of the Modern Games – Edited by Kevin Young and Kevin B. Wamsley, 2005
Volume 4:	Tribal Play: Subcultural Journeys Through Sport – Edited by Michael Atkinson and Kevin Young, 2008
Volume 5:	Social and Cultural Diversity in a Sporting World – Edited by Chris Hallinan and Steven J. Jackson, 2008
Volume 6:	Qualitative Research on Sport and Physical Culture – Edited by Kevin Young and Michael Atkinson, 2012
Volume 7:	Native Games: Indigenous Peoples and Sports in the Post-Colonial World – Edited by Chris Hallinan and Barry Judd, 2013
Volume 8:	Sport, Social Development and Peace – Edited by Kevin Young and Chiaki Okada, 2014
Volume 9:	Sociology of Sport: A Global Subdiscipline in Review – Edited by Kevin Young, 2016
Volume 10:	Reflections on Sociology of Sport: Ten Questions, Ten Scholars, Ten Perspectives – Edited by Kevin Young, 2017
Volume 11:	Sport, Mental Illness, and Sociology – Edited by Michael Atkinson, 2018
Volume 12:	The Suffering Body in Sport: Shifting Thresholds of Pain, Risk and Injury – Edited by Kevin Young, 2019
Volume 13:	Sport and the Environment: Politics and Preferred Futures – Edited by Brian Wilson and Brad Millington, 2020
Volume 14:	Sport, Alcohol and Social Inquiry: A Global Cocktail – Edited by Sarah Gee, 2020
Volume 15:	Sport, Social Media and Digital Technology: Sociological Approaches – Edited by Jimmy Sanderson, 2022

Volume 16: Doping in Sport and Fitness – Edited by April Henning and Jesper Andreasson, 2022

Volume 17: Athletic Activism: Global Perspectives on Social Transformation – Edited by Jeffrey Montez de Oca and Stanley Thangaraj, 2023

Volume 18: Gambling and Sports in a Global Age – Edited by Darragh McGee and Christopher Bunn, 2023

Volume 19: Emergent Sociological Issues in Family and Sport – Edited by Steven M. Ortiz, 2023

Volume 20: The Postcolonial Sporting Body: Contemporary Indian Investigations – Edited by Veena Mani and Mathangi Krishnamurthy, 2024

Volume 21: The Mediating Power of Sport: Global Challenges and Sport Culture in China – Edited by Enqing Tian and Nicholas Wise, 2024

Volume 22: Towards a Pacific Island Sociology of Sport: Seeking New Horizons – Edited by Yoko Kanemasu, 2024

Volume 23: Cultures of Sport Hazing and Anti-Hazing Initiatives for the 21st Century: Stepping Across the Millennium – Edited by Jay Johnson and Jessica W. Chin, 2024

RESEARCH IN THE SOCIOLOGY OF SPORT   VOLUME 24

SPORT IN KOREA: CULTURE, POLITICS AND POLICY

EDITED BY

EUNHA KOH

Inha University, Republic of Korea

United Kingdom – North America – Japan
India – Malaysia – China

Emerald Publishing Limited
Emerald Publishing, Floor 5, Northspring, 21-23 Wellington Street, Leeds LS1 4DL

First edition 2025

Editorial matter and selection © 2025 Eunha Koh.
Individual chapters © 2025 The authors.
Published under exclusive licence by Emerald Publishing Limited.

Reprints and permissions service
Contact: www.copyright.com

No part of this book may be reproduced, stored in a retrieval system, transmitted in any form or by any means electronic, mechanical, photocopying, recording or otherwise without either the prior written permission of the publisher or a licence permitting restricted copying issued in the UK by The Copyright Licensing Agency and in the USA by The Copyright Clearance Center. Any opinions expressed in the chapters are those of the authors. Whilst Emerald makes every effort to ensure the quality and accuracy of its content, Emerald makes no representation implied or otherwise, as to the chapters' suitability and application and disclaims any warranties, express or implied, to their use.

British Library Cataloguing in Publication Data
A catalogue record for this book is available from the British Library

ISBN: 978-1-83753-897-3 (Print)
ISBN: 978-1-83753-896-6 (Online)
ISBN: 978-1-83753-898-0 (Epub)

ISSN: 1476-2854 (Series)

INVESTOR IN PEOPLE

CONTENTS

About the Editor   *ix*

About the Contributors   *xi*

Introduction – Sport in Korea: Culture, Politics, and Policy   *1*
Eunha Koh

PART ONE

Chapter 1   A Glass Escalator Leading up to the Stage: The Hidden Gender Advantage for Men in the Dance World   *9*
Sangwoo Nam

Chapter 2   Consuming Sports as a Popular Content of Korean Reality Television Shows: Reading the Sport Media Issue Under the Umbrella of Multiple Approaches   *25*
Yoonso Choi

Chapter 3   Changing Meaning of Nationalism on Team Korea: Focused on the Korean National Soccer Team   *43*
Wanyoung Lee

PART TWO

Chapter 4   Critical Reflections on "Sport Ethics" Discourse in Korean Society   *63*
Hee Jin Seo and Kiwoon Kim

Chapter 5   The Role of Korean Sports Governance in Ending Sports Violence   *79*
Hanbeom Kim and Seami Lim

Chapter 6 Athlete Activism in South Korea: Limitations and Challenges *97*
Seongsik Cho

Chapter 7 Sports and the 4th Industrial Revolution *119*
Jungrae Lee and Sora Kim

PART THREE

Chapter 8 Development of Sport Policy in South Korea: Historical and Institutional Analysis *135*
Taehee Kang and Sun-Yong Kwon

Chapter 9 Development, Sport Diplomacy, and Soft Power in South Korea *153*
Dongkyu Na

ABOUT THE EDITOR

Eunha Koh is a Visiting Professor of Sport Science at Inha University and the founder and CEO of Sport Insight, a sport policy consulting company based in Seoul, Korea. Her research has focused on nationalism and globalisation in Korean sport, women in sports and their representation by the media and national sport policy and politics. Throughout her career at the Korea Institute of Sport Science and at Sport Insight, she has worked with policymakers and sport organisations, publishing over 60 technical reports on sport governance, sport development and sport diplomacy. Her recent research focuses on Korean national sport policy concerning mega sport events and legacy building. She is currently a Vice President of the Korean Society for the Sociology of Sport and the Korean Association of Physical Education and Sport for Girls and Women. She is also a past Vice President of the International Sociology of Sport Association, the international body in her field.

ABOUT THE CONTRIBUTORS

Seongsik Cho is a Professor of Sport Management at Hanyang University, Seoul. He obtained his BA and MA in Sociology from Yonsei University, Seoul, and PhD in Sports Studies at the University of Iowa, IA, under the supervision of Dr Susan Birrell. His research has focused on cultural studies of sport media and critical approaches to gender, race, nationalism and globalisation in sports. His areas of teaching include sociology of sport, sport and the media, globalisation of sport and sport management. For his teaching efforts, he has received the Best Teaching Award twice from Hanyang University. Dr Cho has also contributed to the development of the critical epistemology branch of Korean sport sociology by introducing feminist cultural studies, publishing research papers based upon critical paradigm, translating Richard Giulianotti's book, *Sport a Critical Sociology*, into Korean and organising several international conferences in Korea, presented by internationally recognised sport sociologists.

Yoonso Choi (PhD, University of Illinois at Urbana-Champaign) is an Assistant Professor in the Department of Sport Sciences at the University of Seoul, Seoul, South Korea. She has studied female body representation through the media (especially on television). Also, she has been interested in interrogating sport policies related to gender equality and improving the rights of marginalised populations such as people with disabilities, the elderly and the children and women from multicultural families in Korean society. Recently, she has focused on looking at the process of cyborgfication embodied through people in wheelchairs' participating in sports.

Taehee Kang is a PhD in the Department of Physical Education at Seoul National University, Seoul, Korea. His research interests encompass sports policy and the dynamics of a sports and leisure society. He received a Master's degree focusing on the efficient utilisation of sports facilities within the public sector and was actively involved in related research endeavours at the Korea Institute of Sports Science. With his interest on sports policy and the publicness, he consistently engages in numerous research initiatives. Recently, he published a thesis on emerging trends in leisure studies and actively contributed to national research projects aimed at evaluating the efficacy of sports policies in the context of digital technology advancements.

Hanbeom Kim is an Assistant Professor in the Department of Sport Science at Hankyong National University, Ansung, Korea. His research interests are mainly focused on social development through sport, and he focuses on conducting practical research that can help sport play a greater role in our society. He is trying to diagnose our society through the academic tool of sociology of sport and suggest various directions for our society based on this. As part of this, he emphasises the importance of good governance as an effective support system for sport policy, and this manuscript was written in this context. In addition, he is also involved in research projects related to Korean sports clubs, anti-doping, sports culture and student-athlete issues in South Korea, which have broadened his academic perspective on various issues in Korean sport. Recently, he has become interested in the ICT transformation of sport and strives to be a Researcher who can proactively respond to the ever-changing academic environment.

Kiwoon Kim is a Research Professor in the Institute of Sports Convergence, at Konkuk University, Chungju, Korea. His research interests include social theory, local sports, sports spaces and marginalised classes in sports. Recently, he has been interested in discrimination and alienation of people with disability in the sports space focused on their physicality. And in this regard, he is carrying out basic study for the development of a Korean sport space guidelines for disability. Also, he is participating in various national research projects related to sports policy. The most representative cases underway include research on the dual career development of student athletes and spreading culture for gender equality in sports.

Sora Kim is a Physical Education Instructor at the Korea Army Academy at Yeong-Cheon, Korea. She received a PhD from the Kyungpook National University in June 2023, specialising in Sports Sociology. The dissertation title is the sports socialisation process and challenges of elementary school students through virtual reality sports classes. Her research interests also include social networking, sports in the era of high technology and social culture.

Sun-Yong Kwon is a Professor in the Department of Physical Education, Seoul National University, Seoul. His research interests include social, cultural and historical aspects of sports and leisure, sports policy and development and sports in international relations. He has published articles in various scholarly journals including *International Review for the Sociology of Sport, Sport in Society, The International Journal of the History of Sport* and *International Journal of the Human Movement Science*. He has also co-authored book publications in Korean including *Sport and Social Theories, International Sport Governance and Globalization*. He is a former President of the Korean Society for the Sociology of Sport and served various professional roles in the organisation. He also served as an advisory board member and is currently the Vice President of the International Association of the Sociology of Sport.

Jungrae Lee is currently a Professor of the Department of Kinesiology at Kyungpook National University. She is currently the Senior Vice President of the Korean Society for the Sociology of Sports and is passionate about academic activities. She is interested in sports culture and has written many papers related to phenomenology. They have a perspective on problems from a critical point of view rather than a structuralist point of view and have conducted various studies on this. She is interested in the changes in sports that have emerged from the recent Fourth Industrial Revolution and is trying to approach them from various perspectives.

Wanyoung Lee (PhD, Hanyang University) is a Research Fellow in the Department of Sports Policy at the Korea Institute of Sport Science (KISS). His research interests include sports policy, nationalism, sports society and culture. Recently, he has been studying sports spaces with interest, with a particular interest in the elements of the placelessness of stadiums. The latest research related to this includes a study on 'Professional Soccer Fields Viewed Through Ralph's Theory of Placelessness', and a study on discrimination against the disabled that occurs in public sports centres is underway using Martina Löw's social space theory. In addition, he is actively participating in national research projects related to sports policy as well, and the most representative cases underway include research on spreading culture for gender equality in sports and preparing codes of practice to prevent sexual harassment and violence in sports.

Seami Lim is an Assistant Professor in the division of Sport Science at Incheon National University in South Korea. A former tennis player, her research interests include elite sport systems, coaching policy and Korean sports clubs. She mainly focuses on social issues and policies in elite sport and is also interested in the culture of elite sport. She has worked on several projects related to sport policy, proposing policy solutions for the development of elite athletes. She is also conducting research to diagnose various phenomena in elite sports and establish a basis for a sports system that can provide a better environment for athletes. In the future, she will work on research projects involving coaches, referees and governing bodies related to elite sports and propose various policy alternatives related to the elite sports environment.

Dongkyu Na is a Senior Research Fellow in the Asian-Pacific Research Center of the Institute of Global Affairs at Kyung Hee University in Seoul, South Korea. He received his PhD in Sociocultural Studies of Human Kinetics from the University of Ottawa, Canada, in June 2021 with specialisation in the politics of sport for development, sport diplomacy and international studies. He worked as a Research Fellow at Inha University in Incheon, South Korea, and taught as an Exchange Lecturer at the Middle East Technical University in Ankara, Türkiye.

Sangwoo Nam is an Assistant Professor in the Department of Sport Science at Chungnam National University. His study centres on the sociology of sport and policy, social philosophy and cultural studies. He has authored over 50 articles on gender, social theory, policy, leadership and subcultural studies in the *Korean Journal of Sport Sociology*. He authored a Korean textbook titled *Social Issues and Debates in Sport*, with the fourth edition being published in 2021. He is currently engaged in the development of textbooks focused on sport policy, sport ethics and sport coaching.

Hee Jin Seo is a Professor at the Department of Sport and Health Science, Konkuk University, Chungju, South Korea. His research interests include youth sports, sports policy, sports governance and sports media. He has recently been very interested in research on unethical practices such as corruption and sexual violence in the Korean sports world and in improving the efficiency of local sports administrative organisations. Also, he has published articles in various scholarly journals, and he recently published a study on the symbolism of the Olympics in South Korea in *the International Journal of the History of Sport*. He is former President of the Korean Society for the Sociology of Sport and he serves as a professional member of various sports organisations including the Ministry of Culture, Sports and Tourism in Korea.

INTRODUCTION – SPORT IN KOREA: CULTURE, POLITICS, AND POLICY

Eunha Koh

Inha University, Republic of Korea

KOREAN SPORTS GOING GLOBAL

With the increasing popularity of K-pop and K-drama, South Korean culture has recently stepped into the spotlight with growing interest from the public and academia. Although the emergence of South Korean sports celebrities on the global stage began in the mid-to-late 1990s, the recent success of Korean sport stars is seamlessly coupled with the global surge in interest in K-pop, K-drama, and K-food, creating a multifaceted wave of Korean cultural influence worldwide. Sport stars like Son Heung-min in the English Premier League (EPL) and Hyun-Jin Ryu in Major League Baseball (MLB) excel in their sports and play pivotal roles in increasing the visibility and appeal of Korean culture. Their athletic achievements parallel the explosive popularity of K-pop groups like BTS and BLACKPINK, K-dramas such as Squid Game, and the global fascination with Korean cuisine. This synergy amplifies Korea's cultural impact, fostering a deeper appreciation and interest in Korean culture, from its entertainment to its sports stars.

During the past two decades, there has been a growing number of scholarly publications on East Asian sports, including book publications (Bien-Aimé & Wang, 2022; Hong & Zhouxiang, 2020; Horne & Manzenreiter, 2002), especially on Japanese sports (Kelly, 2018; Nakayama, 2006). There have been sociological studies analyzing Korean sports (Bridges, 2012; Hong, 2011; Kwak et al., 2018; Lee, 2015; Merkel, 2008), but they fall short of matching the global interest in Korean culture, including sports. Moreover, it is rare to find a comprehensive book dedicated to sociologically examining Korean sports in depth. This is also primarily true of the domestic Korean situation. Sociology of sport in Korea has more than 30 years of history with a nationwide academic society and undergraduate/graduate programs (Koh, 2016). However, despite an extensive volume of research done in the field domestically, there has been little effort to collect and publish them in a book to introduce them to the global audience.

With the growing interest in Korean sports and its social significance from academia and the public, this volume intends to bring together research on the social, cultural, and political aspects of Korean sports today. To this end, this volume is designed as a collection of three distinctive themes: (1) sport culture and consumption in 21st century Korea, (2) key issues and controversies in Korean sport, and (3) Korean sport policy and its impact on shaping the Korean sport structure and process. A total of 9 chapters were written by authors who have been actively working in the field of sociology of sport in South Korea. The topics of each chapter are subjects that the authors have focused on and are currently the most vigorously debated in the sociology of sport in South Korea.

CULTURE, CONTROVERSIES, AND POLICY

Part One of this volume deals with Korean sport culture, where sport has become a consumer culture and provides spectacles from stadia to screens and from competition to entertainment content. As spectatorship has shifted to diverse media platforms such as YouTube, portal sites, cable TV, and OTT, there is a growing tendency of selective consumption of sports content of specific teams or leagues while, at the same time, nationalism and regionalism are still strong when watching football or baseball games. Another clear Korean trend is that sports have become an enormously popular form of entertainment across all media. During the last decade, many reality TV shows have broken the boundary between sport and non-sport media content where sport celebrities challenge to compete in other sports, nonathletes compete in team sports with famous sport figures as their coaches or sport stars become full-time entertainers. Yoonso Choi and Wanyoung Lee deal with interrelated themes of nationalism, consumerism, neoliberalism, and in the context of contemporary Korean sport culture. Choi critically examines the ways in which sports as the content of popular reality TV shows in South Korea is consumed in the Korean media market, while Lee explores the changing meanings of the "nation" and "nationalism" perceived by football fans using the notion of "civic nationalism." Finally, Nam uses the term "glass escalator" to examine the organizational advantages afforded to male performers in the female-dominated dance industry.

Part Two deals with various Korean sports issues that have attracted public attention and criticism. First, Heejin Seo and Kiwoon Kim examine ethical issues in Korean sports ranging from doping to match-fixing and from violence to organizational corruption. By analyzing the sociocultural context, the authors discuss the use of sports as a tool to reestablish approved sports values and regain public trust. Hanbeom Kim and Saemi Lim raise the issue of the value and roles of collegiate sports by examining current dimensions such as conflicting roles of student-athletes, the decline of college teams, and the role of the Korea University Sports Federation (KUSF). In Chapter 6, Seongsik Cho's critical analysis of the limitations and challenges of athlete activism continues the analysis. Cho suggests several ideas on individual, institutional, and governmental levels to promote athlete activism in Korea. Finally, Jungrae Lee draws attention to what may be called the Fourth Industrial Revolution and changes in sports in Korea.

Part Three emphasizes that the government's sport policy has largely shaped Korean sports since the 1980s. Sport policy in Korea has four central pillars: promotion of people's sport participation; elite sport performance enhancement; development of sport industry; and international sport relations and sport diplomacy, with emphasis on specific sub-themes according to political regimes (Ministry of Culture, Sport and Tourism, 2020, 2022). Part Three starts with Taehee Kang and Sunyong Kwon's chapter on the history and development of Korean sport policy centering on the concept of policy paradigm with an in-depth analysis of paradigm shifts in sport policy in congruence with the nation's broader political and economic contexts: industrialization, democratization, and globalization. Drawing on the conceptual frameworks of sport diplomacy and public diplomacy, Na analyses the tripartite blending of sport, diplomacy, and development at both the national and international levels and the historical transformation of Korean sport diplomacy during the course of Korea's politically guided development practice.

As a collective, the chapters in this volume offer a comprehensive understanding of Korean sport culture and structure and open up new avenues for sociological research in the field of sports. This, in essence, paves the way for future research on Korean sports, a prospect that we hope will inspire and motivate scholars from diverse backgrounds to contribute to this evolving field.

THE FUTURE

The planning of this book started in 2022, when I was invited to edit a volume on Korean sport for the Research in Sociology of Sport Series. It was a challenging but rewarding process to edit the first book on the sociology of sport published in English by Korean sport sociologists. As I conclude the introduction, I would like to share the following points with the readers.

First, I would like to mention the importance of the role and status of sport sociologists in Korea. Since the establishment of the Korean Society for the Sociology of Sport (KSSS) in 1990, the sociology of sport has seen significant quantitative and qualitative growth over the past 34 years. Within South Korea, it has become an integral subject in physical education departments and is considered a core academic discipline. Internationally, KSSS has actively engaged in scholarly exchanges with other countries and has been an active national member of the International Sociology of Sport Association. However, despite this progress, research conducted by sports sociologists based in Korea has not been widely recognized abroad. I hope this book addresses this gap by introducing current research conducted in Korea. Focusing on the Korean context, it aims to broaden the scope of the sociology of sport, which has historically been North American and European-centric, and stimulate more discussion from various parts of the world.

Secondly, I would like to emphasize the importance of engaging in sport policy, not only because the landscape of Korean sports has been shaped by state-led policy but also because sport sociologists have participated in the process of designing, implementing, and evaluating sport policy as researchers, administrators, or evaluators. In doing so, the subdiscipline of the sociology of sport in Korea has established itself as a core subject both in university curricula and the national teacher/sport instructor license system, which is in direct contrast with the recent relative decline of sociology of sport mainly in North America (Andrews, 2015) or criticism of it being "decorative sociology" (Rojek & Turner, 2000). The recent annual congresses and special seminar themes highlight significant areas within sports sociology and Korean society in general. Key topics include the social expansion of knowledge (KSSS, 2020), pressing issues in Korean sports, such as athletes' rights and gender inequality in the sports labor market (KSSS, 2021, 2024), and the societal role of sports, such as the background and purpose of the establishment of National Sports Committee and the role of sports in the era of polarization (KSSS, 2022, 2023). I hope these efforts to address practical issues continue and such examples also become an excellent influence globally.

Lastly, I want to draw attention to the upcoming 2025 World Congress of Sociology of Sport, which is scheduled to be held in July in Seoul, Korea. This event is particularly significant as it marks the second occasion since the 2001 International Sociology of Sport Association Congress was renamed as the 1st World Congress of Sociology of Sport and was held in Seoul, Korea. I am excited about its potential and look forward to ongoing contributions from the authors of this book and Korean sports sociologists, fostering the continuous advancement of sports sociology in Korea. This event will not only showcase the progress of Korean sports sociology but also provide a platform for global recognition and influence.

REFERENCES

Andrews, D. (2015). Assessing the sociology of sport: On the hopes and fears for the sociology of sport in the US. *International Review for the Sociology of Sport, 50*(4–5), 368–374.

Bien-Aimé, S., & Wang, C. (2022). *Perceptions of East Asian and Asian North American athletics.* Springer.

Bridges, B. (2012). *The two Koreas and politics of the global sport.* Brill.

Hong, E. (2011). Elite sport and nation-building in South Korea: South Korea as dark horse in global elite sport. *International Journal of the History of Sport, 28*(7), 977–989.

Hong, F., & Zhouxiang, L. (2020). *The Routledge handbook of sport in Asia.* Routledge.

Horne and Manzenreiter. (2002). *Japan, Korea and the 2002 World Cup.* Routledge.

Kelly, W. (2018). *The sportsworld of Hanshin Tigers: Professional baseball in Modern Japan.* University of California Press.

Koh, E. (2016). Sociology of sport: Korea. In K. Young (Ed.), *Sociology of sport: A global subdiscipline in review. Research in sociology of sport* (Vol. 9, pp. 75–91). Emerald Publishing Limited.

Korean Society for the Sociology of Sport. (2020). Sociology of sport meets the society: Social expansion of knowledge addressing sports. In *2020 KSSS Annual Congress.* November 27, 2020, Online seminar via zoom.

Korean Society for the Sociology of Sport. (2021). Asking the future of sports. In *2021 KSSS Annual Congress.* November 26, 2021, Online seminar via zoom.

Korean Society for the Sociology of Sport. (2022). Current status and future of athletes safeguarding and their rights. In *2022 KSSS Special Seminar*. July 22, 2022, Online seminar via zoom.

Korean Society for the Sociology of Sport. (2023). Sports in the era of polarization. In *2023 KSSS Annual Congress*. November 24, 2023, Chungju, Korea.

Korean Society for the Sociology of Sport. (2024). National Sport Policy Committee: Backgrounds and sociological outlook. In *2024 KSSS Winter Workshop*. February 15, 2024, 2023, Chungju, Korea.

Kwak, D., Ko, Y., Kang, I., & Rosentraub, M. (2018). *Sport in Korea: History, development, management*. Routledge.

Lee, J. (2015). Examining Korean nationalisms, identities, and politics through sport. *Asia Pacific Journal of Sport and Social Science, 4*(3), 179–185.

Nakayama, M. (2006). *Japan, sport and society*. Routledge.

Merkel, U. (2008). The Politics of sport diplomacy and reunification in divided Korea: One nation, two countries and three flags. *42*(3), 227-249.

Ministry of Culture, Sport and Tourism. (2020). *White paper of sports*.

Ministry of Culture, Sport and Tourism. (2022). *White paper of sports*.

Rojek, C., & Turner, B. (2000). Decorative sociology: Toward a critique of the cultural turn. *The Sociological Review, 48*(4), 629–648.

PART ONE

CHAPTER 1

A GLASS ESCALATOR LEADING UP TO THE STAGE: THE HIDDEN GENDER ADVANTAGE FOR MEN IN THE DANCE WORLD

Sangwoo Nam

Chungnam National University, Republic of Korea

ABSTRACT

The purpose of this chapter is to use the metaphor of a "glass escalator" to examine the organizational advantages afforded to male performers in the female-dominated dance industry. It illustrates how the benefit mechanisms in the dance industry about male performers function with gender dynamics. The findings indicate that the glass escalator, an organizational advantage for male dancers, operates primarily through three fundamental mechanisms: (1) structured scarcity, (2) automated possibility, and (3) symbolized legitimacy. Male scarcity in dance results from a disparity between the masculinity demanded in dance and the socially constructed gendered representations of dance. This disparity made it difficult for male dancers to access the dance world, resulting in a structure that discriminated against dancers. Following this structure, the dance domain discusses the "potential" of male dancers to ensure their survival and continuity, perpetuating "positive discrimination" such as private instruction and lessened admissions-related competition. In the meantime, members of the dance world rationalize positive discrimination by equating men with the messiah leading the development of the dance industry.

Keywords: Dance world; glass escalator; structured scarcity; automated possibility; symbolized legitimacy

INTRODUCTION

The "glass ceiling" concept serves as a visual representation of the discriminatory barriers encountered by women belonging to minority groups within predominantly male-dominated organizational structures. The concept, initially introduced in the realm of organizational sociology, has subsequently prompted scholars to conduct systematic investigations into the obstacles faced by numerical minorities in organizations, specifically regarding their country of origin, ethnicity, race, and gender (Adams & Funk, 2012; Alessio & Andrzejewski, 2000; Cotter et al., 2001; Maume, 1999). The studies mentioned above centered their investigation on the quantitative construct of organizations wherein men constitute the majority and women constitute the minority, thereby addressing the core issue. As Jackson and O'Callaghan (2009) and Powell (1999) have posited, women have encountered various forms of inequality throughout their journey inside an organization, starting at their initial entry and continuing through the process of socialization and adaptation to the organizational culture, ultimately affecting their prospects for advancement to higher positions.

However, gender inequality can appear ironically in the reverse situation, where women outweigh men. This suggests that males who are minority in female-friendly or female-dominated sectors are more likely to be "advantaged" rather than "disadvantaged" in terms of job prospects, wage levels, and advancement potential (Alegria, 2019; Budig, 2002; Kullberg, 2012). The "glass escalator" describes a situation in which men have a relative advantage when women are outnumbered (Williams, 1992). The premise is that individuals in the majority group struggle to climb the organizational staircase for taking an advantage, while those in the minority group enjoy organization benefit by riding the escalator. If the "glass ceiling" is a barrier that exists for a minority of women in a majority of men, the "glass escalator" is a benefit that exists for a minority of men in a majority of women. It is a mechanism of gender inequality found in all areas of society (Alegria, 2019; Budig, 2002; Dill et al., 2016; Lloyd, 2019; Price-Glynn & Rakovski, 2012; Wingfield, 2009).

First, consider the world of music. Although music was one of the liberal arts for women before the 19th century, women were rarely given the opportunity to perform on stage. These fewer opportunities were because playing loud instruments, grimacing while playing, and holding a hefty instrument between their legs on stage were considered unfeminine (Lloyd, 2019). For these reasons, men were more likely to join orchestras despite women now dominating the music profession. Only 1.2 out of every 10 members of the Vienna Philharmonic Orchestra are women, while men hold 85% of the highest-paid principal and associate principal roles (Kang & Noh, 2012). Men have a "hidden advantage" in the music industry for whatever reason.

A similar pattern can be noticed in the nursing profession. As is commonly known, women outnumber males in the nursing profession. This trend is because qualities such as compassion and kindness are highly required in that domain. According to the Korea Nursing Association, there would be just 12,676 men in South Korea in 2021, accounting for 3.37% of the total 394,662 nurses. Of course, it is a worldwide trend that male nurses are only 7.5% of all nurses (Ratcliffe, 1996). It is because male nurses are more likely than females to have an equal rapport with physicians, trust formation, spontaneity, positivity, and proactivity (Chen et al., 2013), to be able to perform tasks that women find difficult (Blau & Tatum, 2000; Floge & Merrill, 1986), to be more comfortable with female physicians, and to have an advantage in areas where masculine roles are considered necessary (e.g., department of anesthesiology and psychiatry) (Park & Choi, 2014).

Glass escalators are also working at elementary schools. Although elementary school is often a female-dominated environment, men are more likely to hold administration roles. According to the Ministry of Education's 2019 Education Statistics, the proportion of female teachers in elementary schools was 71.1%, 70.1% in middle schools, and 53.5% in high schools, while the proportion of managers represented by principals was 51.5% in elementary schools, 72.1% in middle schools, and 88.9% in high schools. These data indicate that men are more likely than women to advance up the organizational ladder in elementary school. Men have an advantage over women in the teaching profession because the expected social roles in the teaching profession differ by gender, and the evaluation criteria of job performance, teaching behavior, and leadership reflect predominantly masculine traits (Ahn, 2019; Lee & Yoon, 2006; Oh, 2003). Men in primary schools have a "hidden advantage."

These phenomena contradict the basic assumption of the gender inequality mechanism imposed on minorities due to quantitative dominance. The glass escalator phenomenon suggests that we must examine gender disparity in terms of social structure and the qualitative characteristics embedded in gender. The important thing is that more research still needs to be conducted to explain the mechanics underlying this tendency. According to Williams (2013), who revived the glass escalator concept, sociology must investigate how the intricate entanglement of several interacting factors working in the workplace (or in any given world) might provide relative benefits to individuals who are minorities. This trying could be a good starting point to add another perspective to the research on gender inequality that has been discussed in the sociology of sport (Balish et al., 2016; Claringbould & Knoppers, 2012; Fink, 2016; Forsyth et al., 2019; Hindman & Walker, 2020; Lagaert & Roose, 2018; Nam, 2019a; Ryan & Dickson, 2018). As a result, using the case of the dance world in South Korea, this chapter illustrates how the glass escalator phenomenon emerges, is maintained, and is structurally rooted.

THEORETICAL BACKGROUND

Much of organizational theory in sociology argues that women are victims in organizations because they are a minority. Organizations are built with cultures, leadership attributes, and hierarchies molded by the male majority, making it difficult for women to enter, adapt, and even advance within the organization. All of these challenges for women in masculine culture – "invisible barriers to women's advancement based on attitudinal or organizational bias" (Morrison et al., 1987, p. 12) – have been referred to as the glass ceiling, a phenomenon in which women appear to be able to climb upward because they cannot see the barrier but hit a wall every time they try. This compelling concept reflects the paradox that something is impeding women's progress. However, it has to be better understood because it acts at the level of invisible culture or norms while not discouraging women from pursuing organizational challenges (because the opportunity for progression to the top of the organization is evident).

Since the glass ceiling, organizational sociology has created various glass metaphors. "The glass cliff," for example, is a metaphor for scapegoating women in times of organizational crisis by promoting them to leadership or responsibility positions, a typical criticism of the glass ceiling in businesses (Ryan & Haslam, 2007). "The glass cage" refers to organizations as iron cages packed with bureaucracy under the rationalization of society, which nowadays prioritizes openness, making all organizational members' private lives transparent (Gabriel, 2005). There is also the "glass escalator" metaphor (Williams, 1992), by which a few men working in a women-dominated organization can quickly ascend to a higher position than most women. Other metaphors discussed include the "glass traveler" (Kullberg, 2012), who is loyal to an organization and works only a limited number of hours, exploiting gaps in expertise rather than spending excessive time at work, and the "glass runway" (Stokes, 2015), a metaphor for the high value of men, particularly male homosexuals, in the female-dominated field of fashion design. The glass metaphor has been shown to be an effective study tool in organizational management for visualizing power processes and consequences related to social identities such as gender and race.

These metaphors aid in explaining gender dynamics in organizations with a high gender concentration. Male admission into female-dominated organizations like social work, fashion, primary schools, and nursing has recently received attention in organizational sociology (Perra & Ruspini, 2013; Torre, 2018; Wingfield & Myles, 2014). The glass escalator, the subject of this study, is also a notion that has been widely used in these investigations. As Lupton (2006) summarized, sociological study on this topic has been organized around three major themes: firstly, to investigate the individual dispositions (psychological and physiological) of men entering occupations that men avoid; secondly, to explicate the mechanisms by which men are allocated to extra jobs due to social (internal) demands on them, such as quotas for male teachers in elementary school; and thirdly, to investigate case studies of men entering female-dominated organizations to capitalize on their relative scarcity in the organization. In the sporting context, we may apply the sociological theory to female-dominated and male-minority sports such as figure skating, rhythmic gymnastics, and golf course caddies as an occupational realm.

Given the hypotheses mentioned above, it is vital to inquire about the intriguing structures intricately woven inside the realm of the dance world we are currently delving into. Moreover, what areas of inquiry can we direct our attention toward, and what specific inquiries can we formulate and present? As previously said, it is evident that the dance industry is predominantly associated with femininity. Within the global framework, it is evident that the male population constitutes a tiny proportion, approximately 25%. Consequently, it is reasonable to assert that men hold significance. Scholars in dance, such as Clegg et al. (2019), have provided a concise overview of the phenomenon. There are certain obstacles for men seeking to pursue careers in dance, particularly in disciplines such as ballet or modern dance. Paradoxically, however, men often encounter relative ease in gaining admission to university dance programs or securing prominent roles on dance stages. This phenomenon has led to a pervasive form of "positively discriminatory treatment" toward male dancers, necessitating significant modifications to dance curricula and pedagogical approaches to address the prevailing influence of masculinity within dance classes (Christofidou, 2018). With this in mind, the present study posits a theoretical proposition suggesting that most female dancers adhere to established norms that tacitly accept the unconventional mechanisms of privilege favoring male dancers within the dance community. This acceptance is rooted in the understanding that the manifestation of gender-based privilege within organizations is a socially constructed phenomenon rather than an inherent one. Furthermore, the perpetuation of these mechanisms relies on the voluntary or coerced consent and agreement of individuals within the group and continuous socialization processes.

Based on the sociological assumptions made earlier, the reality of the dance realm, and the author's assumptions, the five following theoretical propositions explain how the glass escalator mechanism works in the dance domain. Firstly, in a patriarchal society, it is common for organizations to prioritize masculinity to demonstrate their value and sustainability (Evans, 2004; Hultin, 2003; Kimmel, 2000), which is likely to be observed within the realm of dance; secondly, individuals within these realms will acknowledge the preeminence of masculinity inside the institution and attribute a specific significance or interpretation to the duties, assignments, and efforts linked to it; thirdly, the glass escalator phenomenon may occur within the dancing community as individuals engage in routines influenced by the underlying structures containing values and meanings; fourthly, during this process, most members will gradually adapt to and potentially endorse the unquestionable masculine privilege that exists inside the realm of dance; and finally, it will serve as an epistemological basis that confers symbolic significance upon men in a dance world and perpetuates the conventional structure.

DANCE GLASS ESCALATORS: HOW DO THEY WORK?

The gender-based advantage bestowed upon male dancers, a minority within the dance community, acts through three distinct methods. First, the paucity of male dancers can be attributed to the incongruity between the dance industry's expectations of masculinity and the socially manufactured gender norms associated with dancing. Consequently, this incongruity perpetuates a sense of entitlement to gender-based advantages. Second, the dance industry in South Korea assigns significant value to male dancers by emphasizing their "future potential," which is crucial for the business's sustainability and sustains a form of "positive discrimination" through diverse interactions. As a result, male dancers can benefit from gender advantages within this context. Third, within the dance community, there exists a representation of male dancers and their masculinity as indispensable for the long-term viability of the dance industry. This portrayal grants them symbolic capital and rationalizes preferential treatment, perpetuating gender-based advantages. In this analysis, we will examine these three mechanisms in further detail.

Structured Scarcity: The Scarcity Value of Male Dancers Shaped by Gender Mismatch

The initial catalyst for the glass escalator phenomenon within the realm of dance was a condition known as "structured scarcity." It was widely acknowledged that there existed a prevailing belief that dance was a field with a lower representation of men. This belief was considered a fundamental assumption for female-dominated professions such as nursing, librarianship, and social work. This assumption posits that dance is predominantly associated with femininity, making it a domain primarily occupied by women or individuals with feminine tendencies (Cha & Oh, 2018; Park & Kim, 2012; Risner, 2007). Consequently, it is socially expected that men would exhibit less interest in this activity. According to Migdalek (2015), dance has historically been perceived as a "feminine and somewhat questionable pursuit for males" (p. 76). The issue at hand is the enduring presence of a scarcity of male individuals, which has assumed the status of a structure within the realm of dance over an extended period. This is why we call the lack of men in the dance realm "structured scarcity.'

The phenomenon of structured scarcity is pervasive in a global context. According to Burt (2007), the issue of unease toward male dancers has been a prevalent concern in Europe since the 18th century, and it is evident that gender discrimination against male dancers continues to persist today (p. 7). This phenomenon can be attributed to the strong association between dancing and femininity within a societal context characterized by established gender roles and activities. In this particular scenario, males will inevitably encounter disputes during their decision-making process, regardless of their proficiency or aptitude in dancing. The "Billy Elliot syndrome" refers to when a male individual experiences internal conflict regarding engagement in dance due to familial or societal gender expectations, despite having a natural inclination toward ballet. This phenomenon highlights the significant influence of socially constructed gender norms on the initiation of young individuals into the field of dance (Holdsworth, 2013, p. 170). The dancing world is characterized by socially manufactured concepts of gender, which result in men being positioned as a structural minority.

In contrast to prevailing societal gender biases, the field of dance is in great need of male dancers, particularly those embodying traits associated with masculinity. This is the point at which the disagreement emerges. A paradox arises when society perceives dance as a predominantly feminine activity, leading to the misconception that masculinity is superfluous within this realm. However, internally, there is a profound necessity and appreciation for masculine attributes in dance. This phenomenon is because onstage practice and stage composition in dance need to grow more to accommodate individuals of both genders. One perspective posits that the embodiment of masculinity, as exemplified via the maximization of masculine physique or the expression of movement by the male body, has assumed a crucial role in theatrical performance.

Furthermore, within the realm of dance, the proficiency of a dance company is evaluated based on a range of stage compositions that effectively integrate the masculine attributes of male dancers. Consequently, stage directors and choreographers find themselves in severe need of male dancers. Including female dancers cannot effectively substitute for the portrayal of masculinity in theatrical performances. The prevailing norms of masculinity within the performing arts industry establish a limited number of male dancers as possessing a unique, indispensable quality. This limited availability grants them a privileged position or, more specifically, a distinctive attribute, enabling them to ascend the ranks of the dance profession (Wright, 2013).

In summary, the phenomenon known as the glass escalator within the dance industry can be attributed to the limited presence of men resulting from societal gender norms. This inadvertently creates a structural contradiction or a discrepancy between demand and supply within the dance world. Specifically, the inclusion of masculine elements on stage is deemed necessary by the dance community, thereby establishing masculinity as a prerequisite for stage composition. The expression of masculinity onstage, characterized by energy and strength, serves as a fundamental means of preserving, reinforcing, and even commemorating the position of male dancers within the predominantly female dance community (Evans, 2004; Lupton, 2006; Simpson, 2009). Dance companies that possess this invaluable resource of masculinity are spared from the feelings of inferiority and uncertainties regarding their organization's sustainability that are experienced by those lacking this resource.

Automated Possibility: The Existence of a Male Dancer Who Is Treated as a "Possibility to save the Organization"

The discourse of "automated possibility" that its members, primarily professors and choreographers, have established regarding male dancers is the second mechanism driving the glass escalator in the dance community. This discourse serves as a rhetorical foundation for rationalizing the unequal treatment of male dancers, as they are perceived to possess the capacity to contribute significantly to the creation of theatrical performance. Male dancers are esteemed for their limited presence in the dance industry with minimal initial exertion, and it is only after the community acknowledges the perceived advantages of their scarcity that they are afforded opportunities for advancement. Of course, the scarcity of male dancers is a result of an excess supply of female dancers. Based on these situations, two discourses shape the mechanism of automated possibility: the potential for advancement that male dancers, by gender, can bring to the organization and the anticipated benefits that the organization can get from their involvement.

Let us initiate our discussion by contemplating the phenomenon wherein male individuals within the dance world frequently encounter preferential treatment or presumptions of superior aptitude and potential, which parallels patterns observed in numerous studies conducted in diverse disciplines. As mentioned earlier, the research indicates a prevailing perception that men possess greater ambition and are more suitable for leadership positions than women (Bosak & Sczesny, 2008; Dashper, 2012; Kimmel, 2000). In dance, there is a prevailing assumption that men possess an inherent talent and greater capacity for growth. However, this argument can be considered a superficial rationale. The fundamental rationale for this is the perception that males possess an inherent value that cannot be replicated. The notion of structured scarcity pertains to the perception of male dancers as possessing inherent value by professors and choreographers, primarily attributable to their gender, which is an immutable characteristic. Consequently, there is a concentrated emphasis on enhancing their skill sets. This phenomenon persists even in cases where female dancers may indeed have higher abilities. The matter pertains to the appraisal of male dancers, which frequently revolves around their perceived "potential" rather than their foundational skills. This dynamic engenders a sense of detachment and introduces biased criteria for assessment within the realm of dance.

The evaluation being founded on "potential" suggests that the evaluation structure for male dancers is lenient. The dance world's tacit agreement that men are scarce and have high developmental potential has given rise to two perceptions: first, "they must be selected because they are scarce," and second, "they must be selected because they have development potential, even if their current talent level is low." While female dancers are evaluated rigorously on their foundational skills, physique, character, and academic performance, male dancers are evaluated solely on their "gender." This flexible, potentially progression-focused evaluation structure provides male performers with numerous benefits. Even with a late start, it is easy for them to enrol in college, which is a notable advantage. Even in competitions crucial for university admissions, males have a competitive advantage.

The second assumption of the automated potential mechanism is about the "expectation" of the benefits male dancers will bring to the organization. This expectation is grounded on the notion that the active participation of male dancers in external activities will enhance the visibility and reputation of the dance group, resulting in both real and intangible advantages for the organization. Underlying this belief is the possibility of good scores in competitions (concours) in which male dancers participate and the favorable "stage evaluations" and "creative support fund" that can be obtained as they just exist in the dance troupe. Especially concerning concours, male dancers prepare extremely diligently, to the point of risking their lives, because they anticipate some benefits like military service exemptions and subsequent advantages in dance troupe activities and salary increases. Even such diligent preparation does not automatically link to winning prizes in the contest, but the assumption based on a vague belief in the future ultimately symbolizes male dancers in the dance world as entities with potential.

Regarding stage composition, male dancers also contribute to the overall artistic value of the dance company. They contribute to the stage's differentiation from other dance companies, and a differentiated stage allows the dance company to secure additional creative assistance grants. In order to satisfy both the spectators and the performers, a proficient dance company must curate a stage production that showcases a harmonious blend of male and female dancers. In this blend, male dancers have a significant role in the diverse repertoires of the stage, making substantial contributions to enhancing the overall quality of performances. For example, having a male dancer, rather than a female dancer in male attire, stand at the center of the stage in a performance that needs to highlight masculinity can lead to increased audience engagement, positive evaluations from the judges, and ultimately, secure the dance troupe's ability to continue performances. As a result, stage directors and choreographers hold them in high esteem.

In conclusion, the inherently assumed possibility for male dancers is associated with the benefits of stage composition diversity, ease of competition entry, employment benefits, and active dance company promotion. This causes other dance community members to perceive discrimination against men positively. It is, in a word, "positive discrimination." In particular, this affirmative discrimination manifests in various forms in the dance world, the most representative of which is private lessons from professors. Male dancers who enrol in art institutions begin to demonstrate their distinctive presence in the center of the practice room, and private lessons from professors in the center of the stage foster the rapid development of male dancers. Male dancers can easily obtain a position on the stage, whereas female dancers cannot, even after sprinting and jumping hundreds of times. In this way, male dancers can reach the main stage more quickly and comfortably than their female counterparts, despite starting later, due to the consistent opportunities for skill development.

Symbolized Legitimacy: A Misconception Structure That Maintains the Benefits of Male Dancers

The third mechanism of the glass escalator is a structure of misperception known as "symbolized legitimacy." This cognitive system contributes to the perpetuation of extant practices in the dance world regarding male dancers. It is referred to as a misperception structure because female dancers acknowledge that male dancers' advantaged benefits are appropriate, awarding them symbolic capital. "Symbolic capital is misunderstood as capital, regardless of its form of realization; as it is recognized, it exercises symbolic violence and imposes itself as an authority demanding recognition" (Bourdieu, 1978, p. 18). In other words, the capital operates "when any form of capital acquires legitimacy based on the erroneous understanding and recognition of the members in the field where it circulates (Nam, 2019b, p. 39)."

The symbolized legitimacy that operates in the dance world is formed by a consensus that the masculinity of male dancers is necessary, both on stage and in society, and that it must exist despite being irrational for the sustainability of the dance world, despite receiving discriminatory treatment and criticism from female dancers. The phenomenon of false agreement arises due to the ongoing experience of female dancers with the structured scarcity and mechanized potential of male dancers, which they concurrently externalize through encounters in the everyday life of the dance community. There are three common misconceptions among female dancers regarding male dancers. Firstly, there is a belief in the indispensability of male dancers' duties; secondly, female dancers assume that male dancer is identified with the dance realm; and lastly, there is a perception that preferential treatment toward male dancers is an uncontrollable convention.

The first misconception operates through female dancers acknowledging "irreplaceability," expressing the erroneous thought that "I cannot do what men do." While this may at first glance seem like a shared recognition of the facts as they are, it needs to be corrected. At its core, the dance industry's positive discrimination against male dancers is driven by "few (men) versus many (women)," with one side being a less competitive blue ocean market and the other being a more competitive red ocean. The real issue lies in the societal gender representation that obstructs men's entry into the world of dance and the neglectful strategies of the dance world in making efforts to amend this. It is to overlook the essence of the matter to presume that we must accept that a male dancer can do what a female dancer cannot. However, leaving aside the structural issues, many female dancers feel justified in climbing the stairs of competition, while male dancers can effortlessly take the escalator to center stage.

The second misconception concerns the female dancer's "willingness to align with the organization." This misunderstanding leverages male dancers in a primarily symbolic position. Despite the reprehensible preferential treatment afforded to male dancers, the consensus to align them closely with the identity of the organization is underpinned by a pervasive sense of anxiety. Absent this inequitable treatment, the realm of dance might face challenges in securing approval and advancing further, potentially impeding the professional development of female dancers. For example, female dancers believe that the differential treatment of male dancers is justified because they believe they are well-suited to various forms of stage promotion and can advance the dance world by responding satisfactorily to socially constructed feminized fandoms. Nonetheless, this second "reasonable belief" is also based solely on the previously mentioned "automated possibility"; in actuality, the association of male dancers' roles with organizational development is an error of overgeneralization.

The final misconception female dancers hold involves the "uncontrollability" of men's and women's career trajectories following graduation from dance departments and the conformity of female dancers to this reality. It is a fallacy that the differential treatment of men in universities is justified by the different "dance markets" that men and women will enter after graduation. In our society, there exists a prevailing expectation that women will predominantly pursue careers as dance instructors for child and adult hobby classes. Conversely, men are commonly perceived as assuming leadership roles in professional hobby courses and university entry classes, often regarded as more intellectually advanced and sophisticated. In South Korea, there is a preference for male dancers in the recruiting process for specialized entry examinations and municipal dancing troupes. Additionally, male teachers are required to teach at art high schools, university entrance exams, and educational programs catering to experienced participants. This reality of distinct postgraduation pathways legitimizes the differential treatment of male dancers in universities for female dancers. However, this constitutes a fallacy that conflates cause with effect. It attributes the purported "professionalism" of male dancers to their preferential and specially favored treatment prior to graduation (the cause). Subsequently, it rationalizes this discrimination by appealing to distinct market demands for male and female dancers (the effect).

In conclusion, this final mechanism of the dance world's glass escalator toward male dancers operates as a kind of misperception structure, which, as described above, is held by female dancers and actively projected onto male dancers. This structure is maintained by the continuance of a field that is already sociostructurally biased toward male dancers (e.g., Meglin & Brooks, 2012) and by the absence of an in-depth discussion of its causes and operating mechanisms. Female dancers, professors, and choreographers are left with the misguided notion that male dancers must be actively managed to ensure that they do not run away, not only because they are a minority in the dance world but also because they are an absolute necessity for stage composition. Eventually, as this structure persists, male dancers acquire symbolic capital within the organization, regardless of whether they desire it or not, and the glass escalator effect acquires sustainability in the dance world.

CONCLUSION

> Once men enter the world of dance, they often encounter comparatively less competition and may easily rise to what are considered "power positions," such as stage managers and choreographers. However, this comes with a peculiar form of privilege, as they must navigate various prejudices due to their unconventional career choice, which contradicts traditional notions of masculinity. In essence, they pay a significant price for their status advantage by confronting these biases (Fisher, 2007, pp. 53–54).

The purpose of this chapter is to use the metaphor of a "glass escalator" to examine the organizational advantages afforded to male performers in the female-dominated dance industry. It illustrates how the benefit mechanisms in the dance industry about male performers function with gender dynamics. The findings indicate that the glass escalator, an organizational advantage for male dancers, operates primarily through three fundamental mechanisms: (1) structured scarcity, (2) automated possibility, and (3) symbolized legitimacy. Male scarcity in dance results from a disparity between the masculinity demanded in dance and the socially constructed gendered representations of dance. This disparity made it difficult for male dancers to access the dance world, resulting in a structure that discriminated against dancers. Following this structure, the dance domain discusses the "potential" of male dancers to ensure their survival and continuity, perpetuating "positive discrimination" such as private instruction and lessened admissions-related competition. In the meantime, members of the dance world rationalize positive discrimination by equating men with the messiah leading the development of the dance industry.

These three fundamental mechanisms are consistent with the organizational metaphor of the glass escalator: the structural mismatch between social gender representations in dance and the masculinity required in the dance world stems from the dearth of male dancers and entitles them to the advantages of the glass escalator. Now, they are prepared to ascend the escalator. Male dancers benefit positively and differentially from the assumed possibilities within the dance organization – the personal and organizational benefits that professors and choreographers expect male dancers to deliver in the future – while female dancers do not. They are now ascending the escalator to the central stage. Interestingly, the symbolic legitimacy constructed around female dancers keeps the dance world afloat despite this discrimination. In other words, female dancers voluntarily legitimize the prevalent positive discrimination against male dancers in the dance industry, acknowledging that they cannot play the role of a male dancer, that women can only advance if men advance, and that the two genders have vastly different paths after graduation. Misconceptions created in the dance world justify false recognition. Due to the symbolic capital generated by these misconceptions, male dancers continue to ascend the escalator with ease and reap the benefits of the dance industry.

This study's scholarly significance is twofold. First, this study contributes to the utility of organizational sociology's favored metaphor, the glass. Similar to the contributions of various "glass metaphors' to organizational sociology discussed previously, the metaphor of the glass escalator has helped visualize the dominance of certain genders within organizations. However, if we do not adequately explain the mechanisms of the escalator metaphor, as we did with the glass metaphor, "these metaphors will eventually fade away somewhat precariously" (Chia, 1996, p. 141). They are likely to become trendy rhetoric before disappearing from academia. This study's use of the glass escalator as a metaphor for the dominance of one gender in the dance world and the resulting intriguing discrimination goes beyond using the concept as a rhetorical device. It provides a concrete illustration of how gender dynamics in the dance world enable male dancers to ride the benefit escalator instead of climbing the competitive staircase. In other terms, it enhanced the usefulness of the concept.

Second, this study contributes to delineating what type of dance world is in terms of the "theorization of the sports world," which aligns with the sociological perspective on sports. Through an in-depth examination of the dance sphere inside Korean colleges, the author discerned an intriguing line of thinking prevalent among members of this community: female dancers possess a keen awareness of the privileges now bestowed upon their male counterparts within the dance realm. Interestingly, they precisely recognize what is wrong with the status quo, but they do not problematize it. Not only do they not criticize it, but they find its discussion unsettling. This study concludes that the dance world is maintained by ignoring the issue of positive discrimination against male dancers by examining these attitudes and behaviors. In other words, the dance world maintains an inherent "inequality habitus" supporting discrimination against masculinity.

In this sense, the glass escalator will persist in the dance world. As stated previously, the structural disparity between socially constructed gender representations and internally demanded conditions of masculinity in the dance world cannot be reconciled. It is highly probable that the insiders will not alter the "structure" (i.e., increase the number of entrants) but will proceed with the "managing the insiders' dimension (i.e., positive discrimination), employing strategies to uphold a microcosm of the patriarchal society by awarding symbolic capital to the male dancers who have already entered the world, and by compelling the majority of female dancers to tacitly consent to these strategies. Consequently, this structure will remain in place, and male dancers in the minority will continue to benefit from the glass escalator because the structure advantages them.

FIVE KEY READINGS

Williams, C. L. (1992). The glass escalator: Hidden advantages for men in the "female" professions. *Social Problems, 39*(3), 253–267.

This article examines the experiences of men working in traditionally female-dominated fields. It draws attention to the fact that men frequently experience career-advancing structural advantages in these fields, including quicker promotions and higher salaries. In order to advance gender diversity in the workplace, it is crucial to acknowledge and confront these benefits, according to the study's findings. This article illuminates a significant concern within the professional sphere and offers insightful perspectives on the experiences of males and females across various occupations.

Kim, D. (2023). Understanding gender inequality in dance sport: Exploring the glass ceiling phenomenon along the career path. *Korean Society for the Sociology of Sport, 36*(3), 45–59.

The study is based on interviews with 10 dance sports veterans who discussed their career paths, from athletes to organizational leaders. It reveals two main types of gender bias: society tends to place men in leadership roles while women are often relegated to follower positions, and ongoing inequality stems from the structure of the dance sports community. The results show that ingrained gender roles have a significant impact on job paths in dance sports, which keeps the professional environment unequal between men and women.

Kelly, C. (2015). Dancing up the glass escalator: Institutional advantages for men in ballet choreography. *Columbia Undergraduate Research Journal, 2*(1). https://doi.org/10.52214/curj.v2i1.4113

The present study investigates the gender imbalance prevalent in the upper ranks of ballet choreography. The author draws attention to the systemic inequities favoring male dancers over their female counterparts. The paper examines the application of Williams' theory to ballet choreography and demonstrates how its success is contingent on some factors, including the preponderance of female experts in the field. The author posits that ballet choreography exemplifies the glass escalator model, which describes the phenomenon of males advancing more rapidly in professions dominated by women.

Brandford, A., & Brandford-Stevenson, A. (2021). Going up!: Exploring the phenomenon of the glass escalator in nursing. *Nursing Administration Quarterly, 45*(4), 295–301.

This article examines the "glass escalator" phenomenon, which states that men advance to leadership positions in nursing and other female-dominated professions faster than women. Although women comprise most of the nursing profession, males frequently occupy lower level leadership positions. Male and female nurses are impacted by the glass escalator, which is examined critically in this article despite its intersection with racism and gender. In order to cultivate a more diverse and equitable leadership environment, healthcare organizations and nurse leaders must have a comprehensive understanding of this phenomenon.

Nam, S. (2019). Theoretical diversification of the concept of "capital": Explaining the capital territories for the development of sociology of sport. *Korean Society for the Sociology of Sport, 32*(4), 35–60.

The glass escalator is a socially widespread phenomenon that is ultimately based on "capital" in a given field. Various ideas of capital remain unexplored in sport sociology, spanning from economic and cultural capital to gender, performance, and subcultural capital. This study summarizes how the idea of capital has been differentiated in the social sciences up to this point.

REFERENCES

Adams, R. B., & Funk, P. (2012). Beyond the glass ceiling: Does gender matter? *Management Science, 58*(2), 219–235.

Ahn, A. (2019). A narrative study on administrator's career transition process of female elementary school teachers. *Korean Journal of Teacher Education, 35*(2), 195–215.

Alegria, S. (2019). Escalator or step stool? Gendered labor and token processes in tech work. *Gender & Society, 33*(5), 722–745.

Alessio, J. C., & Andrzejewski, J. (2000). Unveiling the hidden glass ceiling: An analysis of the cohort effect claim. *American Sociological Review, 65*(2), 311–315.

Balish, S. M., Deaner, R. O., Rainham, D., & Blanchard, C. (2016). Sex differences in sport remain when accounting for countries' gender inequality. *Cross-Cultural Research, 50*(5), 395–414.

Blau, G., & Tatum, D. (2000). Correlates of perceived gender discrimination for female versus male medical technologists. *Sex Roles, 43*(1–2), 105–118.

Bosak, J., & Sczesny, S. (2008). Am I the right candidate? Self-ascribed fit of women and men to a leadership position. *Sex Roles, 58*(9–10), 682–688.

Bourdieu, P. (1978). Capital symbolique et classes sociales. *L'arc, 72,* 13–19.

Budig, M. J. (2002). Male advantage and the gender composition of jobs: Who rides the glass escalator? *Social Problems, 49*(2), 258–277.

Burt, R. (2007). *The male dancer: Bodies, spectacle, sexualities.* Routledge.

Cha, E., & Oh, Y. (2018). Status and tasks of community dance viewed from gender perspective. *Journal of Korean Association of Physical Education and Sport for Girls and Women, 32*(2), 77–98.

Chen, S. H., Yu, H. Y., Hsu, H. Y., Lin, F. C., & Lou, J. H. (2013). Organizational support, organizational identification and organizational citizenship behaviour among male nurses. *Journal of Nursing Management, 21*(8), 1072–1082.

Chia, R. (1996). Metaphors and metaphorization in organizational analysis: Thinking beyond the thinkable. In D. Grant & C. Oswick (Eds.), *Metaphor and Organizations* (pp. 127–146). Sage.

Christofidou, A. (2018). Men of dance: Negotiating gender and sexuality in dance institutions. *Journal of Gender Studies, 27*(8), 943–956.

Claringbould, I., & Knoppers, A. (2012). Paradoxical practices of gender in sport-related organizations. *Journal of Sport Management, 26*(5), 404–416.

Clegg, H., Owton, H., & Allen-Collinson, J. (2019). Attracting and retaining boys in ballet: A qualitative study of female dance teachers. *Journal of Dance Education, 19*(4), 158–167.

Cotter, D. A., Hermsen, J. M., Ovadia, S., & Vanneman, R. (2001). The glass ceiling effect. *Social Forces, 80*(2), 655–681.

Dashper, K. (2012). Together, yet still not equal? Sex integration in equestrian sport. *Asia-Pacific Journal of Health, Sport and Physical Education, 3*(3), 213–225.

Dill, J. S., Price-Glynn, K., & Rakovski, C. (2016). Does the "glass escalator" compensate for the devaluation of care work occupations? The careers of men in low-and middle-skill health care jobs. *Gender & Society, 30*(2), 334–360.

Evans, J. (2004). Bodies matter: Men masculinity and the gendered division of labour in nursing. *Journal of Occupational Science, 11*(1), 14–22.

Fink, J. S. (2016). Hiding in plain sight: The embedded nature of sexism in sport. *Journal of Sport Management, 30*(1), 1–7.

Fisher, J. (2007). Make it maverick: Rethinking the "make it macho" strategy for men in ballet. *Dance Chronicle, 30*(1), 45–66.

Floge, L., & Merrill, D. (1986). Tokenism reconsidered: Male nurses and female physicians in a hospital setting. *Social Forces, 64*(4), 925–947.

Forsyth, J. J., Jones, J., Duval, L., & Bambridge, A. (2019). Opportunities and barriers that females face for study and employment in sport. *Journal of Hospitality, Leisure, Sports and Tourism Education, 24*, 80–89.

Gabriel, Y. (2005). Glass cages and glass palaces: Images of organization in image-conscious times. *Organization, 12*(1), 9–27.

Hindman, L. C., & Walker, N. A. (2020). Sexism in professional sports: How women managers experience and survive sport organizational culture. *Journal of Sport Management, 34*(1), 64–76.

Holdsworth, N. (2013). Boys don't do dance, do they? *Research in Drama Education: The Journal of Applied Theatre and Performance, 18*(2), 168–178.

Hultin, M. (2003). Some take the glass escalator, some hit the glass ceiling? Career consequences of occupational sex segregation. *Work and Occupations, 30*(1), 30–61.

Jackson, J. F., & O'Callaghan, E. M. (2009). What do we know about glass ceiling effects? A taxonomy and critical review to inform higher education research. *Research in Higher Education, 50*(5), 460–482.

Kang, K., & Noh, J. (2012, February 17). Vienna Philharmonic with 95% men, Bucheon Philharmonic with 85% women… Will there be a difference in sound? *Joongan-Ilbo, 27*.

Kimmel, M. S. (2000). *The gendered society*. Oxford University Press.

Kullberg, K. (2012). From glass escalator to glass travelator: On the proportion of men in managerial positions in social work in Sweden. *British Journal of Social Work, 43*(8), 1492–1509.

Lagaert, S., & Roose, H. (2018). The gender gap in sport event attendance in Europe: The impact of macro-level gender equality. *International Review for the Sociology of Sport, 53*(5), 533–549.

Lee, S., & Yoon, Y. (2006). A study on the life history of teaching profession of female elementary principal. *The Journal of Yeolin Education, 14*(2), 209–224.

Lloyd, V. (2019). *Girls at the Piano*. Allen & Unwin.

Lupton, B. (2006). Explaining men's entry into female-concentrated occupations: Issues of masculinity and social class. *Gender, Work and Organization*, *13*(2), 103–128.
Maume, D. J., Jr. (1999). Glass ceilings and glass escalators: Occupational segregation and race and sex differences in managerial promotions. *Work and Occupations*, *26*(4), 483–509.
Meglin, J. A., & Brooks, L. M. (2012). Where are all the women choreographers in ballet? *Dance Chronicle*, *35*(1), 1–7.
Migdalek, J. (2015). *The embodied performance of gender*. Routledge.
Morrison, A. M., White, R. P., White, R. P., & Van Velsor, E. (1987). *Breaking the glass ceiling: Can women reach the top of America's largest corporations?* Pearson Education.
Nam, S. (2019a). A conceptualization of sexism in sport organizations. *The Korean Journal of Physical Education*, *58*(2), 65–75.
Nam, S. (2019b). Theoretical diversification of the concept of 'capital': Explaining the capital territories for the development of sociology of sport. *Korean Society for the Sociology of Sport*, *32*(4), 35–60.
Oh, J. (2003). Women alienation and alternatives in teaching profession. *Andragogy Today: International Journal of Adult & Continuing Education*, *6*(4), 25–58.
Park, H., & Choi, J. (2014). Medical anthropological perspectives about doctor-nurse relationship: In terms of nurse gender role changes. *Journal of Korean Association of Social Psychiatry*, *19*(1), 27–34.
Park, I., & Kim, S. (2012). The students' cognition about dance sport classes. *The Korean Journal of Physical Education*, *51*(1), 193–206.
Perra, M. S., & Ruspini, E. (2013). Men who work in 'non-traditional' occupations. *International Review of Sociology*, *23*(2), 265–270.
Powell, G. N. (1999). Reflections on the glass ceiling: Recent trends and future prospects. In G. N. Powell (Ed.), *Handbook of gender and work* (pp. 325–345). Sage Publications.
Price-Glynn, K., & Rakovski, C. (2012). Who rides the glass escalator? Gender, race and nationality in the national nursing assistant study. *Work, Employment & Society*, *26*(5), 699–715.
Ratcliffe, P. (1996). Gender differences in career progress in nursing: Towards a non-essentialist structural theory. *Journal of Advanced Nursing*, *23*(2), 389–395.
Risner, D. (2007). Rehearsing masculinity: Challenging the 'boy code' in dance education. *Research in Dance Education*, *8*(2), 139–153.
Ryan, I., & Dickson, G. (2018). The invisible norm: An exploration of the intersections of sport, gender and leadership. *Leadership*, *14*(3), 329–346.
Ryan, M. K., & Haslam, S. A. (2007). The glass cliff: Exploring the dynamics surrounding the appointment of women to precarious leadership positions. *Academy of Management Review*, *32*(2), 549–572.
Simpson, R. (2009). *Men in caring occupations: Doing gender differently*. Palgrave Macmillan.
Stokes, A. (2015). The glass runway: How gender and sexuality shape the spotlight in fashion design. *Gender & Society*, *29*(2), 219–243.
Torre, M. (2018). Stopgappers? The occupational trajectories of men in female-dominated occupations. *Work and Occupations*, *45*(3), 283–312.
Williams, C. L. (1992). The glass escalator: Hidden advantages for men in the "female" professions. *Social Problems*, *39*(3), 253–267.
Williams, C. L. (2013). The glass escalator, revisited: Gender inequality in neoliberal times, SWS feminist lecturer. *Gender & Society*, *27*(5), 609–629.
Wingfield, A. H. (2009). Racializing the glass escalator: Reconsidering men's experiences with women's work. *Gender & Society*, *23*(1), 5–26.
Wingfield, A. H., & Myles, R. L. (2014). Still a man's world? Revisiting men who do women's work. *Sociology Compass*, *8*(10), 1206–1215.
Wright, G. (2013). Male dance educators in a female-dominated profession. *Journal of Physical Education, Recreation and Dance*, *84*(7), 14–15.

CHAPTER 2

CONSUMING SPORTS AS A POPULAR CONTENT OF KOREAN REALITY TELEVISION SHOWS: READING THE SPORT MEDIA ISSUE UNDER THE UMBRELLA OF MULTIPLE APPROACHES

Yoonso Choi

University of Seoul, Republic of Korea

ABSTRACT

The purpose of this study is to interrogate the meaning and the prospect of consuming sports as Korean popular media entertainment contents from the sociological perspective. Now, the Korean media are flooded with variety TV shows using sports as their contents. Not only terrestrial broadcasts but also over-the-top (OTT) such as Netflix and Disney Plus telecast a total of 36 sports entertainment programs using various sports including golf, football, fitness, and so on as the contents. In particular, it is interesting that sports-contented variety shows which combine nonsport persons with sports as the contents attract wide popularity. Moreover, it can be observed that athletes, who had made their names in their own sports when they were active ones and honorably retired, appeared as entertainers in sport-contented variety shows and enjoyed their second life as entertainers, not athletes. As such, various kinds of sports have continuously attracted popularity as core contents for variety shows in the Korean media market. On the basis of the background, this study attempts to seek out the answers to the following questions. First, what are the highlight and challenges of the popularity of entertainment programs using sports as their contents in the Korean society? Second, can it be possible to continuously consume sports as popular contents for the Korean media industry? Finally, how can the consumption of sports as the media entertainment contents influence on the topography of the discourse (males- and popular sport-centered) dominating the sports culture in the Korean society?

Keywords: Reality TV shows; sportainment; multiple approaches; Korean sport-themed shows; Korean media industry

INTRODUCTION

BBC News released an article titled "Physical 100: Are K-reality shows the next big thing in Korean culture?" on February 27, 2023.[1] The article analyzes the global popularity of *Physical 100*, a sports-themed reality television (STR TV) show that premiered on Netflix during the first half of 2023, and clarifies how major streaming platforms, such as Netflix and Disney Plus, started acknowledging such reality TV shows' global marketability. Korean reality TV shows are fast becoming a genre that guarantees viewership globally (Choi, 2019). As mentioned in the article, there is currently an abundance of reality TV shows in Korea. In particular, the reality TV shows with sports as their content are currently gaining popularity and viewership. In addition to performing terrestrial broadcasting, over-the-top (OTT) media service platforms, such as Netflix and Disney Plus, are providing reality TV shows as content for various sports, such as golf, soccer, and fitness. Further, the popularity of sports-themed reality TV shows is not limited to Korea alone. Even in the United States, which first started airing reality TV shows, sport-themed reality shows such as Hard Knock and Amazing Race are one of the popular genres in the media market. Therefore, it is interesting to examine how American reality TV differs from Korean reality TV. In particular, what are the differences between Korean and American STR TV shows, which are both highly popular? The most notable difference in STR TV between the two countries is the concept of selecting the genre according to the cast's athletic abilities. In the United States, if a reality TV show features a cast of professional athletes, its preferred format is "documentary," rather than "enter- tainment." HBO's *Hard Knock*, which has been popular since its first airing in 2001, is a prime example. *Hard Knock* shows National Football League players and coaches preparing teams for the next season's matches. For reality TV shows featuring nonathletes as the cast, an entertainment format where individuals compete in "various physical activities" to win a cash prize is preferred. *The Amazing Race*, which has been airing on CBS since 2001, is the most representative example. Hence, in the United States, STR TV shows follow a documentary format, which focuses on gravitas and expertise in sports if multiple cast members are professionals, and an entertainment format, which presents more exciting competitions involving various physical activities if the cast comprises ordinary individuals. However, most Korean STR TV shows focus on the concept of entertainment regardless of the athletic abilities of the cast. They expect to gain viewers' affinity by drastically reducing the expertise and gravitas associated with professional athletes and creating funny or conflict-arising situations among cast members. Earlier, Korean reality TV shows used to adopt American formats and concepts without any changes. However, Korean reality TV shows, particularly those handling sports themes, no longer follow the format and concept of American reality TV shows, despite being originally inspired by Korean reality TV (Kim, 2011).

Against this background on South Korean reality TV's popularity, this study examines in detail how the sports themselves and athletes appearing in STR TV shows are consumed by Korean society. For this purpose, the current status of all the STR TV shows that have been airing in Korea for the past three years is considered, and the factors contributing to the genre's popularity in Korean society are examined, both in terms of the environment and media industry. The reason that I looked at the STR TV shows airing from 2020 to 2023 is due to a significant increase in those kinds of shows during the pandemic. In addition, the ways in which sports as the content of popular reality TV shows is consumed by the media market of Korean society were explored based on the current status of STR TV shows and the search for popularity factors. The discussion on the phenomenal popularity of Korean STR TV shows was considered from an academic and critical perspective, with ideas being borrowed from several scholars. The first discussion analyzed how STR TV, popularly broadcast, continues to perpetuate gender discourse – especially, male oriented discourse – which is one of the classical hegemonic discourses in the sports domain, based on Michel Foucault's discourse theory. The second discussion reviewed how the combination of sports and entertainment benefits us. Additionally, a discussion on how these benefits subsequently limit viewers' opportunity to take sports seriously in the Korean media market was conducted according to the concept of the public sphere proposed by Jürgen Habermas. Finally, the phenomenon of how the Korean media market's STR TV uses sports and athletes as ephemeral and fixed-term material to acquire popularity was examined according to Zygmunt Bauman's liquid modernity concept.

This study discusses how sports and athletes are being consumed as popular content in the Korean media market. The popularity of similar reality TV shows outside Korea is limited. Further, efforts were made to critically examine the hegemonic discourse that has solidified as the sports culture in Korean society and the by-products of the media market created by sports and athletes practicing intact postmodernist characteristics. This critical discussion is expected to be the first step in providing a platform of thought and reflection for sports and their surrounding environment and culture to be valued more in Korean society.

CURRENT REALITY TV SHOWS AND STR TV SHOWS IN KOREAN SOCIETY

In South Korea, the terms "reality TV show" and "variety show[2]" are used interchangeably and, recently, they have together been referred to as "observational entertainment,[3]" rather than reality TV. Even within the academia or the media industry, it is difficult to precisely define reality TV. One of the reasons for this difficulty is the challenge involved in establishing a clear-cut classification system caused by the continuous changes being made to show formats to match social changes (Shin, 2015). Scholars outside Korea interpret reality TV as "factual television," since it borders information, entertainment, documentary, and drama (Hill, 2005), and define it as a commercial genre that blends popular entertainment narratives and real-world discourse, rather than following systematic rules or certainty (Murray & Ouellette, 2004). Although approximately 200 academic studies have been conducted on reality TV in Korea from 2006 to 2023, no clear definition of reality TV could be found, except in the study by Kim and Park (2006). The authors, Kim and Park (2006), defined reality TV as shows that mix representational formats of fact and fiction to induce changes in reality, deliver the process and outcome of these changes as events, and establish a communication pathway between TV shows and the audience. Although reality TV has no consistent definition, some commonalities can be derived from the aforementioned scholars' descriptions of reality TV. Reality TV is fluid because it encompasses many genres, is a hybrid of fact and fiction, and contains entertainment elements that delight viewers. In particular, academic studies (Choi, 2020; Kang & Yun, 2021; Lim et al., 2020) on the reality TV shows recently aired in South Korea are focused on the so-called "entertainment shows," which suggests that the entertainment element is more substantial than the fluid and hybrid elements in modern Korean society's reality TV.

Reality TV shows started gaining popularity in the United States in the mid-1990s and, soon, firmly established themselves as a globally popular TV genre. The format features "ordinary people" and is based on real life, and the shows are produced using "unscripted" stories with the inclusion of an "entertainment element" to the content (Murray & Ouellette, 2004). Reality TV encompasses stories in which "ordinary" cast is tested; made to compete with one another; or required to change their overall lifestyle habits in various subgenres, including date shows, makeovers, contests, competitions, and games. As previously mentioned, the reality TV shows broadcast to date in Korea are similar in content to American reality TV shows because both types of shows are produced using entertainment elements without a script. However, there is one difference between Korean and American shows in that celebrities, TV personalities, or aspiring celebrities appear as the central cast of reality TV in Korea, whereas ordinary individuals are cast in reality TV shows in the United States (Joe, 2021; Kim, 2011). The appearance of celebrities or TV personalities in shows over the general public is seen as a strategy of the broadcasters to gain an advantage in the fierce competition for viewership (Im et al., 2020).

In the last three years since 2020, a total of 48 STR TV shows have been aired. Among them, 37 followed a sport-themed reality show format after excluding one-time broadcasts for mega-events like holiday specials, the Olympics, and the Asian Games (Naver, 2023). All these shows aired in the evening or night between 5 p.m. and 11 p.m. In the sports category, most shows (eight) were on golf; they were followed by four shows having baseball content. Further, soccer, basketball, and Korean wrestling followed golf and baseball with three shows each. Other reality show contents included badminton, tennis, taekwondo, dodgeball, and table tennis. In most cases (14 shows), the cast consisted of TV

Table 2.1. Classification and Types of STR TV Shows.

Classification	Details
Sport	Golf (8), baseball (4), soccer (3), basketball (3), Korean wrestling (3), badminton (1), table tennis (1), mixed martial arts (1), arm wrestling (1), dodgeball (1), tennis (1), taekwondo (1), fitness (7)
Cast	Athletes (retired and current) + TV personalities (14) Athletes (retired) + general public (including youth) (12) Athletes (retired and current) (7) TV personalities (3)
Gender	Male oriented (20) Female oriented (6) Mixed (11)

Source: Naver.
Note: The numbers in parentheses indicate the numbers of shows aired.

personalities (celebrities) and retired and current athletes. There were 20 male-oriented shows, which accounted for more than half of the 37 shows. Table 2.1 summarizes the sports categories, cast, and gender orientation of STR TV shows aired in Korea from 2020 to 2023.

WHY THE STR REALITY TV SHOWS ARE HUGE POPULAR IN KOREAN SOCIETY?

It is necessary to clarify why STR TV shows are very popular in Korean society. The author interpreted the cause of popularity of recent STR TV shows in Korea from two perspectives. The first is the popularity of sports entertainment shows in Korean society from an environmental perspective. The COVID-19 pandemic began in the winter of 2019 and lasted three years and four months until the World Health Organization declared the termination of the Public Health Emergency of International Concern in May 2023. Since the lifting of the highest level of alert against the virus, outdoor sports activities have been increasing in Korean society with the removal of mandatory mask regulations and gradual return of people to their daily lives. However, many sports activities were suspended over the past three years and four months. The suspension of participation in sports activities created restrictions in using social sports facilities in Korea, which limited citizens' sports enjoyment to their homes. This period witnessed the popularity of home training programs and conduction of countless studies on home training (Chi & Kim, 2021; Kim, 2022a; Lee, 2021); further, there was an explosive increase in the spread of home training–related educational videos. Another channel that motivated the citizens to participate in sports, along with home training, during the COVID-19 pandemic was the viewing of sport-themed entertainment shows. Various sports content shows, including those created by broadcasting companies, were created during this period (Jang, 2022). The design and production of sport-based entertainment shows, which presented stories centered on the sporting competitions of retired sports stars, their families, and TV personalities, helped quench the citizens' thirst to participate in sporting events during the pandemic (Jang & Lee, 2022). The prolonged pandemic realized an environment in which it was difficult to produce the so-called "killer content," such as overseas travel shows and *meok-bang*, which is a trend followed by conventional reality TV shows.[4] Subsequently, major Korean broadcasting stations, including cable broadcasting centers, became interested in relatively accessible sports entertainment and invested heavily in production planning. During the pandemic era, the utilization of sports content caused people to stop "playing sports" and start "watching sports"; this increased the popularity of many sports reality TV shows (Kim, 2022c). In particular, Kim (2022b) explains that the mass production of reality TV shows with sports content during the pandemic contributed to expanding the channels that enabled the public to realize their desire to and enjoy exercise simultaneously.

The second is the popularity of STR TV shows from an industrial perspective. First, an explanation of Korean reality TV shows must precede the explanation of the prevalence of sports content to understand the spread of STR TV shows from the industrial perspective. In Korean society, the term reality show is used interchangeably with variety show, which is a show that presents real life with the purpose of amusing viewers. In the 2000s, following the airing of "Survivor" and "Big Brother" in the United States and the growth in global popularity of American reality TV formats, such as "The Amazing Race" and "The Bachelor," the Korean media industry underwent rapid growth by adopting similar formats in the Korean media market and contributed to the growth in popularity of Korean reality TV shows in the Korean market (Hong, 2004). This growth is attributed to the consideration of reality TV format as a media product that guarantees stable viewership and economic advantages to broadcasting producers (Choi, 2020). Broadcasting companies do not need to spend money on developing new TV show formats and can continuously produce "seemingly new" TV shows by using the same format and changing the content alone. Furthermore, reality TV shows are recognized as an attractive media genre that has been consistently guaranteeing high viewership ratings since 2000; these ratings surpass even the viewership rating of dramas, which have traditionally been one of the most prominent genres in the history of broadcast shows (Kang & Yun, 2021). From the broadcasters' perspective, the production of reality shows in a viewer-verified format is a stable strategy compared to the production of dramas, which is characterized by high production costs and uncertain success (Roh, 2015).

If producers are attracted to the reality genre due to its benefits, such as saving production costs and ensuring viewership, what are the reasons for this genre's popularity from the viewers' perspective? Specifically, why do Korean viewers love reality TV shows with sport content? Since the recognition of sports as an attractive and popular media content (Goo, 2011), the territory of sports within the media industry has been expanding to include dramas and reality shows. However, earlier, sports content in shows was limited to the match results that were reported on the news. In addition to the expansion of sports-based reality TV shows, an increasing number of former and current athletes are appearing on reality TV (Lee & Lee,

2023). Earlier, athletes' broadcast appearances were one-time or special events; however, now, they appear as hosts or permanent cast members. Broadcasting companies welcome the appearances of sports stars in shows because this enables audiences to observe the everyday, informal behaviors of the athletes who have given exceptional performances in their respective sport. In addition, the shows highlight the elite athletes' unique spirit and competitiveness and clarify how their natural charm is a strength. Moreover, high-profile sports stars are considered the "ideal cast" for STR TV shows because they are familiar with being in the limelight and have the ability, agility, and endurance (cultivated over years of participating in sporting events) to put on a performance and face any related issues. Lee and Lee (2023) interpret the appearance of current and former athletes in reality TV to be a refreshing experience for viewers, who are generally tired of always viewing celebrities or TV personalities, and clarify that this trend conforms to the needs of viewers.

DISCUSSION

Continuous (Re)production of the Classical Gender Discourse

Unlike other fields, the sports field is dominated by a strong male-oriented culture (Dorer et al., 2020; Merrill et al., 2015; Rahbari, 2017; Richardson et al., 2021). Hence, women have generally faced oppression and discrimination with respect to their participation in sports. However, the women's liberation movement, which was vigorously initiated in the late 1970s to resolve the oppression of women by the patriarchal mindset stemming from the traditional ideology of Korean society, was the cornerstone of expansion of women's participation in sports. Recently, there occurred a shift in the dominant gender image long associated with the sports field, resulting in a sharp increase in the number of female athletes participating in traditionally male-centered sporting arenas (Kim, 2023). Further, male hegemony in sports is not a new concept at all. The situation has improved significantly in recent years, but not by much. Hence, what is the image of women in Korean social media? In particular, what is the image of women in Korean reality TV shows? To find out the answers of these questions, the first discussion analyzed how STR TV, popularly broadcast, continues to perpetuate male oriented discourse, which is one of the classical hegemonic discourses in the sports domain, based on Michel Foucault's discourse theory. Foucault noted that discourse is a form of linguistic activity that is inherently linked to power. Therefore, no discourse can be considered free from power systems. It is conceivable that the male-centered discourse prevalent in the history of sports can become a dominant force in the field of sports. Additionally, this male-oriented discourse has been perpetuated through the familiar television programs to us.

For a long time, the main characters of Korean reality TV shows were men. The male-only entertainment traditions that led to the creation of "Infinite Challenge," "2 Days & 1 Night," and "Knowing Bros" are solid, and the addition of one or two women as mere "seasonings" is considered fortunate (Kim, 2022a).[5–7] Similar to their portrayal in sports, the portrayal of athletic women in the media has been significantly better today compared to the past. For example, "Playing Sister" appeared in 2020, and "Kick A Goal," which has been airing since 2021, ranks 19th on the brand reputation ranking of TV shows in South Korea as on June 2023 (Brand Reputation Index, 2023).[8,9] Today, even in reality TV shows having sports as their content, the proportion of female participation is high. However, TV shows continue to retain their male-oriented culture.

According to the classification of the 37 sport-themed TV shows presented in Table 2.1 by gender, only six of the produced and broadcasted shows have female-centered casts. Among these six shows, four shows – "Kick a Goal" (soccer), "Winning Shot for Tomorrow" (tennis), "Jump Like a Witch," and "Queen of Wrestling" – candidly depict male hegemony in sports. These four shows differ in the sports category, that is, soccer, golf, basketball, and Korean wrestling, alone and follow the identical format of a famous retired male athlete coaching and training female TV personalities and celebrities to participate in competitions. The reason why the author is focusing on the format of such content is to show that the male-oriented culture prevalent in sports is continuously perpetuated in the reality TV genre. The "male trainer–female trainee" dynamic that appears in the aforementioned four TV shows is widely accepted phenomenon in both the Korean sports field and society. The situation is statistically proved, as well, since, currently, 27,226 out of 32,480 athletic trainers are men (84%) and 5,254 are females (16%), which indicate that only 1 or 2 among 10 trainers are women in Korean sports. A careful examination of the gender ratio among trainers in the four aforementioned sports indicates that tennis has a considerably higher proportion of female trainers, with 121 female (26%) and 337 male (74%) trainers (i.e., a total of 458 trainers), than all other sports. Among 571 basketball coaches, 444 are men (78%) and 127 are women (22%). Golf is considered one of the most popular sports in South Korea since Korean professional golfers achieve top rankings in major global events. Nevertheless, only 13% of the active golf coaches in Korea are women. Soccer has a significantly higher proportion of male athletes than all the other three sports. Hence, only 4% of soccer coaches are women (Sports Support Portal, 2023). On this account, is it a global trend for male trainers to overwhelmingly outnumber female trainers in all sports categories? Let us examine the case of head coaches of the FA Women's Super League, which is an English women's soccer league. The proportions of female and male head coaches in the League were 30% and 70%, respectively, in 2011. These figures indicate that the number of female soccer trainers, who comprise 30% of all trainers, in England is much higher than that in Korea. In 2021, the proportions of female and male Women's Super League head coaches were 56% and 44%, respectively; in 2020, the proportion of female coaches became as high as 67% of all head coaches. In other words, the claim that there are only a few female soccer coaches because there are only a few female soccer players can be interpreted as the classical male-centered discourse that continues to dominate Korean sports culture.[10]

Sociologists specializing in sports clarify the cause of the male trainer–female trainee phenomenon from two perspectives. The first is the existence of a glass ceiling for female trainers from a structural perspective. Scholars have found that a glass ceiling exists in the occupational socialization of Korean female coaches and that such a glass ceiling hinders female leaders from advancing to senior positions (Kim & Seo, 2016; Lee, 2020; Son & Yang, 2023). Despite a gradual increase in the proportion of women working in the sports sector, there is still no guarantee of the prevalence of gender equality in leadership positions in institutions, organizations, and professional leagues and clubs. As a result, female athletes often fail to attain trainer positions and end their careers. The second perspective is the prejudice that exists in society against female leaders (Choi, 2023; Lee & Ham, 2018; Ministry of Culture, Sports and Tourism, 2022). The most typical prejudice is that even the best female trainers are limited in leading male athletes in high-level teams or leagues. There are numerous instances of the existence of bias against female coaches. Okja Lee, the head coach of KDB Life Winnus, which is a professional South Korean basketball team, resigned from a managerial position after just one year due to disappointing match results. Similarly, Hyejeong Jo, who led the Seoul GS Caltex professional volleyball team as the head coach, stepped down after one season following unsatisfactory match outcomes. It is necessary to understand whether poor match results were the only reason why these female coaches left the command tower. Sports columnist Byungheon Park (Park, 2022) opines that the reason stems not from their ability to lead but from the prejudice of those in positions of authority who believe that it will be challenging for female leaders to succeed. Perhaps, the appointing authority is prejudiced against female head coaches since it is part of the male trainer–centered sports system of Korea that has long continued undisputed. Since this is one of the primary causes of the male trainer–female trainee phenomenon, most female trainers in Korean society lead youth leagues, and the proportion of those in charge of university and adult leagues remains significantly small. Today, women already face difficulties while coaching university and adult leagues; hence, is it possible for them to coach national teams? The author remains skeptical.

Benefits of the Combination of Sports and Entertainment and the Encroaching Public Sphere of Sports

Laughter plays a vital role in people's lives and helps overcome difficult situations (Bergson, 2018). According to Bergson, in the modern world, the public lives a reality that is difficult to lead without laughter and leisure (Shin, 2015). The media genre that initiates laughter and happiness in the lives of modern people living in South Korea is reality TV shows. However, various types of reality TV shows have been produced since the mid-2000s, and accusations have been made that the competition among these shows contributes to the entertainmentization and commercialization of broadcasting (Lee & Yu, 2016). Despite these criticisms, reality TV shows, which are part of the everyday life of modern people, have become a major aspect of the popular culture of our society by outpacing dramas, which have long maintained high viewership ratings (Shin, 2015).

In particular, the success of STR TV shows in Korea was expected since sports-themed content has the advantage of being easily understood and recognized unlike other types of content. Then, what benefits does the success of these shows bring from the perspective of sports development? The most notable advantage is that these shows have opened up the possibility of expanding society's perspective on sports. Whereas sports media tended to be limited to the broadcasting of matches or game results in the past (Carter, 2011), STR TV shows provide viewers with various stories and contents related to sports today. In other words, the images of nonsports people participating in various sports activities, such as soccer, golf, and basketball, enabled viewers to vividly share their own sports-related challenges and experiences. Based on the earlier focus of sport-themed shows on broadcasting to convey objective facts in sports news and match commentaries, it is deduced that Korean sports culture was centered on "professional sports." However, the popularity of STR TV shows played a significant role in transforming a sports culture based on professional sports to a culture that considers sports a popular cultural activity in which anyone can participate. The images of nonsportspeople "with passion but new to sports" endeavoring to develop skills on STR TV shows help lower the barriers to sports participation. These advantages can also be linked to the liberalization of the press and emergence of specialized cable channels in Korean society in the 1990s, as well as the steady efforts to transform elite sports to everyday sports activities.

Another beneficial effect of the popularity of STR TV programming on sports is explained from the perspective of the sports industry. Most of the current STR TV shows discussed in this study feature former and current athletes. When one or two STR TV shows first aired, the cast mainly consisted of popular or legendary sports stars. Now, however, current and retired athletes who are active in various areas appear on SRT TV shows. Carter (2011) explained that athletes' television appearances are a medium through which individual athletes can practice athlete branding. Athletes who resolutely compete in matches reveal their warm and approachable personalities in STR TV shows and, sometimes, produce a secondary identity in addition to their identities as athletes. In Korea, secondary identities are referred to as "alt" (alternate character), and the alts created by athletes within STR TV shows provide them with an opportunity to reform their lives after retirement. Further, the positive alts created by athletes within TV shows serve them beyond their individual branding and are directly linked to viewers' positive perceptions of the sporting entity.

Are all the effects of STR TV shows on sports development beneficial? The answer is no. Often, the popularity of STR TV shows is a major cause of concern. The biggest issue is that the image of sports consumed in the media, which combines sports and entertainment, is being accepted by the public as content guaranteeing high viewership and revenue, rather than ensuring professionalism and earnestness. For instance, the match with the highest viewership in the 2022 KBO League (a Korean baseball league) season was played between KIA Tigers and Samsung Lions on May 16, 2022. It had a viewing rate of 2.0%. In the same year, the average viewership of baseball-related news broadcasts on all major terrestrial stations ranged from 0.2% to 0.4%, which was lower than the viewership of the live broadcasts of matches (SBS Sports, 2022). In contrast, "Kick A

Goal," a popular STR TV show, ranks 12th in viewership among all terrestrial broadcasts at a viewership of 6.5%.

As explained earlier, the consumption of sports as entertainment can increase society's access to sports as a whole. However, this has initiated serious debates on various aspects of sports that cause social issues and affect the functioning of the media industry. The concerns regarding the popularity of Korean STR TV shows based on the views on the public sphere presented by Jürgen Habermas are as follows: Habermas traced the rise and decline of the public sphere by analyzing the emergence and development of media in modern society (Giddens & Sutton, 2017).[11] As defined by him, the public sphere is the arena of public debate in which issues of general interest are discussed and public opinion is formed (Giddens & Sutton, 2021). Habermas explains the public sphere concept as a regulative ideal that should be pursued by society in the public domain, rather than being a rigorous evaluation of the deliberative discourse on specific phenomena or issues (Habermas, 1962/1989). This public sphere contributes significantly to the democratic resolution of the political problems of the phenomena observed in our society through "public" discussions. However, Habermas (2006) criticized the commercialization of media, particularly the spread of entertainment, since it reduces the public sphere by eroding discussions and debates and weakening public participation in public phenomena. Further, the reduction of the public sphere can cause the public neglect of many sports-related issues that require public discussion, and sports may become merely a tool to provide public entertainment. It is sad that, although the internet is providing a forum for some discussions on sports-related issues and phenomena on behalf of television, meaningful public discussions are not actively taking place because most stories are private and nonpolitical. Yoo (2021) pointed out the positive effects of the proliferation and popularity of sports content, including STR TV programming, in the media industry of South Korea and, simultaneously, criticized media's treatment of sports consumption as an entertainment aspect and humorous element. Further, he strongly criticized this trend as a deterrent to the emergence of sports in Korean media as "earnest journalism." Since television remains one of the key mass media providing guidance to our society, it must fulfill its "public" function. To this end, it is necessary to find a way to prepare continuous discourse on various sports phenomena, rather than considering sports a mere content to entertain the public.

Declining Popularity of STR TV: Media Industry's Consideration of Sports and Athletes as Short-Term Consumer Goods

The popularity of STR TV has persisted in Korean society for many years. However, can the popularity of TV shows with sports as their content in the Korean media market persist in the future? Further, will the popularity of STR TV affect athletes' ability to sustain their newly created identity in the media? In the author's opinion, the answer is no. This section presents scholarly opinion on sports and athletes serving their "usefulness" as short-term consumer goods in the Korean media market based on Bauman's insightful analysis of postmodern society. Bauman (2000) explains that all types of behaviors, conventions, rules, general dependencies, and interactions of the society we live in now that guide us and that we can follow, to which we conform, and choose, are melting away and disappearing. In other words, postmodern society does not maintain form, flows endlessly, can move easily, is lightweight, and is inconsistent (Bauman, 2000). Further, Bauman's idea of modern society suggests that STR TV, which has continuously remained popular in the Korean media market, can be considered inconsistent and unstable media contents in a society that is oriented toward "light capitalism" (Bauman, 2011). In light capitalism, capitalists and laborers endlessly search for profits and work, respectively. This disrupts job stability and causes new jobs to be fixed-term, temporary, or part-time employment (Bauman, 2011). In this modern society, which is oriented toward light capitalism, people's minds change frequently (Bauman, 2000), and "immediate gratification" is considered a rational strategy due to the lack of long-term stability (Jang, 2020).

The Korean media industry has a lineage of content catering to immediate gratification. In other words, other content was already providing immediate gratification to viewers before sports became a popular content in Korean media. Further, before the rise of sports' popularity in the media market, *meok-bang* was favored for many years. "Travel" was consumed as popular content for several years, as well. Although *meok-bang* and travel reality TV shows continue to exist, their popularity does not exceed sports' popularity today. Why did the *meok-bang* and travel shows that had been providing instant gratification to Korean viewers for some time lose their popularity? The answer to this question helps draw the conclusion that sports, which has emerged as a popular content, may also be one of the "short-term" and "temporary" materials that provide immediate gratification to contemporary viewers. Each episode of *meok-bang* and reality TV shows followed a similar format and repeated the use of materials, which eventually bored viewers and failed to satisfy them. At a time when reality TV shows featuring eating and travel lost popularity, sports were recognized as an attractive and efficient media content by broadcasting companies seeking new materials that could provide immediate gratification to viewers (Goo, 2011) and were selected as the next hit reality broadcasting. However, similar to *meok-bang* and travel shows, popular reality TV sports shows repeatedly use similar formats and materials (Kim & Jang, 2018). Specifically, STR TV shows are produced using the sports that are popular in Korean society, such as golf, soccer, and baseball, as regular materials. In terms of format, most STR TV shows are produced in such a way that retired star athletes appear as trainers; assist in the training of nonsportspeople, either ordinary people or celebrities; and play games. Sports have always been considered popular content in the Korean media industry. Once the popularity of STR TV declines, profit-pursuing capitalists will leave this arena in search of new content. Alternatively, the capitalists may have already found the next consumer product for the immediate gratification of viewers.

Naturally, the decline in popularity of STR TV shows will affect the athletes who are the main cast of the shows. In addition to sports as content, athletes, who are the key characters constituting the content, are consumed as temporary workers with no prospects. The Korean media market, particularly STR TV, can be associated with

Bauman's criticism of light capitalism. Broadcasting companies that produce media can be considered capitalists, and athletes, particularly retired athletes who are constantly moving in search of work, can be considered laborers. In postmodern society, individuals' social status is determined by individual decisions. Accordingly, a person's identity is created, rather than given (Bauman, 2000). Many retired and current athletes appearing on STR TV shows create new identities as "entertainers" for life after retirement. Athletes are "striking while the iron is hot" to relieve the anxiety of remaining "surplus humans" enforced by neoliberalism. However, in postmodern society, labor is short term, volatile, and temporary and involves no clear prospects for employment security. The operation of flexible employment systems, such as temporary and part-time work, which is favored by the current Korean media industry, is heralding an economy that induces anxiety (Choi, 2022). Athletes are attempting to find a means of livelihood (*gak-ja-do-saeng*) after retirement and fostering a new identity within this system. In a coincidental, uncertain, ever-changing, and unpredictable society, sports and athletes are merely fluid consumer goods.[12] Since sports comprise a popular content in the Korean media market, academic contemplation and institutional movements on establishing and realizing long-term goals are necessary for the development of sports and the surrounding environment. Further, one should break away from the cycle of sports being considered popular, short-term consumer goods in the Korean media industry.

CONCLUSIONS

This study examined from a sociological perspective the ways in which sports as a content of popular reality TV shows in South Korea is consumed in the Korean media market. As mentioned in the Introduction section, the ideas of Michel Foucault, Jürgen Habermas, and Zygmunt Bauman were adopted to critically examine each phenomenon shown in STR TV shows from an academic perspective.

First, Foucault's concept of discourse helped discuss the persistent gender discourse in sports, which are still perpetuated by STR TV shows. The discourse considered by Foucault (1970) is not merely a set of languages but a system that structures our perception of reality. Micronarratives centered on gender, which have long been continuously produced in the sports field, are being consumed as a trend in the media market, and we, the consumers, come to perceive gender discourse in sports as an unalterable reality and a chosen structure. The gender discourse shown in sports, particularly the status quo of the male trainer–female trainee dynamic, was preserved and transplanted into the media during the creation of STR TV shows. Within these shows, women play the role of learners who "require guidance," rather than assuming the role of leaders. Even in real-life sports settings, women are mostly learners, rather than leaders. Further, even when women are leaders, their roles are limited to leading children. The continuous (re)production of gender discourse in sports is a topic of discussion that is accepted by sports sociologists. Moreover, although numerous sports sociologists have discussed gender in sports, the topic remains controversial in various aspects and lack clear answers. Nonetheless, the reason for selecting the gender discourse observed on STR TV as the main topic of this chapter is that the author – as one of many sports sociologists – wished to highlight the valuable and meaningful discussions that have taken place regarding gender. Hopefully, the author's first discussion, which is brief and unremarkable, will help increase the proportion of female soccer coaches above 50% in Korean sports.

The second discussion was on the benefits of STR TV programming and concerns related to its popularity. Following the enhancement of the freedom of speech and emergence of various media channels in the 1990s, the focus of sports coverage in South Korea shifted from elite to everyday sports. This shift in Korean sports policy promoted the concept of sports for all, and the media industry seized this opportunity to increase the production of reality TV featuring popular sports. Additionally, the sports arena in TV laid out by the media market provided an opportunity for current and retired athletes to create a second identity in addition to their identities as athletes. However, although the increase in Korean society's interest in sports caused by STR TV is a positive outcome, reality TV shows tend to distance various aspects of sports that must be treated as public affairs from the public's attention.

The final discussion in this study explained why STR TV's popularity is not sustainable in the long run and argued that the Korean media industry is using sports as merely a tool for light capitalism. In line with the characteristics of postmodern society, the content of sports is considered short-term consumer goods that provide immediate gratification to citizens, and the athletes' usefulness in the media market becomes temporary when the popularity of STR TV wanes. In other words, both sports and athletes are uncertain content with an expiration date in the media industry of postmodern society. The essence of the author's argument in the third discussion is not to blame the Korean media industry for considering sports and athletes short-term consumer goods. Rather, it was an effort to provide a platform for the concerns that must be contemplated in future to sustain the usefulness of sports and athletes in the media market of postmodern society from a long-term perspective. We should not allow the by-products of the encounter between sports and the media industry to become consumer goods that provide only temporary enjoyment to citizens under the ideology of neoliberalism in the postmodern society in which we live. We must remain vigilant and ensure the appropriate use of sports content, the surrounding environment, and cultural aspects by the media to provide contentment and happiness to people.

NOTES

1. Jean Mackenzie (2023, February 27). "Physical 100: Are K-Reality Shows the next Korean Cultural Trend?"(BBC News). https://twitter.com/BBCWorld/status/1630004403812933633

2. Reality shows are entertainment shows that blend entertainment programs and documentaries. They are often called "variety shows" in Korea. Reality shows are entertainment shows that portray reality; however, their primary purpose is to entertain viewers (Dictionary of video contents: https://terms.naver.com/entry.naver?docId=3350593&cid=58190&categoryId=58190).

3. Observational entertainment falls under the entertainment genre among the categories of TV shows: news, drama, entertainment, and culture. The reason for the term "observational entertainment" is attributed to the fact that the viewers observe the characters' behaviors through a camera rather than seeing the captured reality (Joe, 2021).

4. A shortened term for broadcast shows that primarily show the cast eating food (Naver Korean Dictionary).

5. "Infinite Challenge" was a weekend reality TV show produced by MBC, a Korean terrestrial broadcasting company; it was released in 2006 and remained popular until 2018. https://program.imbc.com/challenge

6. "2 Days & 1 Night" is a weekend reality TV show by the Korean public broadcasting company KBS. It is one of the longest-running reality TV shows; it started in 2007 and is in its fourth season as on 2023. https://program.kbs.co.kr/2tv/enter/1n2d/pc/index.html

7. "Knowing Bro" is a weekend reality TV show produced by JTBC, a Korean cable broadcasting station. It started airing in 2015 and is currently recognized as a popular reality TV show in Korea. https://tv.jtbc.co.kr/jtbcbros

8. "Playing Sister" is a reality show where retired female athletes gather and share their dynamic daily lives. The first season began in 2020 and gained popularity, leading to the airing of the second season in 2021. http://www.imtcast.com/cms/index.jsp?spgmdomain=sportysisters

9. "Kick A Goal" featured female TV personalities and celebrities training and competing under a retired soccer player's supervision. https://shows.sbs.co.kr/enter/kickagoal/main

10. Female Coaching Network (FCN). https://femalecoachingnetwork.com/2021/09/07/more-female-football-coaches-than-ever-before-but-men-still-dominate/

11. The term public sphere is used interchangeably with the phrases public domain and public forum (Giddens & Sutton, 2021).

12. *Gakjadosaeng* means that everyone lives for themselves. It is a suitable term to express the lives of contemporary Koreans living in an insecure society, as indicated by Bauman. An English expression with a similar meaning urges one to "save your own skin."

FIVE KEY READINGS

Foucault, M. (1981). *The orders of discourse. Untying the text: A post-structuralist reader* **(pp. 48–79)(Robert Young (Ed.)). Routledge.**

This book provides a detailed explanation of how Foucault's idea on discourse is closely connected to the power system operating in our society. It reveals that power is implicitly exercised through exclusionary processes such as distinction, prohibition, and rejection in order to maintain the dominant discourse.

Habermas, J. (1962/1989). *The structural transformation of the public sphere: An inquiry into a category of bourgeois society.* **MIT Press.**

Habermas explains the evolution of the public sphere throughout history. He critiques the role of public sphere in contemporary society as a platform for promotion of consumer culture through mass media. In addition, he emphasizes the importance of maintaining and perpetuating the public sphere as a space for critical reflection.

Bauman, Z. (2011). *Collateral damage: Social inequalities in a global age.* **Polity.**

In this book, Bauman examines in detail the relationship between social inequality and its collateral damage such as the words "immediate gratification, short-term, and temporary". In particular, Baumann provides in-depth insights into how the consequences of inequality are permeating our lives as a result of neoliberal globalization.

Murray, S., & Ouellette, L. (Eds.). (2004). *Reality TV: Remaking television culture.* **NYU Press.**

This book, edited by Murray and Ouellette, critically explores the sociocultural impact of reality television as a popular genre in the global media industry from various perspectives. In particular, this book offers a critical perspective on the ways in which neoliberal ideology has played a key role in shaping the current state of reality television.

Carter, D. (2011). *Money Games: Profiting from the convergence of sports and entertainment.* **Stanford University Press.**

Carter's Money games not only analyze how industry stakeholders have monetized through this convergence but also provide readers with answers about how sports businesses can continue to monetize when the boundaries between sports and entertainment are blurred.

REFERENCES

Bauman, Z. (2000). *Liquid modernity*. Policy.

Bauman, Z. (2011). *Collateral damage: Social inequalities in a global age*. Polity.

Bergson, H. (2018). *Henry Bergson premium collection: Laughter, time and free will, creative evolution, dreams & meaning of the war & Dreams* (From the Renowned Nobel Prize Winning Author & Philosopher). e-artnow.

Brand Reputation Index. (2023). *Ranking in June 2023 of entertainment programs brand reputation*. https://brikorea.com/rk/ebr2306

Carter, D. M. (2011). *Money Games: Profiting from the convergence of sports and entertainment*. Stanford University Press.

Chi, D., & Kim, S. (2021). Keyword analysis related to Drone Soccer in e-Sports using the newspaper big data. *The Journal of Sports and Entertainment Law*, *12*(6), 233–239.

Choi, Y. (2019). 'Are you a good female citizen?': Media discourses on self-governing represented in popular Korean weight-loss reality TV shows. *Sociological Research Online*, *24*(1), 154–166.

Choi, Y. (2020). Discussions on beneficial TV Genre: Korean Body-Care TV Programs in the Era of Neo-liberalism. *Journal of Korean Physical Education Association for Girls and Women*, *34*(1), 111–134.

Choi, J. (2022). Understanding Generation Z's 'flex' culture: Focusing on Z. Bauman's concept of 'consumption'. *The Korean Journal of Philosophy of Education*, *44*(1), 139–159.

Choi, Y. (2023). Analysis of research trends on gender equality in the field of sports: Based on sociological perspectives. *Asian Journal of Physical Education and Sport Science*, *11*(2), 117–126.,

Dorer, J., Gouma, A., & Marschik, M. (2020). Intersectionality in sports journalism. *The International Encyclopedia of Gender, Media, and Communication*, 1–8.

Foucault, M. (1970). *L'ordre du discours, Leçon inaugurale au Collège de France du Décembre*. Léditions Gallimard. Jungwoo Lee (Trans.). Orders of discourse, Jungwon Culture.

Giddens, A., & Sutton, P. W. (2017). *Sociology* (7th ed.). Polity Press.

Giddens, A., & Sutton, P. W. (2021). *Essential concepts in sociology*. John Wiley & Sons.

Goo, K. (2011). Possibility and value of sports as culture contents. *Korean Journal of Physical Education*, *50*(5), 57–66.

Habermas, J. (1962/1989). *The structural transformation of the public sphere: An inquiry into a category of bourgeois society*. MIT Press.

Habermas, J. (2006). Political communication in media society: Does democracy still enjoy an epistemic dimension? The impact of normative theory on empirical research. *Communication Theory*, *16*(4), 411–426.

Hill, A. (2005). Reality TV: Performance, authenticity, and television audiences. *A companion to television*, 449–467.

Hong, S. (2004). Reality construction of Television Reality programs: A study on the Television genre formation between fiction and reality. *SBC*, *16*(1), 257–280.

Im, B., Kang, H., & Kim, B. (2020). Celebrities concentration in entertainment programs and online: An exploratory study on celebrities' concentration in Korea. *Korean Journal of Broadcasting and Telecommunication Studies*, *24*(1), 223–253.

Jang, Y. (2020). The predicament of citizenship in postmodern society and the response of citizenship education: Focusing on the Bauman's discourse on postmodern society. *Research in Social Studies Education*, *27*(1), 1–16.

Jang, Y. (2022). Study on trend analysis of sport entertainment contents applying big data algorithm. *The Korean Journal of Sport*, *20*(3), 1–12.

Jang, Y., & Lee, J. (2022). Study on trend analysis of sport entertainment contents applying big data algorithm. *The Korean Journal of Sport*, *20*(3), 1–12.

Joe, C. (2021). Korean reality TV in the age of Covid-19: Social distancing and emotional/sensory closeness. *The Journal of Humanities*, *42*(3), 63–93.

Jung, C. (2012). Sensationalism in online sport journalism. Philosophy of movement. *The Journal of the Korean Society for the Philosophy of Sport, Dance, and Martial Arts*, *20*(4), 283–321.

Kang, M., & Yun, D. (2021). A study on the factors associated with program performances indexes for TV entertainment programs. *Journal of Communication Science*, *21*(2), 86–117.

Kim, S. (2011). The structure of feelings and cultural politics in Korean TV reality shows. *Korean Broadcasting System*, *23*(2), 37–72.

Kim, E. (2022a). The narrative and representations of women's sports in the media – An analysis of the SBS entertainment program women who score goals. *Journal of Women's Studies*, *32*(1), 7–49.

Kim, J. (2022b). Sportainment. Taking over the master bedroom during the COVID 19 Virus era. *Sport Science*, *159*, 60–65.

Kim, K. (2022c). Analysis on home training issue network and topic modeling before and after Corona using media big data. *Korean Journal of Convergence Science*, *11*(2), 39–54.

Kim, K. (2023). Social issues of women who kick soccer balls: YouTube big data analysis. *Korean Journal of Convergence Science*, *12*(3), 1–17.

Kim, Y., & Jang, H. (2018). A study on the similarization of Korean TV programs along with the increase in number of channels-focusing on the formats and materials of TV entertainment programs. *Journal of social Science, Dongkuk University*, *25*(4), 7–30.

Kim, Y., & Park, J. (2006). A study on theories and practices of reality programs. *Korean Journal of Broadcasting and Telecommunication Studies*, *20*(3), 7–48.

Kim, Y., & Seo, S. (2016). A study on expanding measures of the increase of supply & demand for the employment of professional sports woman. *Korean Journal of Physical Education*, *55*(3), 95–111.

Lee, W. (2020). Glass ceiling experience of women's administrator in sport organizations. *Korean Journal of Convergence Science*, *9*(2), 20–33.

Lee, J. (2021). A study on home training market prospect and development plan using big data analysis. *The Korean Journal of Physical Education*, *60*(1), 189–202.

Lee, I., & Ham, J. (2018). Role performance difficulties and overcome strategies experienced by dance sports female instructors. *Korean Society for the Study of Physical Education*, *23*(3), 175–190.

Lee, J., & Lee, Y. (2023). A study on the appearance of sports stars in sports entertainment programs and the success factors of the programs: Focused on in-depth interviews with the producers. *Journal of Speech, Media & Communication Association*, *22*(1), 249–281.

Lee, E., & Yu, S. (2016). Research for vitalizing the exportation of Korean entertainment program format. *International Journal of Contents*, *16*(12), 160–169.

Lim, B., Kang, H., & Kim, B. (2020). Celebrities concentration in entertainment programs and online news: An exploratory study on celebrities' concentration in Korea. *Korean Journal of Broadcasting and Telecommunication Studies*, *34*(1), 223–253.

Merrill, K., Bryant, A., Dolan, E., & Chang, S. (2015). The male gaze and online sports punditry: Reactions to the Ines Sainz controversy on the sports blogosphere. *Journal of Sport & Social Issues, 39*(1), 40–60.

Ministry of Culture, Sports and Tourism. (2022). *Development of networks for gender equality*. Final Report.

Murray, S., & Ouellette, L. (Eds.). (2004). *Reality TV: Remaking television culture*. NYU Press.

Naver. (2023). Sport variety shows in Korea. https://search.naver.com/search.naver?where=nexearch&sm=top_hty&fbm=0&ie=utf8&query=%EC%8A%A4%ED%8F%AC%EC%B8%A0+%EC%98%88%EB%8A%A5

Park, B. (2022, March 30). There are no female supervisors in Women's team sports. *SkyDaily*. https://skyedaily.com/news/news_view.html?ID=154400

Rahbari, L. (2017). Women's agency and corporeality in equestrian sports: The case of female leisure horse-riders in Tehran. In A. Adelman & K. Thompson (Eds.), *Equestrian cultures in global and local contexts* (pp. 17–33). Springer.

Richardson, I., Hjorth, L., & Davies, H. (2021). *Understanding games and game cultures*. Sage.

Roh, D. (2015). Evolution of Entertainment Program Format. *International Journal of Contents, 15*(1), 55–63.

SBS Sports. (2022, October 12). KBO League with spectators for the first time in 3 Years, the ratings go high! *SBS Sports*. https://programs.sbs.co.kr/sports/sbssportsgolf/article/56051/S20000000649

Shin, S. (2015). *Impact of TV entertainment programs on the public-focusing on real variety show programs* (Unpublished doctoral thesis). Dongkuk University, Seoul.

Son, W., & Yang, J. (2023). Occupational socialization and recognition of the glass ceiling of female sports coaches in South Korea. *GRI Review, 25*(1), 107–128.

Sports Support Portal. (2023, October 1). *Enrollment of Trainers*. https://g1.sports.or.kr/stat/stat01.do?gubun=P

Yoo, S. (2021, October 12). A call to action for sports journalism: Need to move beyond sensationalism and practice 'serious journalism'. https://blog.naver.com/kpfjra_/222530685611

Youm, H., Choi, M., & Chung, J. (2022). Analysis of student athletes' viewing experiences on entertainment programs featuring sports players: Focusing on their viewing motives. *The Korean Journal of Sport, 20*(1), 651–660.

CHAPTER 3

CHANGING MEANING OF NATIONALISM ON TEAM KOREA: FOCUSED ON THE KOREAN NATIONAL SOCCER TEAM

Wanyoung Lee

Korea Institute of Sport Science, Republic of Korea

ABSTRACT

Korea was an oppressed country colonized by Japan and is a divided country confronting North Korea. Nevertheless, it has established the capitalism faster than any other countries and has repeatedly underwent acculturation and adaption. In such a society, the national football team has served as a national center. Hence, Korean football fans did not allow any diaspora in organizing athletes for the national football team. They instead forced national athletes to make self-sacrifice for the nation and even asked them to be morally solemn. Their perceptions on the national team, however, seem to be changed. It is, therefore, necessary to explore the meaning of the national football team in terms of changes of the "nation" and the "nationalism." The use of the national team as a measure for pursuing a profit, by escaping from the existing recognition of them as warriors fighting for their country, the adoration for football powers actively accepting naturalized athletes and the active support for our own athletes to advance the European leagues deviate from the existing concepts of the nation and the nationalism, which the Korean society has preserved. This study attempts to explore changes in the meanings of the national football team perceived by football fans based on the concepts of the nation and the nationalism and to predict the future changes in those of it.

Keywords: Nationalism; the national soccer team; decolonization; neoliberalism; ethnic nationalism; civic nationalism

INTRODUCTION

Sports have clearly affirmed national identity in conducting international sports competitions in the name of nations in the modern era (Hoberman, 2020). At the high time during the formation of nations, the hypothetical battles between a nation's team and the opposing team brought together individuals belonging to the community called the "nation" and influenced the formation of a "unified national identity" (Chun, 2010). Sports reflect nationalism, functioning as a tool for entrenching national governance, inculcating patriotism, and practicing diplomacy with other nations. Sports also served as a means of resistance against colonial hegemony and a testing ground for racial superiority in the time when beliefs in national racial superiority were prevalent (Kim, 2010).

As such, sports distinguishes and explains the characteristics and political environment of a nation's constituents, becoming a means for reinforcing nationalism (Arbena, 2022). Nationalism is an ideological framework that endeavors to safeguard the life, traditions, and cultures of a nation and maintain and advance its independence and unity. Therefore, nationalism itself can only be closed off. Gat (2012), in his book *Nations*, defines nations as a collective that possesses a clear consciousness to share kinship and culture and political sovereignty and autonomy. Gat (2012) selects "consciousness of kinship" as the key factor in the formation of a racial/ethnic/national collective rather than a consciousness of bloodline. In this sense, sports and national team athletes serve as a valuable instrument through which citizens of a nation can verify the "consciousness of kinship," and national competitions can rekindle national identity.

In Korean society, the national soccer team is a symbol of national identity and a conduit for the expression of the "consciousness of kinship" domestically and internationally. The Korean Peninsula is a single-ethnic nation that has been under the political and economic influence of neighboring major powers (China, Japan, Russia, and the United States) while being an armistice country that shares a border to the north with North Korea. Geographically located close to major powers while being situated in a closed geographical structure called a peninsula, Korea has utilized sports as an efficient tool to demonstrate its "status," with the national soccer team as the spearhead (Jung, 2009). The Korean soccer team's performance and achievements were a symbol of Korea's national spirit to demonstrate internationally while solidifying national cohesion.

However, the significance of the national soccer team, which symbolizes nationalism, has been rapidly transforming recently. Its value as a symbol of nationalism and solidarity from the "consciousness of kinship," such as the projection of the Korea–Japan and South–North histories, is growing weak. Habermas (2001, p. 121) states, "the fear that globalization's influence weakens the power of the nation is not unfounded." In other words, the globalization paradigm has led to repeated cultural transformation and adaptation in various social spheres while transforming the significance of the national soccer team.

This chapter aims to examine how the significance and symbolism of the South Korean national football team are changing within the context of globalization and geopolitical complexities from a nationalist perspective. Notably, nationalism is not a mere ideology. It is inherently abstract due to its metaphysical characteristic known as "the consciousness of kinship." However, this chapter minimizes this abstract aspect. To this end, this chapter analyzes the changing significance of the national soccer team by focusing on the components of "nationality" as per Gat (2012), who identifies six components of "nationality" – common ancestry, common language, common culture, shared history, shared geographic life base, and solidarity. Among the six, Gat (2012) emphasizes that common culture and solidarity are significantly affected by the political and economic situations within the national society because both constructs are related to social strata and classes, as they "share" certain social facts. Therefore, this chapter intends to explore the meaning and symbolism of the South Korean national football team by discussing the significance of democracy in South Korean society. With this as a foundation, it seeks to analyze the evolving meaning of the South Korean national football team from the perspectives of politics, economy, culture, and kinship (kinship community), all of which are constituent elements of the "nation."

UNDERSTANDING NATIONALISM IN SOUTH KOREA

A "nation-state" emerges when one ethnicity and one nation largely coincide (Gat, 2012). In that regard, Korean society is quite unique because, while there was a time when North Korea and South Korea were considered one nation, the two have remained divided since the Korean War. Korea (South Korea) is seen as a country with strong nationalism. However, Kim (2016) argues that, although the national sentiment of Koreans is strong, their nationalism is weak, to which this author also agrees. The "-ism" terms are ideologies or ideals that have a systematic worldview or sense of purpose, which pertains primarily to the domain of rationality. It is to be noted that the rationality domain combines with feelings and sentiments at times, however, unlike "-ism" concepts, feelings and sentiments are under the domain of emotions, which include vague preferences, affection, hatred, and passion. The boundary between "-ism" and "sentiment" is not always clear.

The discussion on Korean nationalism largely stems from three events: first, the Joseon Dynasty movement to maintain independence; second, the independence movement during Japanese colonial rule and the building of a nation after liberation; third, the discussion around reunification of North Korea and South Korea after their division since the Korean War. However, Kim (2010) argues that the three national-level movement-leading forces mentioned earlier have not become mainstream forces in Korea and have not led the future of Korea: first, during the late Joseon Dynasty, those who sought to protect the nation often had less power than those who wanted to sell out the country; second, independence activists under Japanese rule were often forced to leave the country and could not achieve independence on their own; third, after the Korean War, forces favoring division had more power than those favoring reunification in South Korea. Ever since, the ruling powers or mainstream forces in Korea have shown little interest in achieving external autonomy or conducting autonomous diplomacy.

Korea's past rulers promoted nationalism as a governing ideology. Past presidents such as Rhee Syngman and Park Chunghee used nationalism as a means of governance. The inter-Korean dialogues and reconciliation cooperation policies after the democratization of Korea can be seen as the results of nationalism. Particularly, the progressive governments pursued active cooperation policies with North Korea. Reunification with North Korea was an undeniable task for both conservative and progressive governments.

In contrast, Kim (2010) states that nationalism has never been the ruling ideology in Korea. Except for authoritarian regimes using traditional culture emphasis as a means of strengthening power, nationalism has never been the ideological basis of national policy or the guiding principle of foreign policy (Yoo, 2022). Consequently, considering Korea as strongly nationalistic is an overly exaggerated response. The perceived weakness of Korean nationalism stems from the fact that the Korean people have had to serve or rely on major powers for survival, either alongside or in the gap between major powers, from the past to the present (Kim, 2010). In this process, nationalism had been active at times, leading to resistance against external influence or displays of autonomy. However, Korea had to rely on or serve these major powers for survival. Since the Unified Silla period, Korean dynasties adopted a policy of engagement with major powers as their primary foreign policy approach and, although the official tributary system was abandoned in modern Korea, the dependence on major powers persists (B. C. Park, 2023). It can be said that, for the survival of the nation throughout history, Korea needed major powers more than independence, and this still stands true today.

Contrary to such arguments, Koreans and foreigners emphasize that Korean nationalism is significantly strong (Kim, 2016). The nationalism they are referring to generally means national sentiment or ordinary Korean citizens, rather than nationalism as an ideology, ideals, or national policies (Cho, 2021). Then, why is Korea's national sentiment strong? This is related to geopolitical and demographic reasons. First, the geopolitical reason is Korea's history of depending on major powers and experience with foreign invasions, as mentioned earlier. Such historical and geopolitical factors of depending on major powers, which weakened national identity, also strengthened the national sentiment of Koreans. Second, Korea is a single-ethnicity country, which is rare worldwide. The structural reality, where a country composed of a single ethnicity must survive next to a major power, strengthened the national sentiment of Koreans. In a sense, Korea's weak nationalism is being complemented by strong national sentiment. The reality in Korea is that, while nationalism as a belief, ideology, and policy is weak, the sentiment and self-awareness of national identity are strong (Kim, 2016).

SIGNIFICANCE OF THE KOREAN NATIONAL SOCCER TEAM AND ITS TRANSFORMATION

Politics: The National Football Team Breaking Free From Political Influence

In the 1950s, a tumultuous period marked by the Korean War, Korea was a weak nation; however, even amid the chaos, sports remained a part of Korean history. In 1954, during the 5th FIFA World Cup in Switzerland, Korea was grouped to play against China and Japan. Although it had been more than 10 years since

Korea's liberation from Japanese colonial rule, the anti-Japanese sentiment was strong. The then-president Rhee Syngman stated that "[he] would jump into the sea if [Korea] lost to Japan" (Lee, 2019). During this time when anti-Japanese sentiment was heightened, soccer played a significant ideological role in national politics. Amid the confusion of a newly established nation called Korea, nothing could unite the nation and exude pride in the country and its people better than sports. To the citizens, sports, especially soccer, was a fantasy that combined Korea, patriotism, and the Taegukgi (Korean national flag) (Jung, 2009).

The 1960s saw the continuation of anti-Japanese sentiment along with the rise of North–South confrontation. At the time, North Korea did not emerge on the international stage after liberation, aside from interactions with the Eastern Bloc. However, North Korean soccer was a dominant force in Asia in the 1960s. With the fast-approaching England World Cup in 1966, the Korean government decided to abstain from the tournament, as it evaluated that competition with North Korea should be avoided. The 1970s was a period of military dictatorship under President Park Chunghee. The characteristics of this military regime were the justification of the acquisition of power and the utilization of various resources to divert public attention away from politics (Frantz, 2019). There was no better means than sports to achieve this goal (Jung, 2009). Consequently, soccer, which Korea could win in an Asian competition, came to be loved by all Korean citizens. North Korea's rise into the quarterfinals in the 1966 England World Cup motivated Korea. Soccer teams were created in the military (Army, Air Force, and Marines), as well as by the 12 major banks in Korea and automobile insurance companies, leading to a renaissance of "financial soccer." The Korea Football Association at the time also created "Park's Cup," an Asia soccer tournament with eight participating countries to win points from President Park, typifying how soccer was also a tool to brown-nose the then-sitting president (Chun, 2010).

The 1980s was a period of President Chun Doohwan's reign, who came to power through a coup against the Park government. President Chun also launched professional sports (soccer, basketball, baseball, etc.) to legitimize his acquisition of power and successfully hosted the 1988 Seoul Olympics. At this time, Korea no longer needed to keep North Korea in check, and the latter participated in the 1990 Asian Games for the first time in eight years, as it did not take part in the 1986 Seoul Asian Games. In the process of preparing for this event, there were discussions of a unified North–South team, leading to a thaw in North–South relations. During the Asian Games, the North and South team leaders announced at a joint press conference in Beijing that it had been agreed to hold a North–South Reunification Soccer Tournament in Pyeongyang and Seoul immediately after the Asian Games. Consequently, former adversaries, North Korea and South Korea, were to engage in a friendly soccer match in the name of the North–South Reunification Soccer Tournament. As such, Korea, North Korea, and Japan duly utilized sports for political reconciliation and checks, and the national soccer team was at the center of these efforts (Jung, 2009).

However, since the 2000s, the national soccer team has not been utilized by modern Korea as a political reconciliation or checking tool. This is attributable to the increased focus of Korean citizens on the domestic political turmoil than international politics. The main political debates in Korean society at the time primarily revolved around pro-North or anti-North sentiments, as well as pro-Japan and anti-Japan sentiments. Consequently, the political landscape divided into two major parties, with progressive parties leading toward pro-North and anti-Japan, while conservative parties leaned toward anti-North and pro-Japan (H. S. Park, 2023). This bipartisan system means that the foreign relations landscape with North Korea and Japan can change depending on the party in power, and the utility of sports could also change accordingly. Nevertheless, the current bipartisan system tends to use Korea's relations with Japan and North Korea for the long-term consolidation of power rather than pursuing practical politics that have a purpose.

The lack of long-term efforts for practical national unification resulted in the Korean citizens becoming complacent with partial freedom and a semblance of peace in the relations with North Korea (Kim, 2016). Currently, despite the ceasefire, South Koreans do not perceive North Korea as a significant threat due to the prolonged division between the North and South (Cho, 2021). Moreover, 88% of citizens in their 20s and 30s hold negative views of North Korea, and more than 61% believe that reunification is "not absolutely necessary" (Lee, 2023). Reunification is viewed so negatively because of concerns about the social confusion that would arise if reunification were to occur, such as reunification costs, employment issues, and cultural confusion. When public interest wanes from a certain issue, the political sphere also loses interest in that issue; hence, there was no longer a need to continue North–South exchanges between national soccer teams.

The same applies for Japan. Up until the 1990s, soccer matches against Japan were considered "must-win" games. However, this has not held true since the co-hosting of the 2002 Korea-Japan World Cup. Ban Wooyong, an official cheerleader for the Korean national soccer team, stated the following in an interview: "Recently, [Korea] is not thinking much [about Japan]. That is because Korea and Japan have higher goals" (Sei Yoshiki, 2018). Now, the order to "beat Japan at all costs" is no longer compelling for the Korean national soccer team. Owing to the large bipartisan system, Korean society has seen the relations with Japan shift depending on the party in power – citizens are no longer sensitive to the changes in the political relations with Japan.

Nonetheless, Koreans no longer had much interest in maintaining political relations with Japan because of their perception that Korea was politically and economically ahead of Japan (Cho, 2022). From a purely political perspective, it is widely believed that Korea's positive political development, despite being somewhat confusing, surpasses that of Japan, which, under a single-party system for a long time, has failed to undergo regime changes. This is because the public's judgment on the political sphere has been repeatedly reflected, resulting in a positive development of Korea's politics.

In the past, the symbolism the Korean national soccer team held was mainly anti-Japanese hegemony, which had colonized Korea, and the superiority of the system over North Korea. Modern sports have played a role in reproducing nationalism, and soccer has shown the most powerful performance to this end (Chun, 2010). The success of the national soccer team was a means for Korea to demonstrate its nationalism to the neighboring countries of North Korea and Japan and the entire world. It was an effective means to strengthen nationalism unique to Korea in the complex international political landscape. Nevertheless, currently, Korea does not have to use soccer to surpass Japan. This is also true in the context of relations with North Korea, which adheres to communism under the one-man rule of Kim Jong Un. The Korean national soccer team will no longer be a means to challenge hegemony or for political system competition. Soccer is more likely to become a pure, depoliticized team sport that will be used to showcase the unique characteristics of the Korean nation in the international arena.

Economy: National Soccer Team Transforms From National Champions to Commercial Entrepreneurs

The Korean economy experienced three significant economic crises and an unprecedented period of economic boom from the 1970s to the 2000s. Major economic crises include the oil shock in the 1970s, the period of the "three lows" (low oil prices, low interest rates, and low USD exchange rate) and the yen appreciation in the 1980s–1990s, and the foreign exchange crisis in the late 1990s. Although the Korean economy was hit by oil shock in the 1970s, soccer was the only subject of interest in Korean society (Jung, 2009). At the time, the Korean national soccer team won the Merdeka Cup and the King's Cup in July and November of 1970, respectively, and secured a joint victory (with Burma) in the 6th Bangkok Asian Games for the first time in December 1970. It had created an atmosphere of rising national luck. However, the pivotal occasion that changed the Koreans' perception of soccer was when the Korean soccer star Cha Bumkun was drafted to Germany's Bundesliga. In 1978, Cha joined the West German professional soccer team Darmstadt, becoming the first Korean athlete to play abroad. Cha was the pioneer of the many Korean athletes to follow in his footsteps, such as Park Jisung (Manchester United), Son Heungmin (Tottenham Hotspur), and Kim Minjae (Bayern Munich). Cha was the first Korean athlete to publicize Korea in Europe. Playing among white athletes, Cha was a source of pride for the Korean citizens, and his number, 11, symbolized hope, excellence, victory, and the Taegeukgi (Korean flag) (Jung, 2009). Furthermore, Cha became the model for many corporate advertisements, including men's cosmetics, and his earnings instilled a belief that athletes also could become capitalists. At the time, the monthly salary of the executives of a conglomerate was around US$744, and Cha's annual salaries of US$58,035 and US$111,607 when he signed with Frankfurt and Leverkusen, respectively, proved to the Korean citizens that there was a whole other world out there (Jung, 2009). Even amid the economic challenges of the 1970s, the stature of the national soccer team players rose due to numerous international tournament victories. The overseas drafting of star athletes began to elevate their status, and they were recognized as primary contributors to boosting the country's reputation and earning astronomical foreign exchange income.

In the early 1980s, Korea's economy recorded negative growth due to excessive investments in the chemical industry, the aforementioned oil shock, and the political turmoil under the military dictatorship (Kim, 2023). The government worked to stabilize the economy by taking measures such as freezing financial affairs, industry restructuring, and suppression of wage increases. With the government's strong industrial restructuring policies, Korea's economy regained stability after the mid-1980s. From 1986, favorable conditions were created by the "three lows" (low interest rates, low oil prices, and low USD exchange rate), and over the next three years, Korea saw a rapid economic growth of 12% annually on average. In 1986, Korea also recorded its first current balance surplus of US$4.6 billion. At the time, the sports industry also flourished, with the successful hosting of the 1986 Seoul Asian Games and the 1988 Seoul Olympics. Furthermore, the launch of professional sports in 1982 did not mind conveying the principles of competitive capitalism and market economy to the public, which capital wanted to teach the people. It "normalized" modern society's belief that weak competition will lead to falling behind (MacPherson & Kerr, 2021). The Hallelujah Soccer Team, to which most national soccer players were affiliated, was the first-ever professional soccer team, established in December 1980. This team comprised many star members of the national soccer team. The fact that the star players of this team received US$18,249 as annual salary – a considerable amount at the time – popularized the perception that athletes could become rich.

Korea's economy slumped once again when the "three lows" began to wane in 1989. After the mid-1990s, there was a change in the conditions of the "three lows." The previously stagnant US economy began to improve, causing the USD (yen) exchange rate to rise (decline). Until the foreign exchange crisis, employment was primarily characterized by "lifetime employment." However, after the crisis, there was a paradigm shift. Flexible labor contracts replaced "lifetime employment" as the predominant employment model (Song, 2005). Nevertheless, during moments of crisis, nationalism emerged, almost like a "creation," and was "summoned." At that time, Korean citizens exhibited a voluntary sense of nationalism alongside individualism, aiming to collectively overcome the national crisis (Hong, 2015). A notable example of this was the "Gold Collection Movement" initiated to combat the foreign exchange crisis. In this movement, the entire nation donated their gold to the government, which was then converted into dollars to bolster foreign exchange reserves, igniting a significant wave of patriotism. As a result of these collective efforts, on December 4, 2000, President Kim Dae-jung officially declared, "We have repaid all loans to the International Monetary Fund, and we have completely emerged from the IMF crisis." Subsequently, during the 2002 FIFA World Cup, South Korea's advancement to the semi-finals, occurring immediately after overcoming the foreign exchange crisis, placed the national football team in a situation where they became national heroes (Park, 2008).

Subsequently, Korea's advancement into the semi-finals of the 2002 Korea–Japan FIFA World Cup held immediately followed the end of the foreign exchange crisis, and this timing was sufficient to make the athletes of the national soccer team national heroes (Park, 2008). The athletes who led this excellent national team performance also received offers from European leagues or were drafted to Europe.

The Korean government granted considerable benefits to the national soccer team athletes who made it to the semi-finals. A prominent example is exemption from the compulsory military service. Korea requires all male citizens with Korean nationality to serve in the military, unless they have a compelling reason for exemption. However, the government exempted these athletes from military service. This exemption is a significant benefit for athletes who are about to join foreign leagues because they can continue their professional careers without interruption, which is directly related to their salary increase. Korean fans watched with national pride as these athletes played in foreign leagues (Chun, 2010), while the athletes worked hard in their affiliated teams to raise their market value and upgrade to higher level leagues with higher level teams.

With Korea's advancement into the 2002 World Cup semi-finals, the number of athletes drafted overseas increased rapidly, leading to a change in how national soccer players were viewed. In the past, Cha's contract with Germany's Bundesliga was similar to miners and nurses who went to Germany to earn foreign currency during a time when Korea's economy was tumultuous (Jung, 2009). The stars of the 2002 World Cup semi-finals remain symbolic to this day as entities embodying intersectionality with memories of both national and personal success in a capitalist event called the World Cup and the symbol of Korean society overcoming the foreign exchange crisis together. Ever since, Korea's national soccer team and its players were no longer "warriors" that strengthened nationalism, as in history, but thorough "individual entrepreneurs" prioritizing profit. They are viewed today as entities who are elevating their financial value by utilizing today's nationalism as their stepping stone.

Culture: Significance of the National Soccer Team Changed by Cultural Acculturation in the Context of Toadyism

Korean society has been continuously influenced by the West, starting from the Joseon Dynasty through the foreign policies of the Ming and Qing Dynasties to the acceptance of Western culture since the 1875 Ganghwa Treaty and the beginning of modernization. This leads to cultural acculturation in today's Korean society (Kim, 2016). Cultural acculturation is the unquestioned admiration or reverence of the culture of another society while considering one's culture inferior (Kim, 2022). Flunkysim is not the same as the Korean form of cultural acculturation discussed in this chapter, which is a form of appreciating other cultures and looking down on one's own. This demonstrates the level of difficulty to understand the concept of cultural acculturation from the Western perspective and why no perfect term in English wholly embodies the concept of cultural acculturation. Nevertheless, despite this, when expressing cultural imperialism in Korean, it can be represented as MunHwaSaDaeJuui, signifying the inevitable cultural flattery and subservience that arises in a small country historically influenced by Western powers for a long time.

In Korean society, which tends to acculturate Western societies, the active overseas ventures of Korean soccer players hold various meanings. Particularly since the 2002 Korea–Japan World Cup, many Korean soccer players have played and are playing in overseas premier leagues in the United Kingdom, France, Germany, and so on. These include Park Jisung (Manchester United), Lee Youngpyo (Tottenham Hotspur), Son Heungmin (Tottenham Hotspur), Lee Kangin (Paris Saint-Germain), and Kim Minjae (Bayern Munich). However, many of the South Korean national soccer players compete in the K League (national Korean League) r Asian leagues in China and Japan. Nevertheless, mega sports events involving soccer, such as the World Cup, Olympics, and Asian Games, create a national team, mostly with players in European leagues. This is due to the perception that players in the European league are generally more skilled than those in Asian leagues. Nonetheless, not all players competing in European leagues are superior to those in Asian leagues. Fans have acculturation tendencies, believing that players in European teams are superior in all aspects, including skills, and thus should be selected for the national team.

In 2019, Kim Minjae, who plies his trade in Munich, was drafted to Beijing Guoan on a contract worth 10 billion won for 4 years while playing in the K League with Jeonbuk Hyundai. Fans criticized Kim for being a money-focused player despite his position in the national soccer team because he signed a contract with the Chinese league, which was considered inferior to the K League. Conversely, Ki Sungyueng, the then-captain of the national soccer team, was playing for the United Kingdom's Swansea City and showed a contrasting position when he stated that "the captain of the Korean national soccer team will not go to China." In response to Ki's statement, Kim was criticized while Ki was praised. Owing to his contract with China, Kim was stigmatized as a young player who had no ambition and only chased money. This unquestioning praise of European leagues is a clear manifestation of cultural acculturation (Kim, 2022). Although all professional athletes follow the capital, fans were unhappy with Kim's decision to join the Chinese league, a league considered inferior to the K League, rather than a European league.

Such an acculturation phenomenon has now come to change the significance of the Korean national soccer team (Park, 2019). Since the 2002 FIFA World Cup, numerous domestic players have moved to overseas leagues, resulting in the natural infiltration of overseas soccer culture, including tactics. Players who have been exposed to overseas soccer culture dream of playing abroad. The advancement of media coverage platforms has particularly accelerated the influx and dissemination of overseas soccer league cultures (Peeters et al., 2021). The cultural contact due to the influx of cultures is referred to as cultural assimilation (Adler & Graham, 2017). As Korean fans watch domestic players performing in high-level leagues alongside internationally renowned players, they start to compare the K League with overseas leagues and begin to praise the latter. The influx of overseas soccer culture has naturally led to cultural assimilation.

Cultural assimilation is commonly observed in situations of conquest or colonialism, where the full contact of one social group with a strong dominant society leads to wide cultural changes within the subordinate social group (Chan, 2022). From a global perspective, the Korean national soccer team, considered an underdog, and its fans have undergone a process of cultural transformation as they have witnessed the ventures of famous players from soccer powerhouses. Through this process, the national soccer team players who used to symbolize national pride and nationalism are now watching the lives of famous international players believed to be able to become capitalists and powerful figures. For example, Cristiano Ronaldo dos Santos Aveiro, Lionel Andrés Messi Cuccittini, and Kylian Mbappé Lottin are members of their respective national soccer teams. However, they receive astronomical salaries from their professional teams and continuously negotiate with their team (companies) on the figure. Korean soccer fans perceive them as players who play for the national soccer team and earn high salaries; they no longer view them from a nationalist perspective. Players who have been drafted abroad and demonstrate a successful performance lead affluent lives in both Korea and abroad. Some choose to settle down in the US or Europe after retirement. This demonstrates a departure from the traditional notion of shared territory based on ethnic nationalism. Furthermore, players who play for overseas teams used to be regarded as a symbol of national pride and patriotism. Nevertheless, they are now influential figures who earn good money, are famous, appear in advertisements, and even influence the direction of Korean soccer operations with their opinions. Akin to their counterparts in overseas leagues, Korean national soccer players are also becoming capitalists, global citizens, and influential figures in the world of soccer.

Meanwhile, national soccer team players duly utilize nationalism to maintain their wealth and honor. For example, in interviews after a match with other countries, they speak as if they have played solely for Korea while expressing the burden of traveling long distances for national team duties or pulling up their retirement from the national team to focus on their team overseas, which have not happened in the past. However, fans express disappointment at such decisions, but more fans have come to understand their decisions. The lives of successful players with a strong image of capitalism appeal to Korean fans in the neoliberal era, showcasing that they could decide to do so as capitalists. This demonstrates that the boundary of the "nation" no longer serves as the focal point of national consciousness. Today, excellent national soccer team players are recognized as capitalists who enjoy immense wealth, honor, and power, and they are no longer a means to affirm national identity nor nationalism. This is the transformation in the significance of the national soccer team, through which the change in national consciousness can be observed.

Blood Ties (Kinship Community): Korean National Soccer Team Cannot Break Away from Ethnic Nationalism

The Korean Peninsula has maintained its national identity despite invasions and colonization by neighboring countries in the past. This explains why Korea's culture, identity, and national consciousness have remained consistent for over a millennium. Gat (2012) suggested that if Korea's collective identity had not been politically important, such consistency for a long period could not have been maintained against such powerful neighbors in the pre-modern era of nation-states defined by elite dominance and class divisions. Hobsbawm, a modernist theorist and historian, also argues that Korea, along with China and Japan, is an extremely rare case of a historical nation composed of entirely or almost entirely homogeneous people (Duncan, 1988).

The ethnic homogeneity of Korean society is also visible in the composition of the Korean national soccer team. A naturalized player or one with dual nationality has never been selected for the Korean national soccer team. Conversely, neighboring countries, such as China and Japan, show civic nationalism rather than ethnic nationalism when forming their national soccer teams (Zmire, 2021). Ethnic and civic nationalism are concepts created by Hans Kohn and are useful in explaining nationalism to this day (Kohn, 2017). Civic nationalism is about belonging to the same community, nation, and territory, while ethnic nationalism is rooted in shared bloodlines and kinship (Bugge, 2022). Civic nationalism is equated with the moderate Western European liberal model, exemplified by countries such as the UK and France, while ethnic nationalism is equated with the Central and Eastern European model, often marked by xenophobia and a focus on shared ethnicity (Gat, 2012). Civic nationalism, based on liberalism in the theory of social contract, acknowledges a shared national identity with racially and culturally diverse groups (ethnic groups).

Korean society is amid the tide of globalization. However, simultaneously, the ethnic nationalism inherent in Korean society plays a significant role in discussions about the accommodating attitude of Korean football. It is particularly meaningful when selecting a player who has been naturalized. The Korean national soccer team has engaged in this discussion in the past. However, naturalization requests have been rejected based on the player's skills or their incompatibility with the "national sentiment." How does this work in other countries? France, a country that has grown based on civic nationalism, has selected diverse naturalized players for the French national soccer team. To improve their performance for the 1998 France World Cup, France selected various immigrant players, such as Zinédine Yazid Zidane (Algeria) and David Sergio Trezeguet (Argentina). When France won the France World Cup, Zidane became a symbol of social integration beyond soccer (Nurfauzi et al., 2022), which marked the beginning of soccer gradually breaking away from emphasizing pure-bloods.

Germany is another country that has shifted away from the idea of pure-blooded nationalism. Up until the 20th century, Germany was stubborn about Germanic pure-blood nationalism (Zmire, 2021). The regulations of the German Football Association at the time stated that only persons born from German parents could become a part of the national soccer team. However, after their elimination at the quarterfinals of the 1998 France World Cup, Germany broke away from pure-blood regulations and actively embraced the descendants of immigrants. Notable immigrant players include Gerald Asamoah (Ghana) and Mesut Özil (Turkiye).

Notably, the disappearance of pure-blood nationalism in national soccer teams in Europe is merely a part of bigger societal changes. It is not solely due to the countries' pursuit of better results in soccer matches but because of the increase in immigrant generations coming to Europe in search of jobs and the resulting increase in the number of people with parents with different nationalities. Such changes in societal structures lead to the selection of immigrant players for the national soccer team. Meanwhile, Korea is a country that takes pride in its single ethnicity and unique alphabet, Hangeul (Kim, 2010). Finding foreign players who wish to be naturalized or bi- or mixed-racial players who can fluently speak the Korean language is difficult. Additionally, Korea's status as a divided nation and the mandatory military service requirement for male players pose significant obstacles to the naturalization of these athletes. Therefore, the determination to represent Korea's national team and a strong commitment to the national flag often take precedence over individual skills in the selection of naturalized players.

In Korea, an athlete can pursue either regular naturalization (acquiring citizenship through a process, fulfilling certain conditions) or special naturalization (allowing dual citizenship for excellent foreign talents recognized to contribute to national interests). Many naturalized players partake in ice hockey and table tennis because of the limited pool of youth players and the government's support with athletes at a national level, such as granting special naturalization for players, because professional leagues in these sports have been launched recently. However, for a naturalized player to be selected for the national soccer team, the player would have to be granted special naturalization due to the absence of a Korean player for an "excessively" weak position, or the player would have to have been regularly naturalized, fully assimilated into the Korean culture and values, positively aligned with national sentiment, and willing to go to serve in the Korean military.

Nevertheless, similar to France and Germany, Korea is likely to face an increase in immigrants and the conflicts associated with immigration in the near future. In terms of population, which is the nation's driving force, Korea has a lower birth rate than Germany. Korea's birth rate is 0.7, and Korean society is expected to become an aging society, surpassing Germany, by the year 2040 (Lee, 2013). Therefore, Korea will also have to consider embracing immigrants for its future. However, there are two major issues. First, there is no government agency that can proactively lead immigration. As Korea never had to consider the transition from ethnic to civic nationalism, there was no need for an administrative agency to manage immigrants. Second, there is a sense of wariness and distancing toward immigrants due to ethnic nationalism. Ahn (2023) calls such distancing "Koreantalism." Derived from "orientalism," this term represents the seriousness of the prejudices and stereotypes that Koreans hold against immigrants.

Considering this current structure of Korean society, ethnic nationalism in the Korean national soccer team composition will likely continue. Nonetheless, the era of multiculturalism has officially begun in Korea. To apply civic nationalism in the national soccer team, the Korean people must adopt a more flexible attitude and administrative support for the acceptance of various ethnicities. Only 4% of the Korean society are immigrants, and Korea must break away from Koreantalism and consider a more open perspective toward immigration to solve

Korea's low birth rate and aging society issue (Kim, 2023). This can be accelerated by selecting immigrant players for the national soccer team. It takes longer than expected for a changed mindset to result in institutional changes. If soccer, a nationalistic sport, can be the first to break down the wall of ethnic nationalism to move toward civic nationalism and embrace immigrants, the Korean national soccer team's performance will be enhanced, and the acceptance of immigrants by the Korean society can be accelerated.

NATIONAL SOCCER TEAM: A SYMBOL OF CIVIC NATIONALISM

This chapter examined the significance of the national soccer team amid the changing politics, economy, culture, and community of Korean society, focusing on nationalism. No other sport openly reflects nationalist sentiment in Korea like soccer does. Fundamentally, soccer represents nationalistic sports in Korean society. Therefore, players of the national soccer team are warriors who represent the nation. However, in today's globalization era, the Korean national soccer team's significance can no longer be explained solely from the perspective of ethnic nationalism, which is the prominent form of nationalism in Korea. As discussed above, the national soccer team used to be a means to demonstrate superiority in North–South Korean relations, as well as a symbol of anti-Japanese sentiment. Nevertheless, today, the national soccer team is merely a group of individuals who seek wealth through overseas league participation based on patriotism. Furthermore, the regulations for selecting players for the national soccer team have a seemingly simple system of immigrant acceptance to maintain its collective status. Nonetheless, underneath, it sets a fluid condition of reflecting national sentiment, which is a hidden mechanism to reject immigrants whenever necessary to maintain ethnic nationalism.

As such, the Korean national soccer team today is a subtle blend of ethnic and civic nationalism, whereof the latter combines national identity with liberalism. Based on citizenship, civic nationalism is grounded in a series of integrated political values rather than in a traditional ethnic culture. In other words, it hopes that the acceptance of immigrant players into the team remains under ethnic nationalistic views, while civic nationalism applies to the overseas advancement of Korean players. This dual form of nationalism is ultimately linked with issues related to democracy. Excessive nationalism infringes upon freedom and hinders the development of democracy (Blühdorn, 2020). This implies that inappropriate nationalism does not contribute to the development of a democratic society that is based on freedom. As Korea experienced Japanese colonialism and prolonged military dictatorship following the Korean War, there was insufficient time for proper nationalism and democracy to take root. Korea's economy may be one of the most advanced worldwide, but the country's sense of inferiority of small and weak countries and an unfriendly sense of nationalism persist (Chun, 2010).

Nevertheless, civic nationalism that reflects proper nationalism is necessary in Korean society, which is facing a multicultural era alongside globalization. This civic nationalism should also be applied to the selection of players for the national soccer team because the latter acts as a compass of nationalism for Korean society. To this end, Korea must break away from the conservative perspective that applies ethnic nationalism to the selection of players for the national soccer team. The same applies for players who have been naturalized. If the players meet the requirements under the naturalization law, they should be selected solely based on their skills regardless of their race. If national sentiment becomes a problem, Korea must endeavor to establish a social consensus standard, and the accumulation of such experience will undoubtedly impact its society's acceptance of diversity in terms of nationalism.

FIVE KEY READINGS

Gat, A. (2012). *Nations: The long history and deep roots of political ethnicity and nationalism.* **Cambridge University Press.**

Nations, authored by Azar Gat and Alexander Yacobson, is the product of their deep dissatisfaction with the way that the study of nations and nationalism is currently framed. The book explores the conflict between countries, the roots and history as the basis of nationalism, and the relationship between political nation and nationalism.

Anderson, B. (1991). *Imagined communities: Reflections on the origin and spread of Nationalism.* **Verso.**

Anderson, the author, says that the reason people are willing to sacrifice for their nation is because they imagine it as something they were born under a destiny, like kinship and homeland. He viewed the nation as a cultural and historical meaning rather than a political one, and Anderson's this perspective provides a perspective on the nation that needs to change in Korean society, which has entered a "multicultural & multiracial society".

Chun, J. H. (2010). *Kick the football if you are a man of Joseon.* **Purunyoksa.**

This book, authored by Chun Jung-Hwan, was written to provide a broader understanding of the Korean colonial era. He used soccer to illustrate the nationalism and nationalist mass society of Korean society in colonial times.

Jung, H. J. (2009). *Sports Korea Fantasy.* **Kaemagowon.**

The author sheds light on modern and contemporary Korean society through sports, holding the viewpoint that "sports are a reflection of society." The contents of this book are organized around people and events that imply the era of modern and contemporary Korean society, and it introduces the influence of sports heroes of each era on Korean society.

Kim, Y. M. (2016). The concepts and tasks concerning Korean Nationalism. *Journal of Korean Political and Diplomatic History, 38*(1), 217–247.

While emphasizing the need for a uniquely Korean nationalist ideology, the author says that along with the need for national unification and external independence, national exclusivity and closure must be alleviated. Explaining the boundary between nationalism and national sentiment, this paper elaborates on Korean nationalism and toadyism with specific examples.

REFERENCES

Adler, N. J., & Graham, J. L. (2017). Cross-cultural interaction: The international comparison fallacy? *Language in International Business: Developing a Field*, 33–58.
Ahn, M. H. (2023). Countries that have actively accepted immigrants... How about Korea? *Dong-A*. https://www.donga.com/news/Society/article/all/20230817/120749689/1
Arbena, J. L. (2022). Nationalism and sport in Latin America, 1850–1990: The paradox of promoting and performing 'European' sports. In *Tribal identities* (pp. 220–238). Routledge.
Blühdorn, I. (2020). The dialectic of democracy: Modernization, emancipation and the great regression. *Democratization*, *27*(3), 389–407.
Bugge, P. (2022). The history of the dichotomy of civic Western and ethnic Eastern nationalism. *National Identities*, *24*(5), 505–522.
Chan, C. S. (2022). Culture and identity. *Hong Kong History: Themes in Global Perspective*, 157–180.
Cho, E. H. (2021). Koreans' National Self-Esteem and China's 'New' Northeast Project. *The Korean Association of Humanities and the Social Sciences*, *45*(2), 59–82.
Cho, C. H. (2022). Japanese politics worse than Korea, the cause of the 'lost 30 years'. *Money Today*. https://news.mt.co.kr/mtview.php?no=2022080912411276955
Chun, J. H. (2010). *He's a Joseon man. Play football*. Purunyoksa.
Duncan, J. B. (1988). The formation of the central aristocracy in early Koryŏ. *Korean Studies*, *12*(1), 39–61.
Frantz, E. (2019). The legacy of military dictatorship: Explaining violent crime in democracies. *International Political Science Review*, *40*(3), 404–418.
Gat, A. (2012). *Nations: The long history and deep roots of political ethnicity and nationalism*. Cambridge University Press.
Habermas, J. (2001). *The postnational constellation: Political essays*. MIT Press.
Hoberman, J. (2020). Sportive nationalism and globalization. In *Post-Olympism* (pp. 177–188). Routledge.
Hong, S. G. (2015). Responses to the Asian Economic crisis and the future of the Korean developmental state. *Kookmin Social Science Revies*, *28*(1), 23–62.
Jung, H. J. (2009). *Sports Korea Fantasy*. Kaemagowon.
Kim, D. K. (2010). Forming and contexts of nationalism in sport: A new perspective. *Korean Society for the Philosophy of Sport, Dance & Martial Arts*, *18*, 39–59.
Kim, M. K. (2016). The concepts and tasks concerning Korean Nationalism. *Journal of Korean Political and Diplomatic History*, *38*(1), 217–248.
Kim, K. L. (2022). Takahashi Toru's Study of "Joseon" and the discourse of Sadaejuui. *The Review of Korean History*, *145*, 295–332.
Kim, K. P. (2023). The rise and development of the platform economy in South Korea. *International Journal of Asian Studies*, *20*(2), 575–589.
Kohn, H. (2017). *The idea of nationalism: A study in its origins and background*. Routledge.
Lee, J. S. (2013). *Foreign capital in economic development: Korean experiences and policies*. KDI School of Public Policy and Management.
Lee, S. H. (2019). If you lose to Japan, you'll fall into the ocean. *Goyang Newspaper*. http://www.mygoyang.com/news/articleView.html?idxno=51921
Lee, S. W. (2023). 61% in their 20s and 30s "Unification is not essential"... More disliked by China than by North Korea. *Yonhap News*. https://www.yna.co.kr/view/AKR20230423025000005
MacPherson, E., & Kerr, G. (2021). Sport fans' responses on social media to professional athletes' norm violations. *International Journal of Sport and Exercise Psychology*, *19*(1), 102–119.
Nurfauzi, A., Mahendra, M. R., & Putra, F. A. R. (2022). European football and multiculturalism: An analytical approach on the involvement of immigrant descent footballers in European football as the reflection of diversity of European society. *Jurnal Sentris*, *3*(1), 27–48.
Park, B. H. (2008). The economic development discourses of sports mega-events in Korea. *Korean Society for the Sociology of Sport*, *21*(4), 789–812.
Park, J. I. (2019). Is it okay as it is, the language socialism in public institutions. *Inha press*. http://www.inhapress.com/news/articleView.html?idxno=8413

Park, B. C. (2023). A study on 'Strategic Competition' and countermeasures with neighboring countries on the Korean Peninsula: Focusing on the concept of 'Strategic Competition' by the U.S. Joint Forces. *Korea Research Institute for Strategy*, *30*(2), 7–45.

Park, H. S. (2023). Political Polarization and the democracy within political parties: How to reform the candidate nomination process? *Journal of Bolobal Politics*, *16*(1), 83–103.

Peeters, T. L., Mills, B. M., Pennings, E., & Sung, H. (2021). Manager migration, learning-by-hiring, and cultural distance in international soccer. *Global Strategy Journal*, *11*(3), 494–519.

Sei Yoshiki. (2018). *Soccer and Nationalism*. Bogosa.

Song, T. J. (2005). The post-financial crisis labor market in Korea: Has its flexibility improved? *Journal of Economic Theory and Econometrics*, *16*(3), 99–131.

Yoo, H. S. (2022). A study on the characteristic 'segmentation' of Korean nationalism. 哲學論考, *4*, 5–52.

Zmire, Z. (2021). The impact of ethnic nationalism and nouveau-riche nationalism on foreign wives' citizenship in South Korea. *Korea Observer*, *52*(3), 483–511.

PART TWO

CHAPTER 4

CRITICAL REFLECTIONS ON "SPORT ETHICS" DISCOURSE IN KOREAN SOCIETY

Hee Jin Seo and Kiwoon Kim

Konkuk University, Republic of Korea

ABSTRACT

Sports ethics is a growing concern in Korean society, marked by recent revelations of unethical behavior in sports ranging from doping and match-fixing to violence and abuse of power. These incidents prompt critical reflections on the state of sports ethics in Korea and the need for reforms. Key challenges are the intense pressure to win in Korean sports culture, often leading to a focus on short-term success over ethical considerations, and the lack of transparency and accountability in Korean sports organizations. Numerous instances of corruption and abuse of power within these organizations have been reported, which have contributed to a lack of trust among the public. This study examines these challenges and social contexts of sports ethics discourse in Korean society, aiming to provide valuable insights for fostering a more ethical and inclusive sports culture.

Keywords: Sport ethics; ethics discourse; triumphalism; compressed modernity; sport violence; corruption

INTRODUCTION

Since the 1960s, South Korea has experienced rapid growth across its social institutions, including politics, the economy, and culture, following a period of social chaos during the Korean War in the 1950s and the postwar era. South Korea's gross domestic product (GDP) per capita has increased over 100-fold, from $297 in 1970 to approximately $30,000 in 2022 (Bank of Korea, 2023). The nation's GDP per capita is among the top 10 worldwide, with its import and export market share achieving noteworthy growth by entering the top eight positions. Seoul, the capital left devastated by the Korean War, ranks seventh globally in terms of urban competitiveness (Jung, 2023). Furthermore, the phenomenon of the Korean Wave, fueled by the success of the Korean boy band BTS and Palme d'Or-winning film *Parasite* at the Cannes Film Festival, serves as a prime example of South Korea's cultural expansion.

However, Chang (1999, 2016) pointed out that the concept of "compressed modernity" is responsible for the adverse effects in contemporary Korean society, which has been described as a risk society.[1,2] The rapid economic growth witnessed over the past 50 years has undoubtedly been remarkable. However, it has given rise to heightened uncertainties and risks that pose a threat to people's lives and result in instability and inequality in numerous aspects of society. South Korea's current ranking as the top Organization for Economic Co-operation and Development (OECD) country for occupational accidents, traffic accidents, and notably, suicide rates (OECD, 2021) exemplify the instability in Korean society.

This disproportionate societal shift also impacts sports, as South Korea's rapid economic and sporting growth has made it a "sporting superpower." Since 1948, South Korea has consistently participated in the Olympic Games as an autonomous nation. Furthermore, it has frequently hosted major international sporting events, such as the 1986 Asian Games, 1988 Summer Olympics held in Seoul, 2002 FIFA World Cup Korea/Japan, 2011 World Athletics Championships in Daegu, and, most recently, the 2018 Winter Olympics held in Pyeongchang. Hosting international sporting events has received active support from the national government due to the belief that it can improve the country's image and status (Jung, 2008; Park, 2008; Yim et al., 2013).

Sports were introduced into Korea from the West in the early 20th century. However, during the 36 years of Japanese colonization, sports in Korea came to function as a means of national pride and resistance (Park, 2022; Park & Kim, 2012). Following Korea's liberation in 1945, sports in the country followed an elite-oriented growth trajectory in line with the socio-emotional climate and political situation of the time. During that period, sports were considered a highly effective means of strengthening national unity and harmony, particularly amid turmoil such as war and dictatorship under the military regime. Consequently, there was limited opportunity for sports to integrate into society and for people to establish their own culture and history. Sports have been actively utilized and developed for this purpose (Kim & Seo, 2022). Therefore, in this process of growth, Korean sports have been considerably affected by its relatively weak historical and cultural background, resulting in a performance-driven culture devoid of the well-established Western sociocultural sports culture. This has led to several challenges.

Similarly, Korea's "compressive modernization" has fostered a society of risks, which is also reflected in Korean sports. Since the early 20th century, the introduction of modern Western-style sports into Korean society has sparked numerous ethical debates. Typical examples include assault by coaches, sexual crimes in training camps, corruption in entrance exams, match-fixing, and infringement of athletes' right to learn. However, in recent years, the "unethical" aspects of Korean sports have garnered significant attention as crucial social issues. The idea of "winning at all costs" that led to the growth of South Korean society and sports devalues the fundamental principles of sportsmanship and fair play. Additionally, instances of match-fixing, collusion, drug use, irregularities in athletes' military service, and biased selection of athletes contribute to eroding societal trust in the integrity and fairness of the sports system (Seo, November, 2011, 2019). The "#MeToo" revelations of a short-track Olympic gold medalist in 2019 initiated the sports MeToo movement in Korea. Shim Suk-hee, a prominent national short-track speed skater, disclosed that she had been enduring continuous sexual assault by her coach since her teenage years. She highlighted the difficulty in speaking out owing to the hierarchical structure of coaches and athletes. This revelation sparked significant shock within the Korean sports community and across Korean society at large. It brought to light the unethical realities prevalent within the sports world (BBC News Korea, 2019).

Discourse comprises a compilation of objective and shared meanings, ideas, value systems, and interpretations related to a particular subject (Giddens & Sutton, 2021). It refers to a narrative that has the potential to induce change. Furthermore, Jürgen Habermas defined "discourse" as a process enabling groups or individuals to methodically seek rational solutions to a problem through thorough discussions (Habermas, 1981). From this perspective, resolving the current moral quandary in Korean sports requires an exploration of the ethical discourse that has emerged during the rapid development of sports as a means to achieve political goals without considering its rich culture and historical context. Therefore, we shall scrutinize the key concerns and social context of sports ethics discourse in Korean society, with an emphasis on the "state-led sports culture" and "pressure structure of winning" as the principal facilitators of the rapid growth of Korean sports. It is anticipated that this chapter will present justifications for advocating universal values and ethical conduct in sports and fostering a more inclusive sports culture.

THE INEVITABLE SOURCE OF UNETHICAL BEHAVIOR IN KOREAN SPORTS

The "compressive modernization" concept elucidates the volatile nature of social change in South Korea. It is not an exaggeration to state that unethical issues in Korean sports today are rooted in compressive modernization. Industrialization and compressive modernization during the 1960s under a development dictatorship resulted in the "inevitable unethicality" of Korean sports due to a performance-oriented ideology (Kim & Seo, 2022; Mangan & Ok, 2013). Numerous immoral issues, including match-fixing, human rights violations, infringements on the right to education, violence, and organizational privatization, have emerged owing to the adoption and propagation of false ideologies in Korean sports and the prioritization of growth and performance over ethical considerations, as depicted in the ethos of "winning at all costs." State-run sports and the meritocracy-based, result-oriented elite sports system are at the core of this compressive growth engine in Korean sports. Therefore, this article aims to offer insight into the sociocultural context of ethical issues in Korean sports.

State-Led Elite Sports and the Promotion of National Prestige

The development and diffusion of sports culture follow several paths. These routes primarily entail the spread of elite sports culture to the public domain, rather than the integration of popular sports culture into elite or professional sports (Green & Houlihan, 2005). Korea's sports culture is focused on elite sports influenced by powerful political and economic ideologies. South Korea's elite sports system developed rapidly owing to swift political changes and economic growth centered on the military regime during the 1970s and the 1980s (Korea Institute for National Unification, 2019). These were the primary driving forces behind the rapid expansion of Korean sports.

Throughout the Cold War, the state's paradigm of leading the development of elite sports to justify political ideologies was dominant. It is widely acknowledged that communist states in Eastern Europe, the United States, and the former Soviet Union have used elite sports to demonstrate their ideological superiority (Boyle & Haynes, 2009; Coakley & Pike, 2014). South Korea has followed suit. Following a military coup in 1961, the Third Republic (President Park Chung-hee) employed a highly centralized, state-controlled strategy to further social progress rather than ones based on democracy and citizen participation. Sports were also subject to this approach.

During that period, the government implemented institutional and legal modifications that were crucial for the expansion of Korean sports. The National Sports Promotion Act was passed and promulgated in 1962, with the aim of "enhancing the populace's physical education, promoting their fitness, and encouraging a vigorous and joyful existence" (Korea Ministry of Government Legislation, 2023). This legislation laid the groundwork for the evolution of Korean sports. The ostensible purpose of the program was to prepare for the 1964 Tokyo Olympics and promote and strengthen elite sports. The establishment of the National Training Center in 1966 and the adoption of the "Physical Fitness is National Strength" slogan in the 1970s exemplified the objectives of the National Sports Development Programme. The military regime saw international success in elite sports as a way to improve national competitiveness and prestige, uphold the legitimacy and superiority of the social system, promote national dignity, and gain an advantage in political confrontations between the North and the South (Kim & Seo, 2022). The "elite sports orientation" in Korean sports during that time resulted from a sports nationalism policy featuring strong nationalist tendencies (Mangan & Ok, 2013) combined with a sanctity ideology.

South Korea's Fifth Republic (1981–1988), led by President Chun Doo-hwan, seized power through another military coup after the events of October 26, 1979.[3] After President Park Chung-hee's death, the Korean populace, hopeful for an end to dictatorship and the onset of democracy, was deeply disappointed and angered by the emergence of another military regime. In an attempt to reduce dissident pressures and stabilize the regime, President Chun pursued various sociocultural policies. The promotion of the 1986 Asian Games and the 1988 Seoul Olympics exemplifies this effort within the field of sports policy. Against this backdrop, the National Sports Promotion Act, foundational to the development of Korean sports, was completely revised in 1982. During this period, the core of the law's revision was to emphasize the goal of "contributing to national prestige through sports." Therefore, "promoting national prestige" was set as the ultimate purpose of the national sports policy. Subsequently, Korean sports development revolved around the elite sports system to promote national prestige. Consequently, elite sports were recognized as a highly effective policy strategy during the military regime. Additionally, by endorsing a sports policy focused on elite sports, the military regime simultaneously pursued its immediate objectives, such as national pride and social cohesion, as well as its potential objectives, such as regime preservation and the legitimization of the current military government (Kim & Seo, 2022).

Elite sports in South Korea have been legitimized by prioritizing the net function of promoting national development and ensuring international competitiveness. However, the amalgamation of political and economic ideologies focusing on growth first and national unity has resulted in elite sports being not self-sustaining and intrinsically restricted, with many unethical issues emerging in the blind spot of state control. The military regime's pursuit of extensive growth in sports policies, driven in an authoritarian manner, overlooks the opportunity to establish a foundation for grassroots sports.

Consequently, the compressed growth of Korean sports provided a time–space limitation in which the essential and moral values of sports such as sportsmanship and fair play that supported modern sports in Western society could not establish themselves socioculturally. From the 1980s until now, for example, athletes have been trained simply for medals, living around the clock in state-built training centers to fulfill the government's goal of "promoting national prestige through sports." In the process, moral values of sportsmanship and fair play have been lost, athletes have been deprived of their freedom by experiencing coach violence, and young athletes have even been deprived of their right to learn. As previously stated, South Korean society is at risk owing to its failure to acknowledge the significant political, economic, and social challenges of intense growth from a strategy of rapid economic development. Similarly, the state-run elite sports system in South Korea is a primary cause of the lack of a healthy sports culture founded on moral values, leading to the widespread prevalence of unethical conduct in all sports fields, including elite sports, school sports, and community sports.

Triumphalism and School Athletic Club Culture

A "growth-first" approach, emphasizing speed and efficiency inherent in South Korea's modernization process, has extended to sports, establishing an ethos that prioritizes victory.[4] Since the 1986 Asian Games and 1988 Seoul Olympics, the South Korean government has actively promoted the development of elite sports to position the country as a "sports powerhouse." Consequently, a "victory mentality" has become the prevailing ideology within the country's sports culture. This section elucidates that this triumphalism or credentialism originates from the culture of the school athletic clubs.

The policy's emphasis on elite sports with a winning mentality has resulted in a decline in school and community sports activities. Consequently, the Korean sports system has adopted the pyramid structure with the school athletic club forming its base, rather than a structure centered on developing national team players through sports for all. This represents the country's pursuit of becoming a leading force in sports dominated by elite sports. The pyramid structure comprises three tiers: school, life, and elite sports. Typically, school sports are an invaluable platform and opportunity for entry into lifelong sports while simultaneously providing the essential athletic resources required for professional sports (Ha et al., 2015). Nevertheless, in South Korea, school sports have functioned as a subordinate system of state-led sports development aiming toward "national development." From elementary school to university, the "school athletics clubs" began to be fostered as this functional group that trains only little professional athletics.

The inception of the Special Admission System for University Athletics in 1972 marked the beginning of a flawed school sports culture.[5] This system aimed to identify students with exceptional sporting abilities and provide a framework for training athletes with superior qualities from primary, middle, secondary, and tertiary education institutions to consistently enhance their performance and serve as representatives of the nation in diverse global competitions. Therefore, it became commonplace for student-athletes to participate in training and games during regular class hours. In other words, these students perceived the training center as more familiar than the classroom. It sought to develop capable sports leaders. Athletes were allowed to enroll in universities regardless of their academic performance as long as they met the university's performance standards. The stated purpose of the system was to foster athletic talent by selecting exceptional athletes; however, it ultimately marked the inception of a government-led sports policy that sought to create a network of elite athletes to promote national pride.

Athletes were able to enter and graduate from university based solely on their sporting achievements, even at the cost of forgoing academic studies. They were also guaranteed "military service benefits" and employment, incentivizing athletes and their primary socializers in terms of sports to abandon normal school life and focus solely on athletic performance to advance to higher education.[6] This system encouraged the prioritization of athletics over academics. Academic development for student-athletes encompasses not only knowledge acquisition but also the acquisition of societal roles and functions as well as career development (de Subijana et al., 2015). The athletic culture in Korean academic departments adversely affects socialization by infringing student athletes' learning rights and imposing a perception of them as athletes. For example, in 2017, a minimum grade point average system was introduced, requiring that student-athletes achieve at least 50% (elementary), 40% (middle school), and 30%

(high school) of their end-of-semester grade point average to maintain eligibility for competition. The system permits athletes to pursue their careers by forcing them to only if they are forced to meet academic standards.

This distinct athletic culture prioritizes success achieved through meeting performance objectives to advance to higher levels, often overlooking unethical practices such as cheating, biased officiating, and violence (Young, 2019). Student-athletes, coaches, and even parents may become captivated by this "performanceism" and endorse the flawed culture. Consequently, a detrimental pattern is perpetuated wherein cultural traits, termed "island culture," within athletic departments are transmitted to successive generations because of their insularity (Lee & Nam, 2021).

South Korea's So-Called "Four Evils of South Korea"

Discourse refers to a collection of universal meanings, ideas, values, and interpretations that gather in a social structure around a topic or story with the ability to effect change (Kirk, 2010). Hence, what is the universal value system related to sports ethics in Korean society? This section explores crucial issues that comprise the discourse on sports ethics in Korea within its historical and cultural framework.

Sports is grounded in just and equitable competition wherein individuals observe fair play and attribute significance and worth to both the process and the final outcome. However, the emphasis on performance in Korean sports has caused several problems that contradict its core values, including fair play, integrity, and fairness. For example, the problem was that many coaches, parents, and some athletes defended corporal punishment as actions with good intentions, calling the instrument of punishment "the rod of love" and claiming that such actions were unavoidable to "win the game." Additionally, "Bribe" transactions have been actively carried out to enter high schools and universities, which guarantee success as athletes.

Notably, these issues manifest in various ways, both at the individual level among athletes, coaches, and parents as well as in national sports culture. Athletes face violence, including sexual assault, corporal punishment, profanity, and deviant behavior, from an early stage. The Korean sports sector is plagued by a range of corruption and criminal practices, such as match-fixing, assaults on referees, poor recruitment and scouting practices, and the privatization of sports organizations.

In 2015, the South Korean government designated unethical conduct in the elite sports system as the "four evils of sports" (Seo, 2019). In 2014, a parent's suicide followed an incident (The Kyunghyang Shinmun, 2014) where a referee showed bias toward the opposing team during the selection of the Seoul Taekwondo team for the high school division of the national championships. This incident involved association officials and the chairman of referees manipulating the match after receiving bribes from the parents of the opposing player. The government acknowledged corruption (including match-fixing and biased judging), (sexual) violence, eligibility irregularities, and privatization as significant issues in sports; dubbed the "four evils of sports;" and initiated institutional efforts to eliminate them. While minor issues in sports existed previously, this incident prompted the government to directly define and regulate unethical behaviors in the sports world.

Athletes and coaches tend to establish hierarchical relationships in South Korea's elite sports system. As the sports system prioritizes winning and performance, leaders wield unlimited power. Violence against athletes is frequently employed as a tool to foster endurance as a requisite element for triumph. In other words, there exists a societal perception and culture of recognizing violence as a highly efficient means of achieving optimal performance and securing medals for athletes, a notion even embraced by athletes themselves in pursuit of success. According to the National Human Rights Commission of the Republic of Korea data from 2019, 15.7% of K-12 student-athletes encountered verbal abuse, 14.7% experienced physical abuse, 3.8% experienced sexual abuse, and 2.4% of elementary school student-athletes endured sexual abuse.[7] The perpetrators of this physical abuse were coaches (44.7%) and managers (14.1%) in positions of authority. This signals toward various issues related to human rights abuse in the elite sports system. Eventually, these problems were exposed through the sports #MeToo campaign that spread in Korean society in 2018. The #MeToo campaign originated in South Korea in 2018. However, in 2019, a well-known South Korean athlete in the short-track discipline revealed a case of sexual misconduct, leading to the #MeToo campaign in sports gaining momentum. Shim Suk-hee, a famous Korean short-track skater and national team player, said that she had been continuously sexually assaulted by coach Cho Jae-beom at a skate field and a Taereung National Training Center (managed by the government) since she was a teenager. This made "human rights violations for victory only," which had been tolerated in the sports world, an issue and created public opinion on structural changes in the sports world to solve the problem.

Furthermore, upon examining the Sports Corruption Reporting Center's case handling status in 2018, it was found that out of a total of 810 cases, excluding unspecified instances, such as embezzlement and misappropriation, organizational privatization accounted for 251 (31%) cases. This number is significantly higher than that of other forms of sports corruption (Ministry of Culture, Sports and Tourism, 2019). The prevalence of corruption in Korean sports indicates that organizational privatization is a prominent factor. This is because of structural issues that commonly overlap with individual internal problems, including entrance exam irregularities and match-fixing. In 2010, an illustrative instance highlighting the issues associated with the privatization of national sports teams occurred when family members of the former acting president of the Korean Curling Federation were appointed as coaches for local curling teams in South Korea. Despite lacking expertise in curling, they received various unjustified privileges solely because of their familial connection to the association's president. These privileges included bypassing proper procedures, receiving national coaching allowances, and participating in overseas travel as national coaches. Furthermore, in 2020, Choi Sook-hyun, a triathlete, tragically took her own life after reporting multiple incidents of assault and abuse perpetrated by her team's head coach, captain, and team training coach. Her team operated under a structure wherein coaches wielded absolute power, creating an environment where they could dictate the appointments of team doctors, coaches, and captains based on personal relationships. This eye-opening event illustrated the pervasive issue of privatization within Korean sports organizations (Kim, 2010).

Concerns of match-fixing and favoritism in school sports persist. This is because school sports in South Korea serve as a means to gain admission into higher education institutions rather than for pure amateurism. The system that determines athletes' admission into universities based on their achievements and rankings in national competitions specifically creates incentives for cheating. Recent instances have implicated various parties in corrupt practices, including bribes accepted by athletes (and occasionally their parents) from coaches, trainers, and even university sports officials (Jung, 2015). While the Sports Ethics Center was established in 2020 under the Ministry of Culture, Sports and Tourism as an independent organization committed to safeguarding athletes' human rights and eliminating irregularities in sports, the eradication of corruption from the sporting world is likely to be an arduous journey.

Critical Discourse and Practice for the Restoration of Ethics in Sport

South Korean sports have improved international competitiveness within a social framework characterized by compressed modernity and an ideology of national superiority. This ideology granted legitimacy to the government's utilization of sports as a political tool to promote South Korea's global standing and national identity. However, the sports world's emphasis on "winning at all costs," encompassing a unique club culture and "silent cartels" supported by a special admission system, has generated a structural contradiction. While yielding apparent positive results, the structure harbors internal unethical behavior. Particularly, the "silent cartel," or closed structure, which failed to address unethical issues as significant concerns for victory and neglected to penalize perpetrators, was identified as a significant challenge. Eventually, in recent years, despite legal and institutional measures aimed at combating corruption and efforts to transform the sports world, elitism has become a prominent issue.[8] This is attributed to the insistence of elite sports leaders, organizations, and parents on the equivalence of the "right to play" with the "right to learn" due to the practical challenges facing student-athletes in balancing their academic and athletic commitments. Under these circumstances, the promotion of ethical values in the Korean sports industry remains an ongoing process, and we must continue to shape conversations toward progress.

Kim et al. (2021) analyzed the social discourse arising from the #MeToo movement in South Korean sports following its emergence in 2019. They identified five social discourses (discourse of postsports elitism, discourse of changing of administrative and supervisory institutions, discourse of reinforcement of legal punishment, discourse of criticism of male domination culture, and discourse of normalization of school sports) emerging from the sports-specific #Me Too campaign. Alongside our analysis, we propose pragmatic solutions to restore ethical values within Korean sports.

> A rigid "pyramid system" and competitive "food chain" create an environment of intense competition for survival, akin to the law of the jungle. The influence of social groups, the drive to succeed, and the lure of financial gain can lead to a cycle of problematic behavior. The influence of social groups, the drive to succeed, and the lure of financial gain can lead to a cycle of problematic behavior. Objective research into more effective scientific training methods takes more effort than simply maintaining the current ways of doing things. Consequently, the "silent cartel" of traditionalists grows stronger. (Lee, 2019)

First, it is vital to break down the nationalistic elite sports system and the phenomenon known as the "silent cartel," denoting the collective tendency and acceptance of immoral and unethical practices within the sports world, driven by a desire for victory, enhanced performance, and better results without publicizing them. The Korean sports community, inclusive of athletes, coaches, parents, and overseeing organizations, has tolerated these problems in pursuit of victory and commendable performance. Ethical concerns persist in Korean sports owing to the lack of focus on grassroots development. Elite sports serve as a covert association of athletes, coaches, parents, teams, and federations entangled in a sexualized framework. The hierarchical organization of sports masks severe internal issues, including (sexual) aggression. These issues have been recognized in various studies (Han et al., 2009; Heo, 2011; Kim et al., 2015, 2019) as instances of complete power discrepancy and structural aggression between players and coaches. Hong (2011) explains how elite sports have been used for nation-building and national glorification in South Korea. In addition, Park et al. (2012) revealed how nationalist elite sports policies, which emerged from the political context of the 1960s and the 1970s, led to educational and life problems for athletes and physical and sexual abuse by leaders. These studies raise awareness of the aims of elite nationalist sports policies and the problems they create.

Second, enhancing the transparency in governance and accountability of sports institutions is crucial. The insufficient role of governing and overseeing bodies, including the government, the Korean Sport & Olympic Committee (KSOC), and sports institutions, has been identified as the major reason for ethical issues in sports in South Korea. In this context, Kim and Kim (2019a) criticized the lack of enthusiasm demonstrated by the KSOC and sports organizations in contrast to the government's dedication to social responsibility and reform, emphasizing the discord between vested interests and reform initiatives in the sports sector. Hong (2020) identified the limitations of the current internal measures of the KSOC, government, National Human Rights Commission, Ministry of Education, and Ministry of Women's Affairs in addressing human rights violations in sports. They emphasized the necessity of creating a separate and independent organization with expertise and credibility in human rights within sports. In 2020, the Sports Ethics Center was established to address the limitations of the relevant institutions and policy needs. However, it is crucial to enhance the accountability of institutions while strengthening their transparent organizational management and supervision functions. The focus should be on fostering responsibility rather than merely enforcing punishment through monitoring. Seo (2019, p. 33) highlighted that "poor governance structures can lead to the award of medals, yet they can also foster a toxic cycle of structures and behaviors, ultimately resulting in corruption within organizations and cheating amongst athletes." Hence, implementing sound governance structures to prevent corruption in sports is the most logical course of action for restoring the sports ecosystem.

Third, stronger legal penalties are required. Kim and Kim (2019b) asserted that existing laws and mechanisms have inadequate power to punish individuals responsible for sexual offenses in sports and to provide protection and assistance to victims. Jeong (2019) emphasized the challenging nature of legal intervention in the closed structure of the sports sector and recommended the validation of leaders' ethics and the enhancement of disciplinary regulations.

> To ensure that the sacrifice of MeToo is not in vain, we must establish robust principles to eliminate sexual assault and abuse in sports and implement a system with severe penalties. Creating a fair society where equal opportunities prevail, processes are impartial, and outcomes are fair is not complex. One only needs to reward the worthy and penalize the guilty. There is no certain method to prevent the reoccurrence as long as the principles are strictly adhered to. (An, 2019)

Fortunately, the 2020 legislative reforms have addressed criticism and established a foundation for preventing gender-based violence in sports while simultaneously strengthening the legal consequences for offenders. The brave disclosures of Olympic medalists highlighted the concealed nature of sports corruption in South Korea and acted as a catalyst for promoting human rights in the sporting realm (Seo, 2019, p. 24). However, it is crucial to remember that robust supervision and penalties are proactive strategies for curbing violence and crime in a society dominated by warmongering.

Fourth, there is a need to shift away from a male-oriented sports culture. The sporting world is firmly entrenched within a male-dominated hierarchy, where "sport equals men" (Brackenridge, 2004). This culture is prevalent across both the East and the West. However, in Korean society, where Confucian traditions remain intact, male dominance is more pronounced.

> To combat sexual violence within the sporting world, it is essential to dismantle the existing gender structure in sports. (Jung, 2019)

Na and Park (2009) reported that the social climate and prejudices against women in athletic activities perpetuate and reproduce gender inequalities. This dominance of men is reinforced by the closed structure and silent cartel of sports, resulting in low gender sensitivity among male leaders. Recently, the Centre for Sport Ethics has enhanced sports ethics education for athletes, leaders, and members of sports organizations to increase awareness of ethics in sports and prevent human rights violations and corruption. Therefore, it is imperative to monitor the effectiveness of education and the ensuing changes.

Finally, it is crucial to establish standardized school sports programs in South Korea. Traditionally, South Korean sports have revolved around school teams. Identifying and nurturing elite athletes relies on the "dream athlete, youth representative, national team candidate, national team" system. Although sports clubs outside schools have practiced certain sports in recent years, primary and secondary schools, which are mandatory, remain under the control and supervision of schools. Numerous instances of training techniques and management strategies that impose limitations on the right to learn school sports have persisted. Specifically, the athletic talent system for bespoke admission to universities and restrictions on athletes' entry to physical education specializations not only reinforce the current regime of training elite athletes but also curtail the career prospects of student-athletes. Moreover, entirely eradicating meritocracy from school sports departments seems unfeasible because coaches' job security depends on their performance. Nonetheless, schools serve a fundamental function in sports socialization, as they are pivotal in unearthing athletic talent and fostering the significance of sports. Therefore, schools should attempt to nurture ethical sensibility among athletes, which must be reinforced through leadership training and practice.

CONCLUSION

This chapter focuses on the discourse on sports ethics, which is an important topic of discussion in Korean society. Corruption, such as match-fixing and biased judgments, (sexual) violence, recruitment irregularities, and the privatization of organizations, which have been referred to as the "four evils" of Korean sport, have continued to occur. These incidents have prompted critical reflections on the state of sports ethics in Korea and the need for reform. One primary challenge in addressing sports ethics in South Korea is the strong pressure to win, which is inherent in sports culture. This pressure often prompts leaders and athletes to focus on short-term success at the expense of ethics. Another issue is the lack of transparency and accountability in sports organizations. The prevalence of corruption and the abuse of power within these organizations are some of the significant reasons for the decline in public trust.

The "compressed modernity" that has worked for South Korean sports has propelled the country to become a sporting powerhouse on the world stage in such a short period. Since the beginning of the 21st century, there have been calls for a paradigm shift in sports. However, the extent and pace of change have been relatively slow. Kim and Seo (2022) reported that:

> In the past, the military regime in South Korea promoted policies that emphasized nationalism, nationalist ideology and individual sacrifice in the name of national interest, but with the consolidation of democracy after the end of the military regime, resistance to such policies intensified and a new moral system centered on fairness, diversity, and individual autonomy was established.

A democratic shift has occurred in Korean sports. However, it will take some time before this change is experienced in all sports. It is questionable whether the country will continue to attract athletes, as it faces a crisis with one of the lowest birth rates in the world.[9] To overcome this problem, creating an athlete development system that is in line with the values of future generations and a sports culture that respects human rights is essential. Ultimately, restoring sports ethics in South Korea requires the combined efforts of all stakeholders. The holistic well-being of both coaches and athletes can be ensured through adequate support. By addressing the root causes of ethical issues and taking proactive measures, Korean sports can regain its status as a bastion of fair play, integrity, and sportsmanship and positively influence the global sporting community through another "Korean wave."

NOTES

1. Compressed modernity refers to a state in which civilizational changes in time and space have extremely condensed aspects, but temporal–spatial heterogeneous elements coexist, and a complex character of civilization is formed and reformed (Chang, 1999, 2016).
2. A theory proposed by Ulrich Beck – the risk society is a new social phenomenon that emerges in highly modernized societies, as opposed to traditional industrial societies, and highlights the different types of risks that arise as a result of human activities (Beck, 1992).
3. The only murder of a sitting president in South Korea's constitutional history.
4. Growth-first policies are those that prioritize "growth," over "distribution or welfare" of the masses.
5. Department of Education (2006, p. 1). Overview of the physical education talent system. Ministry of Education internal document.
6. In South Korea, men over the age of 18 years are required to serve in the military. However, athletes who place third or higher at the Olympics or win a gold medal at the Asian Games may be eligible for alternative service in sports or exemption from peacetime service, allowing them to continue their athletic careers.
7. On February 25, 2019, for the first time, the Intergovernmental Task Force on Human Rights in Sport examined the human rights situation of South Korean student-athletes.
8. In February 2019, the Sports Innovation Committee was established with the goal of strengthening human rights in sports and restoring academic integrity to student-athletes (Ministry of Culture, Sports and Tourism, 2019).
9. South Korea's total fertility rate in 2022 was 0.78, which was the lowest among OECD countries (Statistics Korea, 2023).

FIVE KEY READINGS

Beck, U. (1992). *The risk society: Towards a new modernity.* **Sage.**

The concept of "risk society" presented by Beck is useful in explaining the conflicts and inequalities that emerge in modern society. This book explains the changes in social relations that occur owing to production and distribution as the globalized economy becomes the center of social organization and social conflict. Through this concept, we can focus on the inequality that is prevalent in today's sports organizations and the unethical problems that arise from it.

Young, K. (2019). *Sport, violence, and society.* Routledge.

This book provides new insight and explores sports violence, both on the sports field and off it. It calls for a much broader definition of unethical behaviors in sports to include issues as diverse as criminal behavior by players, abuse of power within sports, and unequal labor practices.

Green, M., & Houlihan, B. (2005). *Elite sport development: Policy learning and political priorities.* Routledge.

This book discusses the emergence, development, and current issues of elite sport in Australia, Canada, and the United Kingdom. Particularly, it focuses on development policy in swimming, track and field, and sailing. Through this discussion, we can obtain policy ideas to create a sustainable sports environment in society.

Chang, K. (2016). Compressed modernity in South Korea: Constitutive dimensions, manifesting units, and historical conditions. In Y. Kim (Ed.), *Routledge handbook of Korean culture and society* **(1st ed., pp. 26–43). Routledge.**

This book provides a definition and core theoretical concepts of compressed modernity in South Korea. It aims to explain the historical meanings of and structural conditions for compressed modernity in Korea from the 1980s to the 1990s. Additionally, it discusses the economic, political, social, and/or cultural changes related to compressed modernity in South Korea.

Tosa, M. (2015). Sport Nationalism in South Korea: An ethnographic study. *Sage Open*, 5(4).

This study explores the history and characteristics of "sport nationalism" in South Korea, with special emphasis on media, postcolonial history of the policies, ritual dimension of sport, and the nonutilitarian aspect of sports with their political and ritual use. Particularly, it examines how different South Korean governments used mega-sport events as political tools.

REFERENCES

An, Y. (2019, January 17). Not enough to get punished. *Dong-A Ilbo*. https://www.donga.com/news/Opinion/article/all/20190117/93738410/1

Bank of Korea. (2023, June 04). Bank of Korea economic statistics system. https://ecos.bok.or.kr/#/

BBC News Korea. (2019, January 09). MeToo: Why the athletic world has been silent on 'MeToo' so far. *BBC News Korea*. https://www.bbc.com/korean/news-46805507

Beck, U. (1992). *Risk society: Towards a new modernity* (published in association with theory, culture & society) Sage Publications Ltd.

Boyle, R., & Haynes, R. (2009). *Power play: Sport, the media and popular culture*. Edinburgh University Press.

Brackenridge, C. (2004). Women and children first? Child abuse and child protection in sport. *Sport in Society*, 7(3), 322–337. https://doi.org/10.1080/1743043042000291668

Chang, K. (1999). Compressed modernity and its discontents: South Korean society in transition. *Economy and Society*, 28(1), 30–55.

Chang, K. (2016). Compressed modernity in South Korea: Constitutive dimensions, manifesting units, and historical conditions. In Y. Kim (Ed.), *Routledge handbook of Korean culture and society* (1st ed., pp. 26–43). Routledge.

Coakley, J. J., & Pike, E. (2014). *Sports in society: Issues and controversies* (2nd ed.). McGraw-Hill Education.

de Subijana, C. L., Barriopedro, M., & Conde, E. (2015). Supporting dual career in Spain: Elite athletes' barriers to study. *Psychology of Sport and Exercise, 21*, 57–64. https://doi.org/10.1016/j.psychsport.2015.04.012

Giddens, A., & Sutton, P. W. (2021). *Essential concepts in sociology*. John Wiley & Sons.

Green, M., & Houlihan, B. (2005). *Elite sport development: Policy learning and political priorities*. Routledge.

Ha, J., Lee, K., & Ok, G. (2015). From development of sport to development through sport: A paradigm shift for sport development in South Korea. *International Journal of the History of Sport, 32*(10), 1262–1278.

Habermas, J. (1981). *Theorie des kommunikativen Handelns. Bd. 1: Handlungsrationalität und gesellschaftliche Rationalisierung*. Suhrkamp.

Han, S., Oh, H., Choi, D., Lee, S., & Kim, T. (2009). The violence in sports through the relationships of power. *The Korea Journal of Sports Science, 18*(3), 271–282.

Heo, H. (2011). Developing Korean guidelines for the prevention of sexual harassment in sports. *Korean Journal of Sociology of Sport, 24*(4), 143–165.

Hong, E. (2011). Elite sport and nation-building in South Korea: South Korea as the dark horse in global elite sport. *International Journal of the History of Sport, 28*(7), 977–989. https://doi.org/10.1080/09523367.2011.563630

Hong, D. (2020). Establishing new sports paradigm and future tasks through the sports reform committee policy documents analysis in South Korea. *The Korean Journal of Physical Education, 59*(2), 285–302. https://doi.org/10.23949/kjpe.2020.3.59.2.285

Jeong, D. (2019). The status of sexual violence in sports and countermeasure. *Law Review, 27*(4), 287–308.

Jung, G. (2008). Reconsideration on the role of sport as political means: The case of 2008 Beijing Olympic Games. *The Korean Civic Ethics Society, 21*(2), 257–280.

Jung, J. (2015, August 17). College sports, this is the only way. *KBS News*. https://news.kbs.co.kr/news/pc/view/view.do?ncd=3131399

Jung, E. (2019, February 10). Rethinking #MeToo in Korean sport. *Hankyoreh*. https://www.hani.co.kr/arti/opinion/because/881691.html

Jung, Y. (2023, January 08). Seoul's 'City Competitiveness' ranked 7th in the world...It's been 5 years since I've gone up to level 1. *Hankukkyungje*. https://www.hankyung.com/article/2023010891491

Kim, J. (2010, October 20). Eliminating organizational privatization of sports organizations... "It is the core of sports reform". *Newswatch*. http://www.newswatch.kr/news/articleView.html?idxno=51465

Kim, K., Choi, Y., & Seo, H. (2021). The #Me too movement and social discourse in sport. *Korean Journal of Sociology of Sport, 34*(2), 51–68. https://doi.org/10.22173/ksss.2021.34.2.4

Kim, B., & Kim, J. (2019a). Sports human rights blind spot: Taekwondo player human rights problems and social responsibility. *The Journal of the Korean Society for the Philosophy of Sport, Dance, and Martial Arts, 27*(2), 35–44. https://doi.org/10.31694/PM.2019.06.27.2.003

Kim, J., & Kim, D. (2019b). Problems and solutions of punishment on sexual violence in the world of sports. *The Journal of Sports and Entertainment Law, 22*(2), 3–23.

Kim, S., Lim, S., & Jeon, W. (2015). The occurrence and basis of sexual violence in elite sports and research of its experience system. *The Korean Journal of Physical Education, 54*(6), 81–94.

Kim, K., & Seo, H. (2022). Tracing two South Korean Olympic pathways: Symbols, conflicts, and integration through global sports events. *International Journal of the History of Sport, 39*(11), 1284–1302. https://doi.org/10.1080/09523367.2022.2133107

Kirk, D. (2010). *Physical education futures*. Routledge.

Korea Institute for National Unification. (2019). *Revitalization of Inter-Korean socio-cultural exchanges through establishment of governance: Focusing on Inter-Korean sports exchanges*. https://repo.kinu.or.kr/retrieve/7858

Korea Ministry of Government Legislation. (2023). *National Sports Promotion Act*. https://www.law.go.kr/LSW/main.html

Lee, Y. (2019, January 10). Elite sports 'private school system' fuels crisis. *Kyunghyang Shinmun*. https://www.khan.co.kr/national/national-general/article/201901102137015

Lee, C., & Nam, S. (2021). *Social issues and debates in sports*. Gungmedia.

Mangan, J. A., & Ok, G. (2013). Beijing 2008: Symbolic hegemonic assertion? South Korean media reactions and responses to the Chinese Olympics. In *Post-Beijing 2008: Geopolitics, Sport and the Pacific Rim* (pp. 108–134). Routledge. https://doi.org/10.4324/9781315868233

Ministry of Culture, Sports and Tourism. (2019, February 8). *The launch of a joint public-private "Sports Innovation Committee" to innovate the structure of the sports sector*. https://www.mcst.go.kr/kor/s_notice/press/pressView.jsp?pSeq=17098

Na, Y., & Park, H. (2009). The present state of Korean female sports Leaders and overcoming of feminist problems. *The Journal of the Korean Society for the Philosophy of Sport, Dance, and Martial Arts, 17*(1), 167–179.

OECD. (2021). *Health at a glance*. https://www.oecd.org/health/health-at-a-glance/

Park, B. (2008). The Economic development discourses of sports mega-events in Korea. *Korean Journal of Sociology of Sport, 21*(4), 789–812.

Park, K. (2022). A Historical study for sports policy on Japanese colonial era. *Journal of Marine Sport Studies, 12*(1), 1–10.

Park, J., & Kim, D. (2012). The historical significance of marathons in Korea. *The Journal of the Korean Society for the Philosophy of Sport, Dance, and Martial Arts, 20*(3), 185–198.

Park, J., Lim, S., & Bretherton, P. (2012). Exploring the truth: A critical approach to the success of Korean elite sport. *Journal of Sport & Social Issues, 36*(3), 245–267. https://doi.org/10.1177/0193723511433864

Seo, H. (2011, November). A sociological approach to fairness in sport. Paper presented at the *Annual Conference of Korean Society for the Sociology of Sport*, Suwon, Republic of Korea.

Seo, H. (2019). A review of the development aspect of sport corruption. *Korean Journal of Sociology of Sport, 32*(3), 22–35. https://doi.org/10.22173/ksss.2019.32.3.2

Statistics Korea. (2023). *Total fertility rate*. https://www.index.go.kr/unity/potal/main/EachDtlPageDetail.do?idx_cd=1428

The Kyunghyang Shinmun. (2014, September 15). *A biased judgment that caused parents to commit suicide, and an organized match-fixing involving the association*. https://m.khan.co.kr/national/national-general/article/201409151434461#c2b

Yim, K., Kim, Y., & Shin, S. (2013). An analysis of involvement, national image, and sponsorship effectiveness by mega sporting events. *Korean Journal of Sport Science, 24*(3), 591–606.

Young, K. (2019). *Sport, violence, and society*. Routledge.

CHAPTER 5

THE ROLE OF KOREAN SPORTS GOVERNANCE IN ENDING SPORTS VIOLENCE

Hanbeom Kim[a] and Seami Lim[b]

[a]Hankyong National University, Republic of Korea
[b]Incheon National University, Republic of Korea

ABSTRACT

In South Korea, many efforts have been made by various sports-related organizations to end sports violence. The causes of sports violence in Korean society can be traced back to structural problems, and it is necessary for related organizations to play an active role as responders to the problem of sport violence. In South Korea, the Ministry of Culture, Sport, and Tourism, the Korean Sport & Olympic Committee, the National Human Rights Commission of Korea, and the Sport Ethics Center are responsible for policy responses to sports violence. The Ministry of Culture, Sports, and Tourism has mainly implemented policies through Korean Sport & Olympic Committee, but in 2020, the Sports Ethics Center was established as an independent organization to promote policies to eradicate sports violence. As an independent organization, the Sports Ethics Center is expected to make a positive contribution to eradicate sports violence in South Korea, but it also has problems such as the lack of disciplinary authority, expertise in investigations, and insufficient investigative personnel. This article suggests future directions for Korean sports organization's response to sports violence: First, a system should be established to effectively promote relevant policies established based on strict standards. Second, an education system that able to maximize the effectiveness of education on eradicating sports violence is needed. Third, effective sports governance should be established to eliminate the current overlapping roles of different organizations. Fourth, efforts should be made to ensure transparency in the process of addressing violence in sport.

Keywords: Violence in Korean sport; Sport Ethics Center; Korean Sport & Olympic Committee; human right; policy response; sports organization

INTRODUCTION: WHY IS THE ROLE OF GOVERNANCE IMPORTANT TO END SPORTS VIOLENCE IN SOUTH KOREA?

A Student-Athlete's Story of Being a Victim of Sports Violence: Two Issues to Consider

> When I was in middle school, I had a coach who was disciplined for violence, and then a few years later, he came back after the discipline was over. When he came back, he didn't use violence, but he made it hard for us in other ways. We talked about it amongst the athletes. I would rather he just hit me. He is bullying us too much.

A few years ago, I interviewed a university student-athlete on human rights. I discovered that the interviewee was a victim of violence featured in a Korean TV documentary program on sports violence. The program showed a coach's serious physical violence and verbal harassment against student-athletes. The coach in the TV documentary used his position of power within the athletic association to coach students through the inhumane tool of violence (and criminal behavior).

According to the student-athlete interviews, the coach was violent toward the athletes not only during training but also in everyday life. After the program was released, disciplinary action was taken against the coach, who did not coach for several years thereafter. About three years later, he returned to work as a coach at another school under the same foundation. While he did not use physical violence, he used corporal punishment through harsh behavior. Student-athletes who experienced this said they would rather be hit, as in the quote above. This shows that many student-athletes are exposed to a culture of violence, and it is surprising that they internalize the culture of violence within athletic teams as their own culture (Kim & Kwon, 2019; Terry & Jackson, 1985).

The above cases were at least seven to eight years old, so they may not be representative of the culture of violence in Korean athletics today. Recent data show that the culture of violence and violent behavior in Korean sports has declined to some extent. However, the problem is that remnants of this violent culture persist in athletic teams. Therefore, the culture of violence in Korean sports is not just a thing of the past but a problem that needs to be addressed in the present.

These examples of student-athletes experiencing a culture of violence raise some questions. First of all, this chapter should reflect on why a culture of violence, which has always existed in some Korean sports clubs, occurs. And we must critically reflect on the Korean context in which coaches who use violence against students could return to coaching.

Reasons for a Culture of Violence in Sports: Power Inequality and Acquiescence

First, this chapter discusses why a culture of violence occurs in sports yet. Since the 2000s, there has been an increase in societal interest in human rights in sports, which has led to a significant decrease in the prevalence of violence in sports, both intentional and unintentional (Jeon & Kwon, 2021; Korean Sport and Olympic Committee, 2018). However, the scars of the past remain, with more than one-tenth of all athletes still exposed to a culture of violence in sports. From a sociological perspective, violence in sports is triggered by excessive power. This culture is perpetuated when those who are supposed to check this power is silent and tolerant of it for the sake of a shared goal (Lim & Kim, 2021; Roberts et al., 2020). With the shared goal of improving performance and the acquiescence of other actors in the athletic team, the leader commits violence, and the leader's authority to commit violence is gradually transferred to seniors, creating a hierarchical culture of violence in the athletic team (Breger et al., 2019; Ko et al., 2006).

This culture of violence in athletics is often tolerated by parents and others with the shared goal of improving athletic performance, which further consolidates the power of coaches. This is particularly true when coaches influence athletes by providing access to higher education and recruitment. It can be argued that the coach in the above case was able to use violence openly because the other players tolerated and acquiesced to the coach's unauthorized power to achieve a shared goal among the players, which was to attend a better school (Solstad, 2019).

Violence appears in sports teams due to the misguided culture governing them. In other words, a poorly formed athletic culture manifests itself as violence. If the mainstream culture of student-athletes is steeped in violence, then the few student-athletes who resist the culture of violence must exist as nonconformists. Previous studies have shown that athletic violence is reproduced through cultural norms. There is a vicious cycle of victimization in athletic cultures. Even student-athletes who believe that violence is wrong may conform to and internalize the culture of violence and become perpetrators of violence in the name of disciplining their peers and classmates (Kim, & Kwon, 2018; Ohlert et al., 2021).

Why Does Sports Violence Repeat Itself in South Korea: Structural Issues

Next, this chapter explores how a coach who commits a violation serious enough to be featured in the media, as in the case above, can return to coaching with impunity. We can assume that the coach was able to return because there was a conspiracy to trivialize the perpetrator's behavior and give the coach the benefit of the doubt. In addition, victims may have turned a blind eye (or forgiven the perpetrator) because of the influence of the coach, hoping to move on to a better school, improve their performance, and so on. Likely, the sport's governing body and the athletic association with disciplinary authority over the coach may have used the coach's influence and connections to provide a rationale for the coach to return to the sport field. These flawed organizational responses and procedures appear to have been driven by a closed culture within the sport that has long been implicit and the perception that sports violence is a necessary evil and acceptable to improve performance (Lim et al., 2019; Roberts et al., 2020).

The perpetrator could return to coaching students because of the weak management system of the sport, the lenient perception of sports violence in Korean society, and the culture within sports organizations where covering up has become a virtue. From 2014 to 2019, the Center for the Reporting of Sports Misconduct handled 349 cases of physical and sexual violence, of which 132 (38%) were suspected of improper handling. Furthermore, 28 cases (8%) were delayed for more than one year without any special reason. In addition, the survey results indicated that, in many disciplinary cases, the sentencing criteria were arbitrarily changed for reasons that are difficult to understand (Sports Human Rights Task Force, 2020).

On the other hand, the notion that the complainant may face harm has brought attention to the prevalent sports violence culture (Cho, 2021). Moreover, during the period ranging from 2014 to 2019, only 1,026 incidents of human rights violations were reported to public institutions, schools, and sports organizations (Sports Human Rights Task Force, 2020). Given that the statistical proportion of athletes experiencing violence in comprehensive usually exceeds 25%, it appears that only a minuscule fraction of student-athletes disclose incidences of human rights violations like violence to external entities surveys (Korean Sport and Olympic Committee, 2018; National Human Rights Commission, 2019a, 2019b).

Now that violence in sport has become a social issue, Korean sports decision-makers need to consider about who should actively approach the problem. The lack of public trust in the eradication of violence within sport society in the past, the argument that Korean sports stakeholders alone can solve the problem internally may be perceived as somewhat unreasonable. It is mainly because the Korean sports community has not shown a clear solution of its own problem (Lee, 2019; Oh, 2020). However, the argument that people involved in sports area should be excluded from the problem-solving discussion because the closed culture of the Korean sports community has created a negative culture, such as the culture of violence in sport, as some people say, is also a somewhat unreasonable misreading of the current situation. In this context, I think that the role and leadership of sports organizations is the solution to overcome the culture of violence in sport. They have real power over internal management and can be the optimal structural point of contact to receive help from outside the world of sport. In other words, the right response to sport violence by sport organizations can be a key point to change the existing negative culture of sport violence and closed sport structures.

POLITICAL ACTION TO END SPORTS VIOLENCE

The Ministry of Culture, Sports, and Tourism's Policy Response to Incidents of Sports Violence

Over the past two decades, academia and media have engaged in discussions on the elimination of violence in sports. The death of elementary school soccer players in a fire in a locked dormitory in 2003 drew attention to athletes' human rights, creating a significant social issue. This sports human right case led to an increased awareness of the rights of students and other athletes. In 2005, the Korean Sport & Olympic Committee conducted a large-scale survey on violence in sports (Korean Sport and Olympic Committee, 2005). The survey report revealed that 78.1% of athletes had experienced various forms of violence, such as verbal and psychological violence, beatings, and harsh treatment, thereby indicating the prevalence of such incidents in Korea's elite sports structure, which favors meritocracy. Policymakers have implemented several strategies to address this issue (Hong, 2019).

From 2008 to 2021, the Ministry of Culture, Sport, and Tourism has made efforts to improve human rights in sport, combat corruption in sport, and eliminate violence in sport (Kim, 2020).

Governments have issued policies to address violence in sports and the human rights of athletes since the mid-2000s (see Table 5.1). In the early 2000s, the issue of violence and sexual assault against athletes became a public concern, and the media began to cover the issue extensively. In 2008, the government announced a plan to eradicate sexual violence in sport to address the problem of violent sexual violence in sport. In 2012, the government announced policies against organizational irregularities and match-fixing as well as sexual violence in sports, and in 2013, it announced comprehensive plan centered on the establishment of governance (centers, punishment standards, management systems, etc.) to eradicate violent sexual violence in sports. In 2014, the government identified match-fixing and illicit admission, unfair judgments, violence and sexual violence, and organizational privatization as the "Four Evils of Sports" and proposed a system improvement plan to eradicate those.

Although these efforts have improved the problem of violence and sexual violence in sports to the certain extent, the government is still very concerned about the human rights of athletes. Therefore, it has promoted various policies from 2014 to 2021. In particular, the Sports Ethics Center was established in 2019 to comprehensively investigate and discipline ethical issues related to sports. It is worth noting that the government has attempted to address social issues related to sports violence and sexual violence, which had been mainly addressed by the Korea Olympic Committee (KOC), through an independent organization, the Sports Ethics Center. The government seems to have placed expectation on the internal self-regulation of the sports sector so far. However, the government's willingness to implement the project through the Sports Ethics Center reflects its recognition of the need for external monitoring and management (Lee et al., 2022; Nam & Yoo, 2020).

Despite these measures, the incidence and perception of sports violence remain unchanged. In addition, it is disappointing that remedial measures are predominantly announced after a major social issue, such as a postmortem visit which has already occurred. These measures appear rushed and aimed at silencing negative media rather than being part of a proactive, step-by-step eradication policy.

The government's role as a control tower is key to eradicating sports violence (Sam et al., 2023). The policies of South Korea have been characterized by top-down rather than bottom-up policymaking, so it is imperative that government agencies such as the Ministry of Culture, Sports, and Tourism, which is the

Table 5.1. Policy on the Elimination of Human Rights Violations in Sport (Kim, 2020).

Year	Policy	Action Plan
2008	Measures to end sexual violence in sport	• Permanent bans for sexual assault leaders • A quota system for female coaches
2013	Measures to eradicate sports violence to create an environment for enjoyable exercise	• Expanding the scope of support for sports human rights centers (disabled and professional athletes) • Establishing disciplinary sentencing standards for each sports organization and applying the zero-tolerance principle • Establishment of a coach registration management system (including disciplinary history) and sharing of disciplinary information between sports organizations
2014	Plan to establish and operate a reporting center for the four major sports evils	• Four major evils in sports (match-fixing and biased judgment, (sexual) violence, entrance examination irregularities, and organizational privatization) • Reporting and handling
2014	Measures to prevent sexual violence in sports	• Expanding sexual violence prevention education and conducting (gender) violence surveys • Establishment of regional centers of the Sports Human Rights Interest Center by region • Promoting a deregistration system for coaches
2016	Measures to prevent athlete violence	• Strengthening disciplinary action against coaches for (sexual) violence - Suspension of qualification for one year or more
2019	Measures to eradicate irregularities in athletics such as (sexual) violence	• Establishment of the Sports Ethics Center (an independent agency dedicated to sports irregularities) • Establishment of legislation on mandatory reporting of (sexual) violence cases • Establishment of human rights counseling center and deployment of female managers in National Training Center
2019	Recommendation to establish a protection/support system for victims of sexual violence in sports and a complete reform of the system for responding to human rights violations by the government and the sports industry	• Review and joint consultation by the Ministry of Education, Ministry of Culture, Sports and Tourism, and Ministry of Gender Equality and Family • Establish an organization to promote human rights and gender equality in sports • Establish a legal basis and secure human resources and budgets
2021	Measures to eradicate violence in school sports and improve human rights protection in sports	• Ministry of Culture, Sports and Tourism and Ministry of Education • Establish principles and standards to ensure that perpetrators are held accountable and that victims can achieve true healing • Victim-centered investigation/resolution of past incidents • Establishment of a shared database of sports violence incidents • Improving the evaluation system that leads to sexualization

highest level of government, make responsible policies with the right direction. On the other hand, if the government adheres to an excessively government-led top-down approach and fails to properly grasp the opinions of the field and related stakeholders, it may result in policy fail (May et al., 2013). For example, in South Korea, "the Sports Innovation Council" was recently established to promote national sports innovation. The Council proposed various directions related to the human rights of athletes, including the elimination of violence in sport and corruption in the sports sector, but the lack of consensus among key stakeholders, including athletes, on the recommendations significantly weakened the momentum of the policy.

Korean Sport & Olympic Committee's Policy Response to Incidents of Sports Violence

In addition to governmental improvement measures, the Korean Sport & Olympic Committee, which oversees overall sports support, has addressed sports violence through various policy responses. As previously stated, the organization initiated a survey in 2005 to assess the status of sports violence. Since then, regular surveys have been carried out and information gathered to implement policies aimed at eradicating violence in sport and promoting the human rights of athletes. Based on the main survey results, 78.1% of Korean athletes experienced sports violence in 2005, followed by 51.6% in 2010, 28.6% in 2012, 32.2% in 2014, 26.9% in 2016, and 26.1% in 2018. Incidents of violence encompassing psychologically (verbal) and physically abusive experiences decreased sharply until 2012, followed by a gradual decline in violence in sport (Korean Sport and Olympic Committee, 2018). This finding implies that although several sports-related organizations have made efforts to increase awareness of violence in sports since 2005, there is a pressing need for a fresh policy approach to uproot the culture of violence prevalent in sports.

In response to the 2005 survey, the Korean Sport & Olympic Committee established its own Athlete Protection Committee and Athlete Grievance Center. In 2008, it enhanced its efforts by creating a specialized department aimed at preventing sexual violence. The Sports Human Rights Center was founded and operates as an action-oriented institution committed to eradicating violence in sports. The Sports Human Rights Center functioned as a venue for lodging complaints related to enhancing the human rights of athletes, with a focus on sports violence. As emphasis was placed on the significance of sports violence prevention education, the Center's operations as a resource for human rights education were also set into motion (Kim et al., 2015).

In addition, the Korean Sport & Olympic Committee has produced a set of guidelines and manuals that may be valuable for professionals in this domain. For instance, the organization created and circulated guidelines for the prevention of (sexual) violence against athletes, specifically targeting athletes, coaches, and parents. In addition, a manual was developed to help coaches solve sports violence issues. The "Athlete Guidance Manual for Improving Sports Human Rights" was produced in 2012 to highlight the significance of coaches in establishing a sports environment that respects human rights. The guidance highlights the importance of leaders playing the roles of educators, counselors, and managers in creating a sports environment that upholds human rights. Customized guidance methods are then presented, specific to each sport (county), to improve human rights in sports, along with tailored guidance for various situations, such as training, competition, and accommodation. Additionally, effective athlete management methods have been outlined (Korean Sport and Olympic Committee, 2012). The manual strives to enhance the sports culture by providing comprehensive and useful direction to leaders. However, its practicality in the field may be slightly constrained, as it does not fully consider the distinct characteristics of different sports.

Although the efforts of the Korean Sport & Olympic Committee to eradicate sports violence have produced some degree of success, the issue has not been fully resolved. Furthermore, critiques of the NOC's reaction to past instances of sports violence indicate the need for a separate, autonomous entity. The Sports Ethics Center, an independent organization dedicated to protecting the human rights of athletes and fostering a fair sports environment, was established in 2021. Subsequently, policies aimed at eliminating violence in sports, previously promoted by the Sports Human Rights Center and the Clean Sports Center in Korean Sport & Olympic Committee, were transferred to the Sports Ethics Center. The Sports Ethics Center is taking diverse measures to eliminate violence in sports through its increased jurisdiction.

The Sports Ethics Center reports, counsels, and educates on sports rights and misconduct. However, the Korean Sport & Olympic Committee, local athletic associations, and Sports organizations by sport have the right to discipline and reward athletes. Each organization's sports fairness committee predominantly exercises authority. If the Korean Sport & Olympic Committee receives a disciplinary recommendation from the Sports Ethics Center or a reporting agency, it transfers the case to the provincial sport's governing body where the incident occurred, except in cases deemed serious or urgent. Furthermore, the sport-specific organization decides whether to take disciplinary action against the national team (Sports Human Rights Task Force, 2020).

In 2020, a report from the Sports Human Rights Task Force highlighted that the Sports Fairness Committee of the Korean Sports Council abides by rigorous processing standards and systems but frequently fails to implement them in practice. The report notes that the Sports Fairness Committee and other organizations within provincial sports councils lack clear standards and only provide one-time punishments and responses. In addition, most members of the Sports Fairness Commission are appointed by influential decision-makers in sports organizations, which limits their ability to ensure independence and impartiality (Sports Human Rights Task Force, 2020).

The effectiveness of policy implementation decreases with each passing week when institutions that play a key role in solving problems fail to perform their roles and gain the trust of the society (Lehtonen et al., 2022). In Korean society, the distrust of sports organizations is quite serious. Whenever there is a social problem related to sport, the Korean Sport & Olympic Committee is often blamed for the problem. Not only that, but many people mistrust the process of solving problems when they arise. This is because Korean sports organizations have often shown themselves to be collectively deviant. Instead of properly punishing those who should be disciplined for nepotism, academic and regional connections, Korean sports organizations have operated in a closed culture, tacitly defending their vested interests. Therefore, instead of monitoring and punishing sports violence through a representative organization (Korean Sport & Olympic Committee), the government wanted to create and operate an organization that could play a role independent of vested interests in the sports sector.

However, despite the negative perception of existing sports-related organizations, this does not mean that an independent body that exclude sports sectors is the answer. The Korean Sport & Olympic Committee has done a lot of work and should be recognized for its efforts. It could also have considered establishing an organization or committee that could play an external role while creating a political climate to eradicate sport violence from within the sport sector. In this context, it can be argued that the policy is problematic in that it attempts to address the issue of violence in sport and human rights through extreme rather than integrated policies (Harvey & McNamee, 2019). With the Sports Ethics Center now up and running, coordinated cooperation with the Korean Sport & Olympic Committee and effective governance, the results of the efforts to eliminate violence in sport could be further expanded.

The National Human Rights Commission's Efforts to End Sports Violence

In addition to the Ministry of Culture, Sports, and Tourism and the Korean Sport & Olympic Committee, the National Human Rights Commission has been active in addressing human rights violations in sports, including violence. In 2009, the National Human Rights Commission conducted a survey on the human rights of athletes (focusing on learning rights, violence, and sexual violence among middle and high school student-athletes), which played an important role in raising awareness of the culture of violence prevalent in the sports. In 2010, it developed and disseminated the "Sport Human Rights Guidelines" and the "Sport Human Rights Charter," which can serve as standards for the promotion of human rights in sport (National Human Rights Commission, 2009, 2010a, 2010b).

In 2019, a special survey on the human rights of student-athletes in elementary, middle, and high schools is conducted to understand the current human rights situation in sports. In total, 14.7% of elementary, middle, and high school student-athletes have experienced physical violence; 33% and 31% of university student-athletes have experienced physical violence and verbal violence, respectively; and 33.9% and 15.3% of unemployed athletes have experienced verbal violence and physical violence, respectively. These findings indicate that adult-athletes can also be victims of sports violence (National Human Rights Commission, 2019a, 2019b).

In 2019, the National Human Rights Commission, together with the Ministry of Education, the Ministry of Culture, Sports, and Tourism, and the Ministry of

Gender Equality and Family, established the Special Investigation Team on Human Rights in Sports to conduct a large-scale investigation into cases of violence and sexual violence in sports. Based on its findings, the National Human Rights Commission made the recommendations to the government and sports organizations (Sports Human Rights Task Force, 2020). First, the need for an independent organization to protect human rights in sport was underlined. The recommendations of the National Human Rights Commission in 2019 served as the reference point called for stronger disciplinary action in cases of human rights violations, which had been promoted in previous policies. In particular, it called for the establishment and promotion of concrete measures to protect the human rights of student and professional athletes.

In addition, the National Human Rights Commission conducted a study on the revision of the Sports Human Rights Charter/Guidelines to revise the contents of the Sports Human Rights Guidelines and the Sports Human Rights Charter, which were established in 2010, so that they can serve as more practical standards (National Human Rights Commission, 2021). In addition, the Study on Case Analysis and Remedies for Sexual Assault/Violence Cases in Sports provided guidance on viewing cases of sexual assault or violence that occur during sports.

The efforts of the National Human Rights Commission to eliminate violence in sport have been very significant in terms of raising public awareness of the issue. It is also very positive that it has approached violence in sport as a human rights issue in our society, not just as a problem within sport, and has made various efforts to improve it. However, the focus on the human rights aspect of the program went too far and did not consider the specificities of the sports policy environment. It is also problematic that the focus on the human rights aspect of the issue tends to exaggerate past human rights problems as current problems, despite the fact that many studies have shown that there have been significant improvements over the past 20 years.

SPORTS ETHICS CENTER AS A RESPONSE SYSTEM TO SPORTS VIOLENCE: FUNCTIONS AND LIMITATIONS

The Role of the Sports Ethics Center in Addressing and Preventing Incidents of Sports Violence

In 2019, the National Human Rights Commission investigated human rights violations such as violence and sexual violence in sports and recommended the establishment and operation of an independent organization that can effectively respond to incidents of sports violence and sexual violence, pointing out insufficient personnel and facilities for victim relief, an inefficient system for handling human rights violation cases, and an inadequate victim protection system in the case investigation process (Sports Human Rights Task Force, 2020). A Sports Ethics Center was established against this institutional background. The Sports Ethics Center was established under Article 18 of the National Sports Act to protect athletes' human rights and promote sports fairness, including the eradication of sports violence and sexual violence (Nam & Yoo, 2020).

The Sports Ethics Center is an organization established and operated with the goal of eradicating sports violence, sexual violence, and sports corruption. With the slogan "Not first, for human rights," the Sports Ethics Center strives to raise awareness of sports corruption among participants, officials and workers in the sports facilities, as well as the public. Specifically, the Center investigates corruption and human rights violations in sports and provides comprehensive psychological, emotional, and legal support to ensure that perpetrators are punished and victims recover.

The role of the Sports Ethics Center in combating corruption in sport is as follows (Sport Ethics Center, 2023). First, the Center receives and investigates reports of corruption and human rights violations in sports and provides assistance to victims. It conducts reports, receptions, and investigations on sports irregularities and human rights violations in general and demands measures such as disciplinary actions from responsible and relevant organizations based on the results of the investigations. It also strives for follow-up management, such as checking the status of the implementation of follow-up measures and plays a role in the eradication of corruption in sports by providing counseling and legal support services to victims of human rights violations and liaising with external professional organizations. Specifically, the Sports Ethics Center runs a system of sports human rights monitors (human rights defenders) who can monitor and advise on the human rights situation to eradicate human rights violations and irregularities in sports. It runs a training course for professional instructors in sports human rights education, including sports violence prevention, so that sports human rights education can be carried out systematically and efficiently.

Second, the Sports Ethics Center makes efforts to investigate irregularities and human rights violations in the sports industry in order to improve the system. It raises awareness of sports ethics and human rights through the deployment of expert personnel and contributes to the improvement of related policies and institutions through the investigations of sports irregularities and human rights violations.

Third, it conducts educational and promotional activities to prevent sports irregularities and human rights violations. It provides education on the prevention of human rights violations and irregularities in sports and develops educational content in cooperation with experts. It also produced and distributed various promotional and educational materials and conducted promotional activities in professional and everyday sports competitions. In particular, we have recently launched a compulsory education course for the prevention of sports violence (Sports Ethics Learn Program) and are working to promote the training of physical education coaches, retraining of physical education teachers, and education on violence prevention, including sexual violence.

Fourth, it operates a disciplinary information system to prevent the recurrence of human rights violations in sports. Through the disciplinary information system, it strives to establish a disciplinary history management system to effectively manage and punish sports misconduct.

As mentioned above, it is necessary to carry out projects with different approaches and perspectives to ensure fairness in sports and protect the human rights of athletes, and the Sports Ethics Center is making significant efforts to achieve its goals at the forefront of ensuring fairness in sports and protecting the human rights of athletes.

Reporting, Counseling, and Investigations at the Sports Ethics Center

Reports received by the Sports Ethics Center will be investigated, and the complainant will receive comprehensive medical, emotional, psychological, and legal support following counseling. Reports may be made through various methods, including email, website, telephone, and mail; in some cases, the Center may provide counseling services without a report. Reported incidents will be investigated and subject to a decision by the Review Committee unless the case is suspended or resolved during the investigation. The outcome of the decision will be categorized as caution, reinvestigation, or dismissal; based on the outcome of the deliberation, disciplinary action will be requested through the Ministry of Culture, Sports, and Tourism, or a complaint will be filed with an investigative agency. After the case is handled, the status and implementation of the measures taken in the case are checked, and victim support is monitored.

As of October 26, 2021, there were 82 cases of sexual violence; 256 cases of violence; 186 cases of human rights violations such as harassment, bullying, and excessive training; and 15 other cases. In terms of corruption, there were 32 cases of organization privatization, 58 cases of embezzlement and misappropriation, 17 cases of match-fixing, 9 cases of admission irregularities, and 485 cases of other types of corruption, with embezzlement, misappropriation, and organization privatization being the most common. Looking at the number of consultations and reports, the total number of consultations was 927, with 563 consultations related to human rights violations and 364 consultations related to sports irregularities, and the total number of reports was 400, with 163 cases of human rights violations and 237 cases of irregularities. The total number of reports and consultations on sports irregularities was 1,327. Thus, an average of four to five people per day are reported and received by the Sports Ethics Center (Sport Ethics Center, 2023).

When examining the number of reports and complaints received by the Sports Ethics Center, it is clear that the number of reports is very low compared to the size of the Korean athlete population. According to the recent 2023 Sports Human Rights Violations Survey (Sport Ethics Center, 2023), 4% to 10% of Korean athletes experience physical or verbal violence, and even if we simply extrapolate this percentage, the number of reports is very small. This shows several problems with the Korean sports culture/environment that hinder the eradication of violence in sports. Firstly, it shows that there is a general fear of reporting and that it is taboo to report a teammate or leader in the culture of the sport. This closed culture is a major reason why athletes experience sports violence and do not receive adequate help from responsible authorities. Another issue is the mistrust that athletes have of the relevant organizations. Athletes have seen time and again that the organizations involved in eradicating violence in sport have failed to do their job. As the interviewee mentioned in the introduction, there have even been instances of coaches being disciplined for violence and then returning to work with impunity. This has caused athletes to lose trust in the organizations involved. In the future, any organization that aims to eradicate violence in sport will need to work to build trust in the organization.

Limitations of Sports Ethics Centers as a Response System to Violence in Sports
As an active response system to violence in sports, the Sports Ethics Center should perform very important roles and functions. To avoid following in the footsteps of organizations with similar functions that have been operated by organizations such as the Korean Sport & Olympic Committee and the Ministry of Culture, Sports and Tourism, it is necessary to clearly understand what society expects from Sports Ethics Center and to diagnose the limitations of the organization. Sports Ethics Center must strive to play the role of a contact zone where all necessary human and material resources can be concentrated to eradicate violence in sports, regardless of whether the world is sports or non-sports (Jamieson & Orr, 2009). In this regard, the Sports Ethics Center is expected to provide an opportunity to eradicate human rights violations and corruption in sports, which have existed in a closed structure, through the operation of an independent dedicated organization.

Through investigative power, the Sports Human Rights Center can request the submission of materials deemed relevant to the investigation of a case and conduct on-site inspections or appraisals of venue facilities or materials related to the case (Nam & Yoo, 2020). In particular, since the Sports Ethics Center is independent of other organizations, it is considered more advantageous in terms of ensuring fairness than organizations that have previously performed similar functions (Sports Human Rights Center and the Clean Sports Center in Korean Sport & Olympic Committee, etc.). However, since the Sport Ethic Center does not have direct investigative powers, and its investigative power is insufficient compared to the size of the case and the target population, it is expected that overcoming these limitations will be key to determining the effectiveness of the Sports Ethics Center.

The Center can play a significant role through its power to bring charges against investigative agencies and demand disciplinary action. However, the lack of disciplinary authority is a limitation of the center. Once a request for disciplinary action is made through the Ministry of Culture, Sports, and Tourism, it is up to the Korean Sport & Olympic Committee or the Sports Fairness Commission of each sports organization to make the final decision on whether to impose actual discipline. In this case, even if the level of punishment is deemed inappropriate, there is no institutional mechanism to enforce or sanction it, so the "disciplinary recommendation" of the Sports Ethics Center may be only a disciplinary recommendation. Therefore, additional institutional measures are required to effectively address this issue.

Besides, there are concerns about the professionalism of the investigations. To investigate human rights violations in sports, including sports violence, it is necessary to quickly secure evidence and judge the reasons for their occurrence. In other words, a practical and effective investigation requires expertise in the investigation itself and on-the-ground expertise that can help understand the closed culture of sports organizations and identify problems. Unfortunately, the number of professionals with the necessary expertise to investigate cases at the Sports Ethics Center remains limited.

CONCLUSION: FUTURE DIRECTIONS IN RESPONDING TO INCIDENTS OF SPORTS VIOLENCE IN SPORTS ORGANIZATIONS

Efforts by organizations such as the Ministry of Culture, Sports, and Tourism, the KOC, and the Sports Ethics Center are urgently needed to effectively prevent sports violence and establish a system for actively responding to incidents. To ensure these organizations can effectively eradicate sports violence, it is necessary to accurately identify the problems and limitations of the current response methods (policies, etc.) to sports violence and, based on this, to establish a response direction that can fundamentally solve the problem of sports violence. In this context, the presenter would like to conclude the manuscript by offering opinions on the problems with the existing response to sports violence incidents and the direction of the response of sports organizations to eradicate sports violence in the future.

The future directions of organizational responses to sports violence incidents can be summarized as follows. First, while many plans to eliminate sports violence have been developed with relatively strict criteria, the willingness of institutions/organizations to implement them seems very low. As mentioned, institutional responses to sports violence have focused primarily on removing social condemnation after an incident has occurred, and it is disappointing that they have been unable to establish a step-by-step plan from a medium- to long-term perspective.

Second, while most measures to prevent sports violence have focused on education, actual education tends to be somewhat formalized. The content and methods of training for eliminating and preventing sports violence should be more practical. Developing guidelines and manuals on human rights in sports and incorporating them into on-the-job training programs is also necessary. As for the content of the training, it should be improved in such a way that it not only promotes the understanding of the prevention and elimination of sports violence but also raises the awareness of human rights in sports, including sports violence, and enhances their skills as actors in the sports field.

Third, the roles of the institutions and organizations involved in the prevention of sports violence are fragmented and overlapping. Currently, there have been some improvements, with the Sports Ethics Center playing a central role as a dedicated institution. However, to eradicate sports violence, it is necessary to establish cooperative governance among government ministries such as the Ministry of Culture, Sports, and Tourism, Ministry of Education, Ministry of Gender Equality and Family Welfare, Korea Sports Federation, Korea Disabled Sports Federation, National Human Rights Commission, and local athletic association, to establish an effective and systematic response system to eradicate and prevent sports violence (Sam et al., 2023).

Fourth, sports-related organizations lack transparency in responding to sports violence. As mentioned earlier, the establishment and operation of the Sports Ethics Center was based on the belief that it would ensure impartiality in responding to incidents of sports violence. This is because previous organizations with similar roles have responded to sports violence with methods and procedures that have been difficult for officials and the public to understand. In other words, the existing similar institutions have lost social trust because they have not ensured fairness in the process of responding to incidents of sports violence. Therefore, sports organizations, including the Sports Ethics Center, should transparently operate all procedures in response to incidents of sports violence and establish a system to win public trust by operating institutional measures to control and monitor them.

FIVE KEY READINGS

Harvey, A., & McNamee, M. (2019). Sport integrity: Ethics, policy and practice: An introduction. *Journal of Global Sport Management, 4*(1), 1–7.

This article highlights the importance of integrity in the management of sport organizations/governance. As an introduction to the *Journal of Global Sport Management*'s special issue on "Sport Integrity: ethics, policy and practice" and this article argues that "integrity" should be on the agenda when promoting sport policy. The papers in the special issue will help you understand the imperative for sport organizations to practice integrity.

Donnelly, P., Kerr, G., Heron, A., & DiCarlo, D. (2016). Protecting youth in sport: an examination of harassment policies. *International Journal of Sport Policy and Politics, 8*(1), 33–50.

This research argues that policies created in response to incidents of abuse against athletes are not working well on the ground. The human rights policy implemented by SPORT CANADA has been adopted by many Canadian sport federations. However, the paper questions the practical effectiveness of this policy, which is somewhat at odds with the direction of the original SPORT CANADA policy and argues that it should be reviewed in the future.

Lee, W., Hannun, D., Choi, Y., & Park, J. (2022). The Olympic movement and safeguarding athletes: Exploring South Korea's journey to protect athletes. *The International Journal of the History of Sport, 39*(3), 308–323.

This study critically examines South Korea's policy on human rights in sport as part of the IOC's Olympic movement. In the same context as the body of this chapter, it presents the efforts, achievements, and limitations of the government and the Korean Sport & Olympic Committee. This study provides a deeper understanding of the socio-structural complexities of implementing sport integrity in the Korean circumstances.

Nam, K., & Yoo, S. (2020). The legal and institutional improvement for establishment of Sports Ethics. *Dankook Law Review (DLR)*, *44*(4), 165–190.

The researcher argues that before the establishment of the Sport Ethics Center in Korea, sports organizations with similar mandates were in operation, but their achievement was somewhat inadequate. Therefore, the researcher proposes the appropriate operation of the Sport Ethic Center and related policies to expand the value of integrity in sports in Korea.

Sam, M., Stenling, C., & Tak, M. (2023). Integrity governance: A new reform agenda for sport? *International Review for the Sociology of Sport*, *58*(5), 829–849.

This study explains the importance of "integrity" as a critical agenda for sport policy and proposes the establishment of an integrity system. It examines the process by which sport integrity has been established as a new national agenda based on Australia and New Zealand ad examples. This research will provide insights into what it means to have sport integrity as a major agenda at the national level.

REFERENCES

Breger, M. L., Holman, M. J., & Guerrero, M. D. (2019). Re-norming sport for inclusivity: How the sport community has the potential to change a toxic culture of harassment and abuse. *Journal of Clinical Sport Psychology*, *13*(2), 274–289.

Cho, S. (2021, December 20). Athletic discipline? The perpetrator will take a break and come back. *HanKook-ilbo*. https://m.hankookilbo.com/News/Read/A2021121018550001454

Harvey, A., & McNamee, M. (2019). Sport integrity: Ethics, policy, and practice: An introduction. *Journal of Global Sport Management*, *4*(1), 1–7.

Hong, D. (2019). Innovation in sport, a challenge for society. *Sport for Us*, *21*, 29–33.

Jamieson, L. M., & Orr, T. J. (2009). *Sport and violence: A critical examination of sport*. Routledge.

Jeon, W., & Kwon, G. (2021). A study on the alteration in the perception structure of violence culture for school athletic club instructor: Based on men's judo. *Korean Journal of Convergence Science*, *10*(3), 94–112.

Kim, D. (2020). 100 days of the centre for sports ethics and the way forward. *Sport Issue and Analysis*, *3*, 1–6.

Kim, S., Jwon, W., & Lim, S. (2015). The occurrence and basis of sexual violence in elite sports and research of its experience system. *The Korean Journal of Physical Education*, *54*(6), 81–94.

Kim, H., & Kwon, S. (2019). Team identity formation and commitment of student-athletes. *The Korean Journal of Physical Education*, *58*(1), 17–28.

Ko, E., Lee, H., Kim, Y., & Jang, D. (2006). *Survey for violence in sport*. Korea Institute of Sport Science.

Korean Sport and Olympic Committee. (2005). *2005 Survey for Violence in Sport*.

Korean Sport and Olympic Committee. (2012). *Athlete Guidance Manual for Sports Human Rights*.

Korean Sport and Olympic Committee. (2018). *2018 Survey for (Sexual) Violence in Sport*.

Lee, J. (2019). Policy response to sports sexual violence accidents and introduction of punitive damages system. *The Korean Association of Sports and Entertainment Law*, *22*(2), 131–152.

Lee, W., Hannun, D., Choi, Y., & Park, J. (2022). The Olympic movement and safeguarding athletes: Exploring South Korea's journey to protect athletes. *International Journal of the History of Sport, 39*(3), 308–323.

Lehtonen, K., Kinder, T., & Stenvall, J. (2022). To trust or not to trust? Governance of multidimensional elite sport reality. *Sport in Society, 25*(11), 2250–2267.

Lim, S., & Kim, H. (2021). Sports, social problems, and sociology of sport: The challenges and possibilities of sociology of sport for social problems. *Korean Society for the Sociology of Sport, 34*(1), 63–79.

Lim, S., Kim, H., Kim, M., & Pak, S. (2019). Experience of anger target and response type of athletes. *Journal of Wellness, 14*(1), 209–218.

May, T., Harris, S., & Collins, M. (2013). Implementing community sport policy: Understanding the variety of voluntary club types and their attitudes to policy. *International journal of sport policy and politics, 5*(3), 397–419.

Nam, K., & Yoo, S. (2020). The legal and institutional improvement for establishment of Sports Ethics. *Dankook Law Review, 44*(4), 165–190.

National Human Rights Commission. (2009). *A Survey on the Human Rights of Athletes*. https://www.humanrights.go.kr/base/board/read?boardManagementNo=17&boardNo=590558&searchCategory=23&page=1&searchType=total&searchWord=%EC%9A%B4%EB%8F%99%EC%84%A0%EC%88%98&menuLevel=3&menuNo=115

National Human Rights Commission. (2010a). *Sport Human Rights Guidelines*. https://www.humanrights.go.kr/site/program/board/basicboard/view?menuid=001003001003003&searchselect=boardtitle&searchword=%EC%8A%A4%ED%8F%AC%EC%B8%A0%EC%9D%B8%EA%B6%8C&pagesize=10&boardtypeid=17&boardid=7605338

National Human Rights Commission. (2010b). *Sport Human Rights Charter*. https://www.humanrights.go.kr/site/program/board/basicboard/view?menuid=001004002001&boardtypeid=17&boardid=7605337

National Human Rights Commission. (2019a). *Amateur Adult Athlete Human Rights Survey*. https://www.humanrights.go.kr/base/board/read?boardManagementNo=17&boardNo=7604962&searchCategory=&page=1&searchType=total&searchWord=%EC%84%A0%EC%88%98&menuLevel=3&menuNo=115

National Human Rights Commission. (2019b). *Student-Athlete Rights Survey*. https://www.humanrights.go.kr/site/program/board/basicboard/view?boardtypeid=24&boardid=7604726&menuid=001004002001

National Human Rights Commission. (2021). *Study to develop a Sport Human Rights Charter Guideline*. https://www.humanrights.go.kr/base/board/read?boardManagementNo=17&boardNo=7607762&searchCategory=23&page=1&searchType=total&searchWord=%EC%8A%A4%ED%8F%AC%EC%B8%A0&menuLevel=3&menuNo=115

Oh, J. (2020, July 06). I've been aware of sexual violence in the sports world, but… The complacent response. *Kukie News*. http://www.kukinews.com/newsView/kuk202007070001

Ohlert, J., Vertommen, T., Rulofs, B., Rau, T., & Allroggen, M. (2021). Elite athletes' experiences of interpersonal violence in organized sport in Germany, the Netherlands, and Belgium. *European Journal of Sport Science, 21*(4), 604–613.

Roberts, V., Sojo, V., & Grant, F. (2020). Organisational factors and non-accidental violence in sport: A systematic review. *Sport Management Review, 23*(1), 8–27.

Sam, M., Stenling, C., & Tak, M. (2023). Integrity governance: A new reform agenda for sport? *International Review for the Sociology of Sport, 58*(5), 829–849.

Solstad, G. M. (2019). Reporting abuse in sport: A question of power? *European Journal for Sport and Society, 16*(3), 229–246.

Sport Ethics Center. (2023a). *Homepage*. https://www.k-sec.or.kr/front/main/main.do

Sport Ethics Center. (2023b). *2023 Sports Human Rights Violations Survey*. Southern Post.

Sports Human Rights Task Force. (2020). *Recommendations to Governments (Including Sports Organisations) to Improve Human Rights Protection in Sport*.

Terry, P. C., & Jackson, J. J. (1985). The determinants and control of violence in sport. *Quest, 37*(1), 27–37.

CHAPTER 6

ATHLETE ACTIVISM IN SOUTH KOREA: LIMITATIONS AND CHALLENGES

Seongsik Cho

Hanyang University, Republic of Korea

ABSTRACT

Athlete activism has developed along with movements for human rights protection and promotion in Western societies. There have been many voices, active behaviors, and social movements that oppose and resist sexism, racism, or homophobia in society and sports. Unlike such sociopolitical occasions in the United States and European countries, neither strong voices nor active behaviors and organized movement against discrimination have existed in Korean society. Recently, incidents of violence at training facilities or athletes' dorm resulted in government policies centered for anti-violence. Structural factors limiting the outbreak and development of athlete activism were analyzed and discussed, including the conservative and authoritarian physical culture, the athletes' lack of awareness of social issues in sports, and the absence of governmental policies to combat and end sexism, racism, and homophobia in sports. Finally, this chapter explores several challenging plans to overcome structural constraints and build up, promote, and develop athlete activism in Korea as follows: First, it is to increase opportunities for student athletes to develop social awareness by normalizing their education and school life; second, it is to abolish the regulations that restrict student athletes graduating from high school to PE/sports/kinesiology major departments of universities; third, it is to greatly expand athletes' social networking and increase their social power. Finally, the chapter argues that the development of athlete activism protecting and promoting athletes' human rights can be an important turning point for Korea to leap forward as a sport democratized and advanced country.

Keywords: Athlete activism; sexism; racism, and homophobia in sports; conservative and authoritarian physical culture; athletes' social awareness; sports policy

Start where you are, use what you have, do what you can. (Rick, 2016, p. 36) Arthur Ashe (American Tennis Player, Gland Slam Champion, Civil Rights Activist)

INTRODUCTION

A tsunami of athlete activism developed along with the American civil rights movement. As both the Black civil rights movement and the feminist movement developed into mainstream social changes, the human rights movement in sports was expressed as athlete activism (Doehler, 2022). That is, athlete activism has been in parallel with the development and promotion of civil rights even though the activism was lagged. As social movements aimed at the abolition of discrimination by gender, race, and sexual orientation have spread across the United States and Western Europe, athlete activism has become part of the collective trend. However, South Korea has had a different story regarding gender, race, and sexual minority, so social movements have not been as active as in the West. There were hardly any dissenting voices from athletes, and there was no collective action at all. Sporadically, there used to be athletes' verbal reactions to violence in sport settings happening around training facilities or athletes' dorm and disabled athlete activism for equal access to sport facilities (Choi et al., 2021). Government policies in Korea have been largely prepared and implemented to prevent violence in sports rather than sexism, racism, and homophobia in sports, or to promote the equal opportunity of sport participation for disabled athletes and people (Ministry of Culture, Sports and Tourism, 2022a).

Athlete activism is strongly related to the social awareness, democratic thoughts, and resistance consciousness of the athletes which are formed through school education and school life (Armstrong & Butryn, 2022). And it is associated with the sociocultural and educational structure and the philosophy and directions of government policy. This chapter introduces and discusses the social, cultural, educational, and political mechanisms that act as limitations to the development of athlete activism and explores the challenges needed for the future growth and development of athlete activism in Korea.

THE CONSERVATIVE AND AUTHORITARIAN PHYSICAL CULTURE

There have been two main dominant cultures in Korea which greatly influence the sport environment and continue to be deeply reflected in the sport culture. One is conservatism, and the other is authoritarianism in physical culture (Nam, 2020; Park, 2018). Korean society has been conservative about gender and race because of its long-standing patriarchal Confucian tradition and the pure-blooded belief of one single ethnic group so that male-superior practices and xenophobia have been powerfully maintained and preserved (Lee et al., 2021; Yuh, 2016). There are some popular proverbs about women which are very sexist but are still shared about among people; "when a woman gets married, she must be deaf for three years and must be mute for three years" (meaning that a woman must be patient when living with parents-in-law); "a woman's fate is tied to her husband"; "when the hen crows, the family is ruined" (meaning that women should not have a voice in the house); "a woman has a good fate in life when she does not know the market day of her village" (meaning that a woman is happy when she lives inside the house without knowing about the outside society) (Yoo, 2019). These conservative and sexist prejudices against women have been strongly working against women's participation in sports and their active roles in sports organizations.

A recent national survey shows that 31.7% of women have never participated in physical activities, as compared to 27.3% of men even if there have been strong campaigns for women's sport participation from public sectors including government, sport organizations, and sport agencies (Ministry of Culture, Sports and Tourism, 2022b). And women's sporting activities are very passive, simple, short, and unorganized; 49.4% of women who answer "I do participate in sports on a regular basis" are primarily involved in walking and running, while the proportion of men is only 25.0%; women's average exercise time is 104.6 minutes per each participation, while men do the exercise for 149.2 minutes; women's average monthly expenditure on sport participation is 65,837 KW, while men's expenditure is 87,750 KW (Ministry of Culture, Sports and Tourism, 2022b). Despite the growing number of women on the Korea Olympic Committee (hereinafter KOC), only 25% of members in 2023 are women, while 41% of International Olympic Committee (IOC) members are women. Among the 30 KOC commissions, two chairs are female, that is, only 6.7% are women while 14 of the IOC commissions, 42.4% are led by female chairs (IOC, 2024; KOC, 2023a).

Gender discrimination is found in many sports. For instance, there is a big difference between men's and women's players in daily allowances for the national soccer team; women's daily allowances (50,000KW, approximately US38$) are half that of men's (100,000KW); women's flight seat class was economy, but recently only some players have sat in business class while all male players continue to use business class (Yoon, 2015). The article title of one newspaper is "Korea Football Association closed their eyes and plugged their ears: Women's national soccer team players play their games for half the money than men"; "why discriminate against women's national team?"; "what is the Korea Football Association doing for women's soccer?" (Do, 2022) These discriminatory practices are often covered by female reporters, not male counterparts who are reluctant to write such articles and even if male reporters try to do, it is not easy to be published as an article. Of course, it seems to be impossible for female soccer players to speak out at all (Kim, 2016).

Given the women's "poor" involvement in sports and less active and less powerful roles in sports politics, feminist-oriented athlete activism is very difficult to generate and develop, and thus no strong voices and movements toward female athletes' equal rights and treatment have existed. The few women with decision-making powers are highly dependent on male power structure so that they are likely to keep an eye on male-majority counterparts or male superiors who have the power to appoint and dismiss. The status quo of male dominance in sport has been unquestionably maintained and preserved. The voices and actions against sexist practices are not supported, are considered as causing trouble and face opposition and even retaliation from existing structures in which male dominance and superiority have been regarded as natural, traditional, and unchallenged (Schmidt et al., 2020). In the absence of such a challenging effort for gender equality from female leaders' side and under the male dominance of sport organizations, it is very difficult for young female athletes even to raise the questions about gender inequality. Hence, no activism led by female athletes has emerged. Many female leaders in sports are assimilated into dominant male-superior practices, and even they don't like feminist voices and actions. There have been only occasional media articles and coverage about gender inequality in sports (Do, 2022; Doo, 2021).

The authoritarian physical culture, heavily influenced by Confucianism, has been working against (female) athlete activism. It has particularly emphasized hierarchy by age and positions (Park, 2018). Sports administrators and those in positions of power are much older than athletes. They greatly dislike the phenomenon of sports becoming a site for gender-political struggles, and for power conflicts between athletes and coaches or between athletes and sport governing organizations (Chung & Won, 2011). They still believe that sports should be free from politics, arguing that fighting is only in the arena, not on the street (Platt, 2018). The influential people in sports organizations sometimes intentionally have ignored political issues around gender because they believe that the status of women's sport and athletes' human rights are improving, and progress will be ultimately made toward achieving gender equality and the promotion of human rights (Kim & Lee, 2023). They are likely to subscribe to views of evolutionary change for gender equality in sports rather than a fundamental reformation to solve the problem of gender discrimination. And they try to avoid the sports world becoming a site for power struggles and conflicts with the existing sport structures deeply rooted in conservatism and authoritarianism. However, potential for change is on the horizon. The authoritarian rule, which has been maintained for 32 years since its creation in 1988, has been eliminated: The KOC and Korea Sports Council in 2020 deleted the clause that "the national team athletes must obey the instructions and orders from coaches" which specified training guidelines for athletes (Do, 2020). The obligatory rule of "obedience" to the coaches' order was a typical symbol of authoritarian physical culture in Korea and a major obstacle to the protection and promotion of athletes' human right. Unfortunately, it wasn't until 2020 that the clause belatedly ended. This shows the reality of sport human rights and justice in Korea and that athlete activism still seems far away and almost impossible in Korea.

The cultural conservatism in Korea in relation to race and ethnicity is centered on mono/homo-nationalism which is based upon the ideology of pure bloodedness within only one ethnic group (Cho et al., 2017; Kim, 2020). It often manifests itself as a xenophobic phenomenon, especially toward Black people or people from Southeastern Asian countries (Cho et al., 2017; Mulyaman & Ismail, 2021). Xenophobia in sport settings have worked for racial prejudices and discrimination against Black athletes who are playing in Korean professional leagues including basketball, baseball, and volleyball (Cho, 2010). When a Korean player's racist behavior occurs, Korean fellow players tend to ignore rather than criticize it or make an issue. In this case, the conservative collectivism among Koreans of the same blood works stronger, so there is no such thing as criticizing each other among Koreans (Chung, 2023). That is, some Koreans believe that chauvinism including racial prejudices is a type of patriotism or nationalism which is strongly promoted through sport environment (Ward & Denney, 2022).

One famous Korean former professional baseball player (A) appeared on an internet radio broadcast and joked about one Black pitcher; "his face is so dark that when he smiles on the mound, his white teeth overlap the ball, so it's hard to hit" (Kim, 2013). Some fans filed complaints to the National Human Rights Commission, claiming that A's comments were racist. The Commission concluded that A's statement is a racist remark and that the club and league should make every effort to prevent various human rights violations. The Commission asked that to prevent similar incidents recurring in the future, education for players and staffs is necessary. He apologized for his remarks, but there was no sanction or punishment from the club and the league. The Korea Baseball Organization's reaction reveals the challenge: The PR manager of the KBO described A's remarks as a "joke", hence there were no plans to warn the players and the team, or to provide education to prevent recurrence (Chung, 2023). Because A admitted that he made a mistake and the National Human Rights Commission decided not to investigate, the baseball community saw the crisis as over. Despite many in the media, including headlines, describing A's comments as "racial discrimination", there was no outcry from the teammates of the Black pitcher. The media criticized the team and the league for their indifference and irresponsibility (Chung, 2023; Kim, 2013).

Black players in a professional basketball league would face racist comments on social media networks. One Black player who became a Korean through naturalization received aggressive racist statements on the internet (Chung, 2020). However, there was almost no active criticism from fellow Korean players. A few Korean players asked fans to refrain from such racist behavior, but there were no organized voices and actions from players against racism. Korean athletes generally demonstrate strong collectivism and solidarity, but they do not exist beyond race or seem very weak between different races when fellow Black players face racism on the court or off the court; the sense of collectivism and solidarity among Korean athletes strongly works with only Korean athletes. The sense of comradeship among players is also strong, but it is difficult to find any unified comradeship on racial issues; many Korean players do not accept any kind of racist comments and behaviors from fans or other players, but they are reluctant to send counter-messages to them and don't protest verbally and physically against racism. The Korean Basketball League prepared a legal response to an aggressive internet attack but then failed to actually proceed with the lawsuit

(Lim, 2020). The League seemed to want to minimize sensitive racial issues by responding passively or only verbally to attacks. Perhaps the team or the league might think that the punishment for racist acts was considered a punishment imposed by Koreans on Koreans rather than punishment for wrongdoing. They believe that players or fans are of the same ethnicity, family, and customers, so both team and league prefer moderate methods such as persuasion and enlightenment rather than strict sanctions and punishment for their racist behavior. When the problem of racial discrimination occurs, the conservative cultural dogma of the same, homogeneous, and pure-blooded ethnic group acts strongly. Political conservatism is overworked because it doesn't like to see racial discrimination issues become political issues (Kim & Jeon, 2017). And when teams and league with power and authority remain silent, it seems that players are not allowed to speak out and protest collectively. Even speaking out against injustices is regarded as preventing the sport from growing in popularity or harming the sports organizations because the conservatism in physical culture values the group as a whole much more than the individual (Watanabe et al., 2017). In the world of Korean sports, the sacrifice of the individual – not to speak out, not to act – is accepted as unavoidable for the sake of the preservation and benefit of the group (Tan, 2015). In these situations, opportunities to initiate and participate in athlete activism against racism are very limited.

Regarding race and sexual orientations, the Korean Government and public sport agencies have not paid attention to issues of discrimination. In 2019, KOC declared the charter of human rights management: Article 5 in the charter is "To not discriminate in employment because of gender, religion, disability, age, social status, or place of origin" (KOC, 2019). There are no words of ethnicity, race, and sexual orientation at all, revealing that conservatism is much greater in the sports realm than in other realms; there is discomfort about inserting the word "race" or "sexual orientation," and it seems that the issue of sexual minorities is not even brought up. The cultural conservatism like patriarchy, racial prejudice, and homophobia has been produced, reproduced, and maintained through sports in Korea. Athlete activism is a movement that rises from the bottom up by athletes, but the prevalence of conservatism and authoritarianism has made it difficult to even start the activism and has tended to make criticism and opposition to discrimination difficult.

ATHLETES' LACK OF AWARENESS OF SOCIAL ISSUES IN SPORTS

In Korea, most student athletes in elementary and secondary schools had attended morning classes and missed afternoon classes for practice and training until the late 2000s when their full attendance was required. On game days, they missed the entire classes without any make-up and tutoring. Athletes were expected to give all their attention to athletics rather than class performance, and thus they had no choice but to neglect school classes. Student athletes' school lives centered around gymnasium, field, training camp, or athletes' dormitory, and they always saw the slogan banners hanging in the gymnasium, and athletes' training camp and dorm ("Failure is the mother of success," "No pain, no gain," "Our great challenge for victory continues," "Blood and sweat must be rewarded," or "Let's not give up to win") (Eo, 2023; Lee, 2011). Student athletes were expected to devote all their efforts and energy to sports. Even their school class assignments were waived because schools and teachers had already acknowledged that student athletes could not study properly. As a result, it was difficult for student athletes to have opportunities to develop sufficient body of knowledge and social consciousness, and to dialogue and discuss with peers (Myung & Chung, 2019).

This phenomenon is due to the special sports structure of Korea which makes it easy to go to college or become a professional athlete if student athletes focus only on sports. As of 2023, Korea has a population of 51 million; there are only 26 high school men's basketball teams, only 12 college teams in division 1, but 10 professional teams which is a relatively large structure, and only 23 high school men's volleyball teams, only 15 college teams, but 7 professional teams. There has been a very high probability that a high school player receives an athletic scholarship at college without meeting the academic minimum requirements. And in basketball and volleyball, the odds of first-division college players being drafted into a professional league range from 40% to 50% (Cho, 2015). Women's basketball and volleyball are structured to go to professional league immediately after graduating from high school, so high school academic records are not required at all. To become a professional player in Korea is not structurally tough and student athletes don't have to think about other alternative career paths besides their sports. Both student athletes' parents and coaches also think that it is much better for the kids to make all their effort and pour all their energy on the court than in the school classroom. This Korean elite sport structure is called as "all-in sports," "very few elite athletes" and "academic abandonment" types (Cho, 2015). Compared to the population size of Korea, there are the very small number of high school and college sports teams, which means that only a small number of elite athletes are involved in sports at highly competitive levels, and they put everything into sports and their sport career. Today college student athletes must meet a minimum 2.0 GPA to be eligible for participation in competitions, but it is common for professors to help student athletes maintain their athletic eligibility and qualifications by lenient grading rather than strict evaluations based on objective standards.

In this sporting structure, it is difficult for student athletes to receive a general education, gain a strong foundation in the knowledge of humanities and social science, be aware of social problems around them, and raise awareness of social issues in sports. Student athletes' mission is to dedicate all of their efforts to success on the field. If gender and racial issues happen in their sports, student athletes might think that it has nothing to do with themselves at all, so they don't have to pay attention to such issues. The training camp system throughout the season which had been maintained for a long time in Korean secondary school and college sports has worked as an obstacle to the development of student athletes' knowledge, social consciousness, and understanding of social realities (Lee, 2011). During training camp, student athletes are treated as semi-professional athletes whose interests are only training and practicing, and they lose the opportunity to encounter the academic environment and to raise and develop the awareness of social issues (Myung & Chung, 2019). In Korea, most male collegiate athletes live together in athletes' dorm for four years so that they eat three meals a day together and play together for their leisure time while sharing a room with three or four fellow student athletes. Within this athletes' dorm culture, it is very difficult for student athletes to form a deep interest in and awareness of social issues including discrimination against female athletes, nonethnic Korean athletes, or sexual minority athletes. Rather, they cultivate a sense of homogeneity with each other as a man, as a Korean, or as a mainstream heterosexual. They tend not to have diverse ideas about the issues about gender, race, or sexual minorities; some student athletes think that the issues regarding gender, race, or sexual minorities have nothing to do with "my athletic career." Finally, they tend to ignore the problems and issues about discrimination in sports.

Limiting high school athletes to PE/sports/kinesiology major departments in college becomes another factor blocking their cultivation and development of social awareness about social problems. When high school student athletes enter college, they don't have the right to choose a department major they wish to enter and are assigned only to PE/sports/kinesiology departments by government regulation. This system is based upon the myth that it is easy for student athletes to combine athletics and studies together once they enter PE/sports/kinesiology departments and that they cannot properly perform their academics in any major other than PE or sports. However, a strong athletic identity within PE/sports/kinesiology departments can lead to negative influence on their academic performance and experiences (Foster & Huml, 2017). Student athletes are not allowed to study science and engineering as a major and cannot major in psychology, philosophy, history, sociology, politics, journalism, economics, or business which many college students study. All their courses are the ones opened by PE/sports/kinesiology departments in which professors tend to give generous grades for their student athletes who need to remain eligible to participate in competitions. Because student athletes cannot study various majors, it is very difficult for them to have the opportunity to acquire diverse knowledge, to expand their view of society, and to develop the awareness of social issues.

Social awareness is seen as an ability that includes leaning into others' perspectives with curiosity, recognizing and acknowledging the inherent strengths in others, demonstrating empathy and compassion, showing concern for the feeling of others, identifying diverse cultural and social norms, recognizing situational demands and opportunities, and creating and promoting a just and caring community (California Department of Education, 2023). During student athletes' college years, their habitus is limited to PE/sports/kinesiology department classrooms, gymnasium, field, and athlete's dorm without receiving academic advice and tutoring. In such spaces, they follow old conservative practices and authoritarian traditions like status quo, age hierarchy, male dominance, and racial and homophobic prejudices rather than being exposed to a range of new ideas and trying new challenges for a society where human rights regardless of gender, ethnicity, race, and sexual orientation will be strongly respected (McGregor, 2022). That is, they have been in an unfavorable environment for forming and developing critical social perceptions and thoughts. Moreover, there are few people around student athletes, who can help to inspire their awareness of social problems and work with them toward solutions. The Sport NGOs in Korea are focusing their jobs and work only on anti-violence in sport and monitoring sports organizations and government policy; the mission of Civic Network for Justice in Sport, a leading prominent sport nongovernmental organization (NGO), is to conduct monitoring activities to ensure the transparency of sport organizations, increase sporting people's human rights (only focusing on activities to prevent athletes from being subjected to violence), and monitor and evaluate government sport policies (Civic Network for Justice in Sport, 2023). The philosophy of the Network is to build the sports world where justice is realized, but there have been no active activities against gender and racial discrimination, and homophobic practices in sports. Given the lack of social awareness among student athletes and the absence of outside help, it seems very difficult for athletes to demonstrate compassion with disadvantaged athletes, and protest sexism, racism, or homophobia in sports through which their fellow athletes are unfairly treated and suffer.

ABSENCE OF GOVERNMENT POLICIES TO COMBAT AND END DISCRIMINATION IN SPORTS

Sports in Korea have always been developed under government policies and initiatives. Since more than 70% of the money for most sports governing bodies and agencies is procured from government budget and public funds like the sport promotion fund, the government has strong power over sport organizations and agencies. Once the government's sports policy is established, sports organizations are structured to align their activities with the government policy. The Sport White Paper published annually by Ministry of Culture, Sports and Tourism includes the increase of sport participation for the underprivileged and the disadvantaged, the advancement of athletic department operation in schools, and the prevention of unethical problems in sport (Ministry of Culture, Sports and Tourism, 2022a). In this government policy, the social alienated groups just include the lower economic class youth and the elderly over 65, not referring to the ethnic minorities or gay people. The improvement for student athletes is centered on anti-violence and their regular class attendance while the policy doesn't cover the action plans for eliminating sexism and racism in school sports. The unethical issues in sport focus on the personal privatization of sports organizations, violence (including sexual violence), corruption in college admissions, and match fixing but the policy doesn't include the education of social awareness about discrimination in sports. The Sport Ethics Center established for the protection of athletes' human rights pays attention to anti-corruption in sports organizations, anti-illegal sports betting, bribing the referee, and anti-fraudulent entrance to the university rather than any antidiscriminatory activities in sports settings (Sport Ethics Center, 2023). That is, the missions of the Center, to ensure fairness in sports and protect human rights, are far from eliminating and abolishing discrimination in sport and establishing fairness aiming for equality regarding gender, race, and sexual orientation. Moreover, the sport policies of the Korean Government related to the athletes' human rights have focused only on both preventing violence and guaranteeing student athletes' right to attend classes in school. Even though they have some action plans about women, children, and youth from multicultural families, the plans are primarily based on promoting the increase in sport participation; public sport clubs and facilities opening more programs for women and young people with both foreign parents, or one foreign parent (Ministry of Culture, Sports and Tourism, 2022a). It doesn't include a strong policy to combat and end sexism, racism, and homophobia around sports environments.

Why doesn't the government policy even declare the elimination of discrimination in sports? There are three possible answers. First, there is no awareness among government policy makers for formulating feminist-friendly policies, anti-racism policies, or even gay-friendly policies which are strongly related to the protection and improvement of human rights in sports (Ahn, 2022; Choi & Seo, 2020; Kim & Jeon, 2017; Lee et al., 2021). Also, even if they know on a personal level that there is discrimination in sports regarding gender, race, or sexual minority, they are reluctant to move to policy formulation and implementation under the strong conservative society. That is, there are big discrepancies between personal and institutional levels. The Korean Government has a ministry for woman, entitled the Ministry of Gender Equality and Family; its main missions for woman include creating policies and action plans to employ more women, prevent sexual and domestic violence, and prevent prostitution; the Ministry doesn't have concrete action plans to prevent gender discrimination in labor markets, educational institutions, or sports settings (Ministry of Gender Equality and Family, 2023).

Second, implementing policies such as elimination of discrimination is seen as admitting that there are many unequal cases involving gender, race, and sexual orientation in Korea. In a situation where the treatment and social status of women and other ethnic groups has improved in society for the last 2–30 years, and severe discrimination against them is gradually disappearing, the government does not feel the need to prepare and publicize explicit anti-sexism, anti-racism, or gay-friendly policies and takes a passive stance on issues and problems arising from discrimination (Kim & Jeon, 2017). There is a big difference between knowing that discrimination is bad and taking action to end it. In Korean society where patriarchy and racism still strongly exist and heterosexuality is regarded as natural and absolute, the Korean Government is hesitant to take the lead in creating and implementing antidiscrimination policies. The government considers the conservative positions held by most of the population on gender, race, and LGBTQ issues. And it hopes that such a social problem is not a big issue and will be easily resolved.

Another reason for the absence of such policies appears to be a political calculation. There are two dominant political parties in S. Korea, the conservative versus the liberal. But both parties declaratively oppose to gender discrimination against women, but they are unable to establish concrete action plans for the elimination of gender discrimination in society (Ahn, 2022). In Korean society, most men, and women in their 40s and older, do not sympathize with the feminist movement, and even some young women consider it radical and do not follow it. Even on the issue of race, people say that racial discrimination is bad, but they have a passive attitude toward an abolitionist policy and penalizing discrimination. In fact, punishment for racial discrimination is also very light. Since Koreans are an ethnically homogeneous nation and value pure-bloodism, the prejudices against foreigners, especially people with darker skin tones, have been strong (Cho et al., 2017). Because the proportion of foreigners residing in Korea (migrant workers from Southeast Asia, foreign students, permanent residents, etc.) among the whole population is only around 4% (more than 95% of the population is one-ethnic Korean), the political parties are burdened with formulating and implementing strong antidiscrimination policies (Yuk, 2016). That is, there is a political calculation that if the party puts forward a strong policy against gender and race discrimination as a major policy of party, it will lose more votes than gain. And in a society where the compulsory heterosexual culture has been strong, it is very difficult for major political parties to come up with policies for sexual minorities like LGBTQ people (Han, 2016). Since the political sectors in Korea don't raise the issues of discrimination against gender, race, and sexual minorities, government policy is indifferent to fighting over these issues and ending discrimination. Accordingly, sports organizations tend to ignore the issues of sexism, racism, and homophobia in sports. Finally, the absence of policies caused by political sectors' indifference and ignorance has been becoming a great limit to the birth and development of athlete activism.

INCREASED OPPORTUNITIES FOR STUDENT ATHLETES TO DEVELOP SOCIAL AWARENESS

Entering the 21st century in S. Korea, social discourses on guaranteeing the right to education for student athletes developed, and from the mid-2000s, active discussions and policy development about the protection of their right to a meaningful education appeared as a key governmental sport policy. As a result, a system was established to regulate and reduce both the training time and the number of days student athletes participate in competitions ensuring that student athletes had sufficient time to attend classes (Lee & Choi, 2018). Many national tournament events which require a lot of travel time and many class absences were eliminated and the league-based regional game operating on weekends was introduced (Cho, 2009). Today, most high school games are held on weekends and during the summer and winter breaks for regional competitions, which allows student athletes to shorten the travel distance and time and enables them to attend as many school classes as possible.

College athletics have been greatly changed; many tournament events were also abolished, and the league-based game operation was implemented to play games in college fields or gymnasiums through which travel time to participate in games was eliminated or largely shortened. And the games are mostly held after 5:00 p.m. on weekdays, minimizing student athletes' loss of classes (Chang, 2010). Some colleges have tried to open as many major courses as possible in the morning rather than in the afternoon and ensure that student athletes can do their athletics while focusing on their academics. When selected as a national team member for Olympics, Asian Games, or World Championship events, they receive a training camp for several weeks at the national training center to prepare for such competitions. If the training camp is held in the middle of semester, however, student athletes might miss classes for a long time. In this case, several PE/sports/kinesiology majors and GE classes are opened within the training center, and they take some classes intensively in the evening and get credits (Korea University Sport Federation, 2023).

Many students have found the status of a true "student athletes" from the long time in the past "athlete students" by balancing between studying and training/competing and combining academics and sports as student athletes (Kim, 2022; Lim, 2023). As a result, today many student athletes attend classes normally and regularly at school and have school lives similar to that of their fellow students. This means that the potential opportunities for student athletes to form and experience basic and general social awareness have increased. In other words, the possibility that student athletes have such a perception and consciousness through their normal school life has increased. Being able to have education and experiences as similar as possible to other students during school years seems that the minimum basic conditions for student athletes to form and develop social awareness have been prepared (Hoffman et al., 2015).

College student athletes take sport social science courses and sport humanities courses offered by PE/sports/kinesiology departments and regularly attend classes because training is scheduled after 3:00 p.m. or because games are held after 5:00 p.m. or intensively during breaks. In classes, they carry out tasks such as class discussions and team projects with PE/sport/kinesiology major students and students with different majors. While most PE/sports/kinesiology departments have reduced major PE skills courses, they have designated internship, sport sociology, sport history, or sport philosophy as required major courses and have newly opened sport marketing, sport and the media, legal issues in sport, sport policy and globalization of sport as electives courses. By taking such courses, student athletes will have ample opportunity to face new knowledge and approaches to sports and society, and greatly expand their epistemology and social awareness about sports in society (Brown et al., 2018). Discussions and joint team projects with other students in a range of majors provide student athletes with new challenges and perspectives that student athletes have never experienced before. These new things help student athletes to form and develop their awareness of social issues and problems related to their athletics of which they were previously unaware. As student athletes come to focus on a range of issues in sports and become aware of the macroscopic society and ideologies related to sports, they may attempt to try a critical approach, experience a critical thinking, and develop their insight about sports and society (Humberstone, 2009).

Recently, many universities are strengthening humanities and social science literacy education to all students including student athletes, and this will also help student athletes to form social awareness which is a basic condition for athlete activism. The philosophy and policy of university emphasizes that most courses are designed to challenge students' existing knowledge paradigm, foster their creative and critical thinking, and apply their critical knowledge to social development, so each class includes the content of critical thinking requirements and practical application for better society (Moore, 2011). If student athletes are more exposed to environments conducive to shaping and developing 'critical' social awareness and consciousness than ever, they are likely to be involved in athlete activism when they or their fellow athletes are treated unfairly or discriminated against because of gender, race, sexual orientations, or any other reason.

ABOLITION OF REGULATIONS TO RESTRICT STUDENT ATHLETES TO PE/SPORTS/KINESIOLOGY MAJOR DEPARTMENTS

South Korea has a unique but discriminatory policy that has restricted high school athletes from going to college only to PE/sports/kinesiology departments. This regulation is undemocratic, greatly limiting student athletes' freedom to pursue knowledge, diverse campus life, and career choices. More than 50% of student athletes drop out of sports while in college, but they must continue to be affiliated with PE/sports/kinesiology departments and neither major change or nor department transfer are permitted (Nam, 2020). In Korea, where the labor market in the field of sports is very narrow and limited, students who quit athletics midway through can't go beyond the field of PE or sports, get a bachelor's degree in PE/sports/kinesiology, and go to find work in a fiercely narrow sport market. A significant number of student athletes, who focused on only athletics in middle and high school and made every effort to athletics after entering college, work as personal trainers in the fitness centers after college graduation because the training methods are a valuable acquired capital for them. As many former athletes and PE/sports/kinesiology college majors work in this small market, however, wages are depressed as the market has an artificially increased labor supply. It is a structure where a lawyer, an engineer, or a medical doctor is not a possible choice for a student athlete. Some student athletes want to continue their study of PE/sport/kinesiology majors or change to interesting new majors, so they can think about going to graduate school. But it is not an easy career path for them who spent a long time in the field or gym and were constrained by PE/sports/kinesiology major boundary; their attempt to pursue other majors is greatly restricted (Nam et al., 2018).

There have been social discourses that student athletes should be given various career options and pathways. The KOC, the leading public sport governing organization, started career support services and vocational education for retired athletes. The KOC opened the career service portal site for athletes, e-center for career support, and is offering a variety of job competency training programs like sports administration, video analysis, asset management, etc. and educating young middle school athletes about their future (KOC, 2023b). However, most career development services are about the field of sports and education programs for retired athletes are basic level, such as vocational preparation education and office skills improvement. Even though they have limitations in providing various social preparation experiences to retired athletes and helping athletes or retired athletes build up social awareness, the KOC's athlete career support project has positive outcome in that it provides new experiences and communications with various fields to retired athletes or young athletes.

Both high school athletes and college athletes should be able to pursue their studies in various subjects and majors while playing sports. They should have the opportunities to think about social issues and problems in sports and to share their diverse thoughts and experiences surrounding sports with various students (Nam, 2020). So, they can pursue their career journey in diverse fields other than sports. When this happens, it is possible for athletes to develop different critical perspectives through their diverse studies, majors, and careers. It is a basic condition for starting to engage in activism and developing activism. If the policy restricting admission to the department of PE/sports/kinesiology is abolished, high school student athletes will have the opportunity to explore a range of career options in college departments, and they will try to think more broadly and deeply about society, making it possible to form social awareness. Student athletes belonging to different departments in college will experience the social, cultural, and academic diversity of the university and have a more active awareness of social issues. There will be no hesitation in developing a critical eye for inequality and discrimination in the world of sports, and athletes will be deeply involved in and taking legitimate action to solve the problem for social justice.

GROWING SOCIAL NETWORKS OF ATHLETES

Many athletes used to build social networks or social relationships with their fellow athletes or fans by sharing their personal and athletic lives and activities in/off the field. Some athletes can speak out, address, and spread their voices and opinions about social issues through Twitter, Instagram, Facebook, or different social network services. Even if an athlete has few followers on social media, it can cause a huge wave and impact if they share the injustice or discrimination cases they have experienced. That is, regardless of the number of followers, an athlete's social media can be fully developed as a social accusation when talking about their experiences of discrimination on social media (Kluch, 2021).

Most people either tend not to share their "bad" experiences like being discriminated against or share them with family member or close friends on social media. In other words, rather than sharing them with many people, some people share them privately with family or close friends. Although the number of people to share with is limited, this use of social media has the meaning of expanding the problems from the personal level to the social level. In the early stages, people tend to be patient when face with such problems and then try to solve the problems on a personal level through family meetings or conversations with friends. The start of activism is made when problems are shared with others at the personal level through social media and the development of activism is greatly expanded when it is transferred to the organizational, political, and legal institutions with the help of families and close acquaintances who have social awareness and consciousness against discrimination (Nam et al., 2018). Due to the routine use of social media and the ease of networking, athletes are more likely to discuss with significant others social injustices they or fellow athletes have experienced and then to share the problems with someone at the institutions.

Some athletic departments of university and sport governing organizations restrict athletes' SNS activity. In Korea, the athletic department of university does not officially regulate the SNS activities of student athletes, but there are unofficial and strong restrictions on content uploaded to SNS. In other words, it is good to upload good news freely, but to refrain from uploading content criticizing organizations and institutions or content that creates social repercussions for the world of sport; even if the contents are about the athlete or what their fellow athletes suffered, there are difficulties in uploading it. In this respect, Instagram or Facebook where many of followers can see the uploaded contents have their limits, but KakaoTalk as a mobile message app most used by Koreans, which has strong personal and relatively selective networking, can become a first step at the institutional level of networking about athlete activism in Korea (Ha et al., 2015). Although it is shared at the personal level, it is sufficiently shared, discussed, and examined at the social level and become a social issue when it is a problem related to human rights violations.

The growth of athletes' social networking means that the power of athletes and their organizational power, which seemed to be trivial, are increasing. Social media has changed the landscape and has become a powerful tool to bring about solidarity, particularly when it comes to athlete activism for social justice (Kluch, 2021; Platt, 2018). Growing social networks of athletes serve as powerful forums where athletes and other people at institutions can discuss and debate challenges for equality and promote action steps for social justice (Sanderson et al., 2016). In the past, the only option was to quietly endure discrimination because their power was weak, but the increased power of athletes through online networking provides diverse and ample options to resist discrimination. The fear of retaliation from the existing power is reduced, and the willingness to protect universal values such as the promotion of human rights and equality in sports is strengthened through expanding networking and resource mobilization while athletes receive support from outside people like civil activists, politicians, lawyers, and civil society people (Nam et al., 2018; Yan et al., 2018). Even if athletes' awareness of protest and activism is not sufficiently formed, athlete activism can occur and develop because social consensus on protest, resistance, and activism is created. Sports fans, more than any other group, view problems from the side of the athletes, so when this networking spreads to fans as well, athlete activism emerges and develops quickly as soon as problems arise.

CONCLUSION

From the perspective of social movement in Korea, the labor movement has been more active and radical than other movements. On one hand, the feminist movement and the anti-racism movement which are related to athlete activism are relatively weakly developed, and the equality movement for sexual minorities is also weakly developed and has been met with a lot of strong conservative reactions. In Korean society, where such social movements are not sufficient to have an influence, athlete activism has been bound to have many limitations. The conservatism and authoritarianism are much stronger in sports fields than in other areas. Sexism and male dominance in sports were easily tolerated and preserved as a long-standing practice in the absence of feminist protest. Cultural chauvinism, often glorified as nationalism, was also easily protected in the sports world, whereby racist practices were produced, maintained, and reproduced and penalties for discriminatory acts against people with darker skin tones were not severe at all. The compulsory heterosexual culture has been maintained and reinforced more strongly around the conservative religious world, including Christianity, whenever the LGBTQ movement occurs and coming out as a gay person requires enormous sacrifices. It has been very difficult for athlete activism to be created, organized, and developed in such Korean society.

For student athletes who do not have enough education and normal student life to form and develop social awareness, athlete activism is bound to be unfamiliar and viewed as a story that only exists in the West. When much space and time in life are limited to the field, gym, camp, and athletes' dorm, it has been very difficult to meet any conditions for athlete activism to occur and develop. The 'athlete-students', not 'student-athletes', focus on only improving athletic performance and winning the games and don't pay attention to social issues in sport. The government's policy has greatly increased the consciousness and action against violence in sport, but the absence of government policy to eliminate sexism, racism, and homophobia in sports has served as a limit to the development of athlete activism. The Korean Government tends to pay attention to conservative public sentiment on issues of gender and racial inequality and homophobic problems. Making political calculations, the government does not implement an active antidiscrimination policy, but verbally declares the words, "human rights protection and promotion" with a passive attitude. As sports governing bodies and organizations follow government policies and are dependent on government power, they don't have any active action plan for antidiscrimination in sports.

Three challenging tasks for the development and vitalization of athlete activism were presented. First, it is to restore the correct identity of student athletes; academics are first, and athletics are secondary. Student athletes will have a similar experience to other students at school, enjoy a normal school life and journey on normal life while having many opportunities to think about social problems as well as social justice in sports. And then they will try to find a good way to solve the problems and reinforce justice. The second is to change the government policy by allowing student athletes to choose their major when entering college. Confining student athletes to PE/sports/kinesiology departments is a very unreasonable idea and restricting academic freedom. The "right to learn" of athletes emphasized by the government is not limited only to attending school class but must include the freedom to choose a major when entering college. Athletes belonging to various departments will have diverse experiences and communications in college life, and their careers after graduation become as diverse as nonathletes' paths. In this process, student athletes will be likely to have a deep interest in social issues and problems around sports and enjoy a lot of opportunities to seek solutions to them. The third task is to increase the social networking of athletes. Athletes are often hesitant to post on social media the problems they and their colleague badly experience. They become afraid of counter-reaction and retaliation. However, an increase in network leads to athletes' increase in social power and a decrease in fear, ultimately by eliciting the support from public opinion and other significant people. And finally, it will play an important role in bringing about antidiscriminatory action plans.

Athlete activism is no longer the exclusive phenomenon of Western sports world. It is a universal necessary activity and social movement for all athletes regardless of sex, ethnicity, race, age, ability, and sexual orientation. Korea shows excellent results in international sports events such as the Olympics, but not so well in the human rights of athletes. Korea should not stay as sports powerhouse but should become a sports advanced country through democratization of sports where the human rights of all athletes are prioritized, protected, and promoted. The development of athlete activism is an important necessary and sufficient condition for sport democratization and sport advancing.

> We have learned that there are tremendous obstacles to change; we know that it takes bravery and courage and perseverance to stand up to them. (Jobs in Football, 2022) Megan Rapinoe (American Professional Soccer Player, FIFA Women's World Cup Golden Boot Winner, Civil Rights Activist)

FIVE KEY READINGS

Armstrong, C. G., & Butryn, T. (2022). Educated activism: A focus group study of high school athletes' perception of athlete activism. In. R. Magrath (Ed.), *Athlete activism: Contemporary perspectives* **(pp. 20–31). Routledge.**

Armstrong and Butryn explore how student athletes perceive, understand, and interact with athlete activism based upon theoretical models such as stakeholder theory and identity theory. They argue that several factors are very important for young athletes to identify with athlete activism and internalize elements of athlete activism in their own identities. The education about athlete activism and athletes' protest is crucial by various stakeholders like agencies and significant others, through which athletes are inspired and aware about activism and protest for justice.

Hoffman J., Kihl, L., & Browning, A. (2015). Civic engagement and activism: Do college students and college athletes differ? *Journal of College and Character*, *16*(2), 75–89. https://doi.org/10.1080/2194587X.2015.1028315

The authors, assuming the negative relationships between sport participation and political involvement at college, try to compare the tendency of nonathlete students and student athletes to have civic engagement and political and electoral voices. The article showed that even though no significant differences between two groups were found in civic engagement and electoral voice, Black student athletes were likely to be reluctant to have electoral voice, and nonathletes' active political engagement is stronger than that of athletes. It suggested that the promotion of volunteerism and the organization of student athletes at campus would play a crucial role in increasing student athletes' levels of civic participation and political voices.

Kluch, Y. (2021). "It's our duty to utilize the platform that we have": Motivations for activism among U.S. collegiate athletes. In. R. Magrath (Ed.), *Athlete activism: contemporary perspectives* (pp. 32–43). Routledge.

Kluch examines various motivations for student athletes to engage in activism regarding their social power and visibility at campus, their status as role models, and their inclusiveness of physical and symbolic environments all of which can be used as the important platform for athlete activism. He argues that athlete activists need to utilize their platform to advance social justice in sports. And he points out that it is important for athletes to receive active programs for developing workshops, drafting a social media plan, and identifying activist partners which are provided from athletic department.

Nam, B. H., Hong, D., Marshall, R. C., & Hong, J. H. (2018). Rethinking social activism regarding human rights for student-athletes in South Korea. *Sport in Society*, *21*(11), 1831–1849. https://doi.org/10.1080/17430437.2017.1421175

The authors investigate how student athletes' activism can outbreak and develop with other groups such as critical academic and journalism community and civic organizations. They argue that the activism of journalist and civic organizations is an important role in increasing public attention for the protection of athletes' human rights. The paper points out that the activism of scholars can directly contribute to empowering civil organizations which support student athletes' human rights.

Yan, G., Pegoraro, A., & Watanabe, N. M. (2018). Student-athletes' organization of activism at the University of Missouri: Resource mobilization on Twitter. *Journal of Sport Management*, *32*(1), 24–37. https://doi.org/101123/jsm.2017-0031

The authors explore how athlete activism outbreaks and develops through social media and to what extent the mobilization of activism is effective in terms of global geography and diverse group cluster. They found that social media mobilizes people who are geographically and ethnically relevant and that social media group clusters show differences between pre-protest and post-protest. The article concludes that protest organization on social media changed from a loosely connected structure to one with a high degree of concentration and that fellow athletes play an important role in bridging and promoting the online protest.

REFERENCES

Ahn, A. (2022, December 3). *Feminist are protesting the wave of anti-feminism that's swept South Korea.* NPR. https://www.npr.org/2022/12/03/1135162927/women-feminism-south-korea-sexism-protest-haeil-yoon

Armstrong, C. G., & Butryn, T. (2022). Educated activism: A focus group study of high school athletes' perception of athlete activism. In R. Magrath (Ed.), *Athlete activism: Contemporary perspectives* (pp. 20–31). Routledge.

Brown, C., Willett, J., Goldfine, R., & Goldfine, B. (2018). Sport management internships: Recommendations for improving upon experiential learning. *Journal of Hospitality, Leisure, Sports and Tourism Education, 22*, 75–81. https://doi.org/10.1016/j.jhlste.2018.02.001

California Department of Education. (2023). *T-SEL competencies: Social awareness.* https://www.cde.ca.gov/ci/se/tselsocialawareness.asp

Chang, J. (2010, March 26). Study together' college basketball league kick-off. *Yonhapnews.* https://sports.news.naver.com/news.nhn?oid=001&aid=0003191208

Cho, M. (2009, December 27). Human rights in sports' takes first steps. *Kyunghyangdaily.* https://www.khan.co.kr/sports/sports-general/article/200912271836515

Cho, S. (2010, August 28). Sport as a socio-cultural catalyst for multicultural development in Korea (Keynote speech). In *International Sport Science Congress of Korean Alliance for Health, Physical Education, Recreation, and Dance.* Gangwondo, Chuncheon, S. Korea.

Cho, S. (2015, June 10). From sports powerhouse to sports advanced country: Proposal for Korean sports system (Keynote speech). In *The 9th Korea Sport Vision Symposium.* Seoul, S. Korea.

Cho, S., Kim, N., & Lee, W. (2017). A study on the manifestation of fans' pure blood identity in the reports of 'Korean (descent)' LPGA players of online newspaper. *Korean Journal of Sports Science, 26*(1), 13–141.

Choi, I., Haslett, D., & Smith, B. (2021). Disabled athlete activism in South Korea: A mixed-method study. *International Journal of Sport and Exercise Psychology, 19*(4), 473–487. https://doi.org/10.108/1612197X.2019.1674903

Choi, S., & Seo, J. (2020). Practicing agency by performing vulnerability: Sexual minorities at the Queer culture festival in Korea. *Journal of Asian Sociology, 49*(4), 501–526. https://www.jstor.org/stable/26979897

Chung, H. (2020, January 15). 'Naturalized basketball player', La Gun-Ah is saying "I receive racist messages everyday". *Newsway.* https://www.newsway.co.kr/news/view?tp=1&ud=2020011519241113094

Chung, Y. (2023, June 26). Racism in sports can't be overlooked. *Labor Today.* http://www.labortoday.co.kr/news/articleView.html?idxno=215832

Chung, J., & Won, D. (2011). The authoritarian policy in South Korean sport: A critical perspective. *European Journal of Social Sciences, 20*(1), 146–157.

Civic Network for Justice in Sport. (2023). *Vision of Civic Network for Justice in Sport.* https://www.sportscm.org/

Do, H. (2020, August 4). Korean Olympic Committee decided to delete 'obedience' clause in training management guidelines. *HuffPost.* http://www.huffingtonpost.kr/news/articleView.html?idxno=99644

Do, H. (2022, March 8). 'Korea Football Association closed their eyes and plugged their ears: Women's national soccer team players play their games for 'half the money' than men. *HuffPost.* http://www.huffingtonpost.kr/news/articleView.html?idxno=117217

Doehler, S. (2022, October 31). 'Shut up and play': A brief history of athlete activism. *OpenLearn.* https://www.open.edu/openlearn/health-sports-psychology/shut-and-play-brief-history-athlete-activism

Doo, K. (2021, October 10). Sport 'WeMeetUp'; for women and by women. *The Women's News.* http://www.womennews.co.kr/news/articleView.html?idxno=215918

Eo, M. (2023, February 16). I went to Jincheon National Training Center. https://blog.naver.com/umg81/223017934704

Foster, S. J. L., & Huml, M. R. (2017). The relationship between athletic identity and academic major chosen by student-athletes. *International Journal of Exercise Science, 10*(6), 915–925.

Ha, Y., Kim, J., Libaque-Saenz, C. F., Chang, Y., & Park, M. (2015). Use and gratifications of mobile SNSs: Facebook and KakaoTalk in Korea. *Telematics and Informatics, 32*, 425–438. https://doi.org/10.1016/j.tele.2014.10.006

Han, J. H. J. (2016, July 4). *The politic of homophobia in South Korea*. East Asia Forum. https://www.eastasiaforum.org/2016/07/04/the-politics-of-homophobia-in-south-korea/

Hoffman, J., Kihl, L., & Browning, A. (2015). Civic engagement and activism: Do college students and college athletes differ? *Journal of College and Character, 16*(2), 75–89. https://doi.org/10.1080/2194587X.2015.1028315

Humberstone, B. (2009). Sport management, gender and the 'bigger picture': Challenging changes in higher education – A partial auto/ethnographical account. *Sport Management Review, 12*(4), 255–262. https://doi.org/10.1016/j.smr.2009.03.004

IOC. (2024). *#GenderEqualOlympics: Advancing gender equality beyond the field of play*. https://olympics.com/ioc/news/genderequalolympics-advancing-gender-equality-beyond-the-field-of-play

Jobs in Football. (2022). *20 Megan Rapinoe quotes to inspire & motivate*. https://jobsinfootball.com/blog/megan-rapinoe-quotes/

Kim, H. (2013, June 29). Human Rights Commission "A's remarks about black pitcher are racist", asking not to happen again. *Kuki Issue*. https://www.kukinews.com/newsView/kuk201306290015

Kim, Y. (2016, August 4). Men's Football is just 'Football', but women's football is 'Women's football?' Sexism in sports world. *The Seoul Economy Daily*. https://www.sedaily.com/NewsView/1L00EXURN0

Kim, H. (2020). Understanding "Koreanness": Racial stratification and colorism in Korea and implications for Korean multicultural education. *International Journal of Multicultural Education, 22*(1), 76–97.

Kim, Y. (2022, July 3). Student athletes studying... Catching 'two rabbits' of sports and academics. *Kyongbukdaily*. http://www.kyongbuk.co.kr/news/articleView.html?idxno=2106134

Kim, J., & Jeon, H. (2017). Anti-multiculturalism and the future direction of multicultural education in South Korea. *Curriculum Perspectives, 37*, 181–189. https://doi.org/10.1007/s41297-017-0025-7

Kim, H., & Lee, W. (2023). The intersectionality of the sports labor market and gender inequality in South Korea. *Sport in Society*, 1–16. https://doi.org/10.1080/12259276.2016.1168156

Kluch, Y. (2021). "It's our duty to utilize the platform that we have": Motivations for activism among U.S. collegiate athletes. In R. Magrath (Ed.), *Athlete Activism: Contemporary Perspectives* (pp. 32–43). Routledge.

KOC. (2019). *Human Rights Management Declaration*. https://www.sports.or.kr/home/010201/0000/view.do?T_IDX=4705652

KOC. (2023a). *Organizational charts*. https://www.sports.or.kr/home/010704/0000/main.do

KOC. (2023b). *Support programs for athletes*. https://welfare.sports.or.kr/

Korea University Sport Federation. (2023). *Normalization of academic administration for student athletes*. https://kusf.or.kr/learn/splayer_bachelor3.html

Lee, H. (2011). The experience process of the student athletes who perform both study and sport; redefining self. *Korean Journal of Sociology of Sport, 24*(1), 1–24.

Lee, J., Cho, S., & Jung, G. (2021). Policy responses to COVID-19 and discrimination against foreign nationals in South Korea. *Critical Asian Studies, 53*(3), 432–447. https://doi.org/10.1080/14672715.2021.1897472

Lee, N., & Choi, J. (2018). Analysis on constructing concepts of university athletes' self-management. *Journal of the Korea Convergence Society, 9*(8), 247–264.

Lim, J. (2020, January 17). La Gun-Ah, 'Victim of racial discrimination', KBL takes legal action. *Nocutnews*. https://www.nocutnews.co.kr/news/5274605

Lim, J. (2023, June 14). 'You can do study and sports at the same time' Choi proved it by winning. *Maekyung*. https://www.mk.co.kr/news/sports/10758928

McGregor, A. (2022). The Anti-Intellectual Coach: The Cultural Politics of College Football Coaching from the New Left to the Present. *Journal of Sport & Social Issues*. https://doi.org/10.1177/01937235221098915

Ministry of Culture, Sports and Tourism. (2022a). *The Sports white paper*. https://www.mcst.go.kr/kor/s_policy/dept/deptView.jsp?pCurrentPage=1&pType=07&pTab=01&pSeq=1827&pDataCD=0417000000&pSearchType=01&pSearchWord=

Ministry of Culture, Sports and Tourism. (2022b). *Survey of national sport participation*. https://www.mcst.go.kr/kor/s_policy/dept/deptView.jsp?pSeq=1691

Ministry of Gender Equality and Family. (2023). *Policy*. http://www.mogef.go.kr/eng/pc/eng_pc_f001.do
Moore, T. J. (2011). Critical thinking and disciplinary thinking: A continuing debate. *Higher Education Research and Development*, *30*(3), 261–274. https://doi.org/10.1080/07294360.2010.501328
Mulyaman, D., & Ismail, A. (2021). Tendentious actions, racism, or bad prejudice?: Examining the relations of ethnocentrism and xenophobia in the contemporary South Korea. *Andalas Journal of International Studies*, *10*(2), 192–205. https://doi.org/10.25077/ajis.10.2.192-205.2021
Myung, W., & Chung, K. (2019). Alienation, reinforcer functions and chain of camp training drawn from Korean male footballers' experiences. *Korean Journal of Sociology of Sport*, *32*(2), 110–127.
Nam, B. H. (2020). Promoting the right to education and dual careers of athletes: Former Korean dropout college student-athletes as social agents to promote critical conflict resolution. *International Journal of the History of Sport*, *37*(17), 1755–1776. https://doi.org/10.1080/09523367.2020.1845152
Nam, B. H., Hong, D., Marshall, R. C., & Hong, J. (2018). Rethinking social activism regarding human rights for student-athletes in South Korea. *Sport in Society*, *21*(11), 1831–1849. https://doi.org/10.1080/17430437.2017.1421175
Park, S. (2018, September 2). *Authoritarianism is No.1 illness in Korean society*. The Korea Herald. https://www.koreaherald.com/view.php?ud=20180829000812
Platt, L. (2018, April 16). Athlete activism is on the rise, but so is the backlash. *Global Sport Matters*. https://globalsportmatters.com/culture/2018/04/16/athlete-activism-is-on-the-rise-but-so-is-the-backlash/
Rick, R. (2016). Good stuff for your heart & mind. https://www.google.co.kr/books/edition/Good_stuff_for_your_heart_mind_a_book_of/cJI_DQAAQBAJ?hl=en&gbpv=1
Sanderson, J., Frederick, E., & Stocz, M. (2016). When athlete activism clashes with group values: Social identity threat management via social media. *Mass Communication & Society*, *19*(3), 301–322. https://doi.org/10.1080/15205436.2015.1128549
Schmidt, E. K., Ovseiko, P. V., Henderson, L. R., & Kiparoglou, V. (2020). Understanding the Athena SWAN award scheme for gender equality as a complex social intervention in a complex system: Analysis of Silver award action plans in a comparative European perspective. *Health Research Policy and Systems*, *18*, 19. https://doi.org/10.1186/s12961-020-0527-x
Sport Ethics Center. (2023). *Sport Ethics Center Articles*. https://www.k-sec.or.kr/front/board/bs/boardView.do?boardSeq=39&pageNo=1&menuSeq=1126&conSeq=2967&keyKind=ALL&keyWord=
Tan, S. K. (2015). The role of Korean collectivism in South Korea's industrialization process. *International Journal of East Asian Studies*, *4*(1), 35–48.
Ward, P., & Denney, S. (2022). Welfare chauvinism among co-ethnics: Evidence from a conjoint experiment in South Korea. *International Migration*, *60*, 74–90. https://doi.org/10.1111/imig.12937
Watanabe, N. M., Yan, G., & Soebbing, B. P. (2017). Market disruption as a regime for athlete activism: An economic analysis of college football player protests. *Sport Management Review*, *22*(5), 600–612. https://doi.org/10.1016/j.smr.2018.08.003
Yan, G., Pegoraro, A., & Watanabe, N. M. (2018). Student-athletes' organization of activism at the University of Missouri: Resource mobilization on Twitter. *Journal of Sport Management*, *32*(1), 24–37. https://doi.org/101123/jsm.2017-0031
Yoo, E. (2019, February 4). "When the hen crows, the family is ruined" ranked #1 on sexist proverbs. *Korea Farm News*. http://www.newsfarm.co.kr/news/articleView.html?idxno=49219
Yoon, H. (2015, April 10). KFA's double standards of football national players... Business class for male but economy class for female. *New Daily*. https://www.newdaily.co.kr/site/data/html/2015/04/10/2015041000036.html
Yuh, J. (2016, September 6). Culture: South Korea, A collectivist society in Confucianism. *PennState Cultural Leadership Blog*. https://sites.psu.edu/global/2016/09/06/blog-entry-culture-south-korea-a-collectivist-society-in-confucianism/
Yuk, J. (2016). The (mis)understanding of race and racism in multicultural Korea. *Korean Journal of Sociology*, *50*(6), 125–145.

CHAPTER 7

SPORTS AND THE 4TH INDUSTRIAL REVOLUTION

Jungrae Lee[a] and Sora Kim[b]

[a]Kyungpook National University, Republic of Korea
[b]Korea Army Academy at Yeongcheon, Republic of Korea

ABSTRACT

The 4th Industrial Revolution changed various aspects of our lives. Those influences also led to many changes in the sports field. The emergence of different wearable devices which adapted Information Technology (IT) played a pivotal role in enhancing the field of sports science. As an example, smartwatches are one of the most popular wearable devices. They monitor an appropriate amount of exercise and manage individual health. These functions reflect people's desire to pursue an individual lifestyle, which leads to a trend of "quantified self." A diversified market related to smart fitness equipment also provided a reasonable opportunity for people to select various training options. Combining online content with fitness equipment created an environment where people compete globally for individual fitness.

As such, the Fourth Industrial Revolution impacted sports field's development but yielded unexpected results. It has been criticized due to taking care of the body relying on machines, misconceptions of figures, and subordination of tools. Like Nomophobia which indicates a fear of being without a mobile phone, No-watchphobia confuses people. Boundaries between sports and game collapse, jobs of personal trainers are threatened, and inequality index of sports participation is enormously broad.

Critical scholars argue the need for in-depth reflection on whether the rationalization of society influenced by the development of science and technology is truly for human happiness and liberation or leads to restraint and alienation. From the critical scholars' perspective, academic concerns and phenomenological considerations should be contemplated based on the aspects of sports sociology.

Keywords: 4th industrial revolution; VR sports; wearable device; digital fitness; smart health

INTRODUCTION

The 4th Industrial Revolution was first mentioned at the 47th World Economic Forum (WEF) Annual Meeting held in Davos, Switzerland, in January 2016. Klaus Schwab, Executive Chairman of the Davos WEF, defined the 4th Industrial Revolution as the next-generation industrial revolution driven by artificial intelligence (AI), robotics technology, and life sciences. In other words, it is a technological revolution that builds on the 3rd Industrial Revolution, combining digital technology, biotechnology, physics, and so forth (Schwab, 2016, p. 18). More precisely, it is a revolution of technological convergence, in which the boundaries between physical, digital, and biological spaces are blurred based on the digital revolution of IT and other technologies, rather than being a revolution of technology industries that had spanned over three industrial revolutions (WEF, 2016).

The 4th Industrial Revolution is characterized by the convergence of digital industry, bioindustry, physics, etc., based on the 3rd Industrial Revolution, using Online to Offline (O2O), Internet of Things (IoT), Big Data, AI, and Cloud Computing, and is hyper-convergent and hyper-connected. A hyper-connected society is one in which everything, including people, things, and media, is connected by networks and the internet (Byun, 2017).

Since the term was coined in 2016, the 4th Industrial Revolution has changed numerous things in our lives. With the rapid development of the IoT, Big Data, and AI, huge amounts of information can be processed in real time, and networked sharing platforms have created a variety of added value. Perhaps the official word "the 4th Industrial Revolution" was only coined at the Davos Forum, but the changes associated with the 4th Industrial Revolution were already happening across our lives.

As the 4th Industrial Revolution spread around the world, countries have strengthened their responses to the social and ethical impacts and risks posed by AI or robots and to the legal system, such as AI algorithm regulations, robotics ethics guidelines, and RoboLaw, to ensure that intelligent information technology can be used as a tool to benefit humans and society (Lee, 2017). These include the National Science and Technology Council (NSTC)'s Regulatory Guidelines (2020), the European Commission's Ethics Guideline for Trustworthy AI (2018), the OECD Committee on Digital Economy Policy's Recommendation of the Council on AI (2019), France's AI for Humans (2018), the UK's Five Principles of Ethics (2018), Japan's Principles for a Human-Centered Society (2018), and Korea's AI Ethics Standards (2020).

The guidelines set forth by each country are a self-serving attempt to minimize the negative impact of the 4th Industrial Revolution. As such, we can recognize that while the 4th Industrial Revolution has many positive benefits in a variety of areas, it also presents various challenges related to human ethics.

The aftermath of the 4th Industrial Revolution also affected sports without exception. The field of sports has converged with core IT groups of the 4th Industrial Revolution, including AI, Big Data, IoT, Augmented Reality (AR), and Virtual Reality (VR), creating new fields of study and markets, which is even leading to employment creation (Kim et al., 2021).

The Korean Society for the Sociology of Sport held an in-depth discussion on the 4th Industrial Revolution and the role of sports through the 2017 Annual Academic Conference. Since then, the studies on the changes in the sports field (Goo & Kim, 2018; Hong, 2019; Kim, 2018; Son & Kang, 2019) and the convergence of sports (Han et al., 2020; Kim, 2019a, 2019b; Cho, 2020) led by the 4th Industrial Revolution have been conducted. Those studies predicted the changes in the sports field by the 4th Industrial Revolution and showed the possibility in terms of how sports can converge with the characteristics of the 4th industry. However, the research has been decreasing over the past three years because they did not show reliable and practical results rather than hasty predictions and possibilities. Thus, it is meaningful to see the association between sports and the 4th Industrial Revolution from the perspective of sport sociology. Also, it is necessary to check the direction for the sports throughout the 4th Industrial Revolution.

This chapter will explore the changes in the field of sports as a result of the 4th Industrial Revolution and what they mean to us.

SPORTS INCORPORATING THE 4TH INDUSTRIAL REVOLUTION

No one really knows what the future holds for us in the aftermath of the 4th Industrial Revolution. It is also impossible to say how this will change the field of sports. What we are seeing and recognizing, however, is that the changes brought about by the 4th Industrial Revolution are certainly significant. In particular, it is important to note that the changes are taking place in a completely different way than the developments we have seen in the past in the field of sports.

If sports before the 4th Industrial Revolution were focused on the availability of manpower and space, sports with the help of AI technical skills are leading technological advancements and developing technologies based on convenience and safety (Kim, 2021).

Elite Sports and Sporting Goods Industries Compete for Contents

It is no secret that the progress of elite sports is based on the development of sporting goods and facilities. Wearable device technology combined with nanotechnology, Information and Communications Technologies (ICT), and IoT has continually evolved sporting goods, and advances in robotics, AI, nanotechnology, and bioscience technologies have further stimulated the manufacturing sector for the development and dissemination of sporting goods. In particular, the transformation of sports brands Adidas and Nike is a prime example of how the 4th Industrial Revolution is transforming sports.

Adidas built its first "Speed Factory" system in Ansbach, southern Germany, in 2015, followed by a second factory in Atlanta, USA, in 2017, to produce customized sneakers that take into account the user's gait, usage environment, etc. (Cho, 2017). The "Speed Factory" system attracted the attention of many people and not just those involved in sports, because robots were in charge of producing customized sneakers. This was a massive game changer. The news was especially welcomed by governments in developed countries, which have been concerned about the damage to jobs and economies caused by factories moving overseas, and was spotlighted as the shift away from low-wage, labor-intensive industries based in Asia.

Nike began its digital transformation with Nike+ (Park, 2020). In 2006, Nike launched the Nike + iPod, wherein a sensor chip is attached to a Nike shoe that is paired to an iPod to manage the user's running information. Nike + has since developed Nike Run Club (NRC), an app that allows users to view their running data like distance and speed on their digital watch. The app allows users to "challenge" themselves by setting their own running goals, assigns levels based on distance run, and provides rewards and a sense of achievement by giving badges or trophies for completing challenges. It also allows users to compare their rankings with others online, establishing competitive relationships to boost their motivation levels and make running more enjoyable. One of the best examples of this is the use of gamification.[1] The company also offers the Nike + Kinect Training app, a game that utilizes Kinect to achieve targeted exercise volumes while being coached by a virtual trainer, which is widely used in fitness centers as well as for home training.

Although the "Speed Factory" system of Adidas, which used robots to produce customized sneakers, was shut down after three years, it was significant in that it predicted how the manufacturing process of sporting goods could be changed by the 4th Industrial Revolution.

In the field of elite sports, the advancement of sports using various contents was already underway even before the term "4th Industrial Revolution" was used. Germany, the winner of the 2014 World Cup in Brazil, introduced a systematic and optimal training method based on the core technologies of the 4th Industrial Revolution, such as the IoT and Big Data, and showed excellent performance, leading many countries to change their sports training techniques (Kim, 2017). In addition, simulation devices that apply VR technology are being used directly to train baseball hitters in batting practice, quarterbacks in American football in tactical training, and professional athletes in golf, tennis, car racing, skiing, volleyball, basketball, soccer, archery, and other sports (Jang, 2018). Not only that, sensors are being attached to elite athletes' uniforms, watch bands, shoes, hats, gloves, bats, clubs, rackets, etc., to collect and analyze information about their movements and changes, which is then used to adopt a personalized training method for each athlete. Also, from accumulating game records using Big Data to managing athletes, such as injury management and systematic training, they are being used not only by the athletes themselves but also by the coaching staff, fronter, and media (Brousell, 2014). This is helping athletes improve their performance as well as increase their chances of breaking sports records.

The wearable devices attached on body of athletes, such as Electronic Performance and Tracking System (EPTS) in soccer, Radio Frequency Identification (RFID) Tag, and Pulse Throw in NFL, help obtain physical data for performance enhancement, game strategy, and physical conditioning. Also, the AI technology in sport broadcasting to collect data from various sensors and analyze them instantly contributed to increasing fans' attention and profit of sports teams in professional leagues. That is, the funds for start-up in sport technology have been increasing since high technology became a focal point in sport field, which led growing the relevant industry. In 2022, the market in sport technology of the world was 159 billion dollars, but the US market anticipated 18% growth per a year, and 792 billion dollars in 2032 (Ahn, 2023).

In fact, escaped from the traditional sport based on feeling and experience, AI can analyze the game data from the sport technology with an objective perspective to make a game plan and set a new record, which leads to practical advancement in sport.

VR Sports Blurring the Line Between Sports and Games

In the past, VR provided gaming-centric entertainment services. Recent advances in VR have led to the popularization of related equipment and products, and VR sports that utilize the technology of VR are providing optimal experiences for sports consumers (Goo, 2023). That said, as VR technology becomes more accessible in the sports arena, it is rapidly spreading across all sports.

VR sports is a representative core ICT convergence sports content in the era of the 4th Industrial Revolution that provides a realistic experience by virtually implementing a real sports environment through a computer program (Yi, 2009). VR sports have the same exercise effect as actually playing sports by creating the illusion of being in the field and have the advantage of being able to enjoy sports regardless of time and place. With these advantages, various sports are evolving into VR sports, eliminating the spatial constraints of stadiums, etc., that used to occupy a large area, and are being reborn as screen sports where one can engage in physical activity while vividly sensing the stadium of each sport in a small space.

VR sports contributed to increasing the market of home training. Home training had a limitation concerning motivation and emotional reactions from competitiveness despite the convenience of home training. VR sports has an enough potential to overcome the barriers. In fact, the increased popularity of Peleton shows how VR sports should be developed.

In Korea, VR sports has been applied to the VR sports classroom in which students in elementary school enjoy throwing and kicking a ball to the screen. According to the 2019 survey for sports rooms, students did not like physical education classes before using the VR sports classroom, but 59.3% of the students began to enjoy the physical education class after using the VR sports classroom and responded that they liked physical education classes (Ahn et al., 2019). As growing popularity and utilization of VR sports classrooms, it has been built in elementary schools by up to 10%, and more installations are expected in Korea.

Meanwhile, signature VR sports include screen golf, screen baseball, screen tennis, screen archery, screen horseback riding, and other contents of various sports are being provided. In particular, with the successful market entry of screen golf and screen baseball and the emergence of VR-based sports theme parks, VR is being recognized as a new business area in the sports industry (Choi, 2019).

Screen golf was first developed by an American golf club manufacturer and introduced in the mid-1990s, but it never caught on. However, in Korea, golf simulators were first introduced in 2001, and since then, the combination of Korea's advanced IT technology and the country's unique "room" culture has made them so popular that the neologism "golf room" was born.[2] In Korea, screen golf competitions have been held since 2008, a golf simulation department was established at the Korea Golf University in 2014, and an internet channel (IPTV, Internet Protocol Television) specializing in screen golf was launched in 2018 (Lee & Kwon, 2021).

The popularity of screen golf in Korea is highly significant. In Korea, golf was perceived as a class-specific sport enjoyed by a certain group of people, making it difficult for the general public to participate. However, screen golf has the advantage of being accessible and free from the restrictions of demographics, location, time, and the number of people, so it has served as a medium to bring those who have experienced screen golf to the actual field. Research on screen golf suggests that screen golf acts as a socializing agent that leads to participation in field golf, reporting that higher levels of satisfaction with the screen golf experience lead to higher levels of field participation. Moreover, lessons on screen golf courses and screen tennis courts are very popular with beginners, and the revenue from them continues to grow.

As a result, screen sports in Korea are expected to continue to evolve due to their universality among consumers, increased accessibility to real-world sports, and diversification of the lesson market and this will not be a case confined to Korea. If each country's sports-limiting factors are approached through virtual sports, the diversification of the sports market will proceed very quickly. It is also speculated that the development of VR technology will herald the birth of a new type of sport, as people will recognize it as a sport, not just a game.

Shifts in the Healthcare Paradigm

Healthcare refers to the full range of health management services, including both traditional medical services that focuses on the treatment of illness and the areas that focus on disease prevention and management. The integration of ICT into the healthcare industry has built a new industrial market called smart healthcare. Countries around the world are adopting smart healthcare ecosystems and are competitively striving to dominate the market in advance. Smart healthcare is characterized by shifting the paradigm of existing medical services to an active preventive level, and in this process, Big Data and AI technologies are being applied to create high added value. In other words, the data generated by individuals is analyzed by experts and fed back into the health management system to provide personalized medical services to individuals, creating added value (Han, 2022).

Beyond medical services, smart healthcare has been welcomed more by those who participate in sports. Sports companies have launched apparel and accessories related to smart healthcare, and a variety of wearable devices are emerging that incorporate IT technology. Wearable devices are revolutionary products for health management that allow users to continuously check the changes in their body by quantifying and quantifying all the data generated in daily life, such as the volumes of exercise and food, heart rate, and sleep for 24 hours via sensors to conveniently measure their body condition (Shin, 2014). According to a report by market research agency International Data Corporation (IDC), unit shipments of wearable devices have been growing steadily since 2014 and are expected to reach $526.8 million by 2024, making it an area to pay close attention to (Yun, 2023). These numbers indicate a paradigm shift in healthcare from diagnosis and treatment to pre-diagnosis and prevention, as wearable devices empower people to rectify their exercise regimens and life habits to suit them, creating personalized lifestyles.

For athletes, wearable devices have been developed based on the characteristics of each sports while smart healthcare systems were focused for nonathletes. Population and generalization should be considered at this point. When wearable devices were introduced, there were many limitations for general people to use. Within not too much time, the limitations became less to be popularized, and better than expected healthcare systems were established.

A wearable device is a combination of the words wearable and device and refers to an electronic device that is designed to be worn or put on. Clothes, shoes, eyeglasses, and watches are some of the most popular, but smart watches are by far the most popular among the public. Smart watches can help users manage their health by checking exercise volumes, managing and modifying their lifestyle, and keeping track of changes in their bodies.

According to a survey by market research agency GFK, the number one reason people use smart watches is to "measure exercise volumes." This is because smart watches allow users to easily see how much they have exercised in a day and receive a variety of other exercise-related information (Kim, 2015). There are studies that prove this. Jordan Atkin, a professor at Duke University in the United States, conducted a survey of 200 women who wear smart bands. The results suggested that they wear their smart bands all the time except when charging and that without them, they feel naked and move less than when wearing them. In addition, 30% of respondents reported feeling guilty if they did not meet a set exercise goal and that physical activity felt like work instead of play afterward (Hong, 2016). Through these findings, Prof Atkin criticized that wearing smart bands was making humans not only suppress their own independent thinking and freedom but also become increasingly dependent on machines. Concerning this argument, the author has also characterized the contemporary man's dependence on smart watches as "no-watch phobia" in a research paper (Lee & Kwon, 2019).

Despite criticisms and concerns, wearable devices are driving the popularization of tracking devices that can analyze biometric data in real time and are propelling the trend of the "quantified self" by aligning with the public's desire to take control of their health in a structured manner and to pursue personalized lifestyles.

The Fitness Scene Replaces Humans

Grafting with ICT, the fitness scene is rapidly evolving into Digital Fitness. According to the "2020 Global ICT Issues Report," the North American digital fitness market, centered on the United States and Canada, was valued at approximately $39.4 billion in 2019, accounting for about 43% of the global market, and is expected to grow at a high average annual growth rate of 31% from 2020 to 2025 (Lee, 2020). As such, the fitness market combined with IT is being analyzed as a long-term change in the industry landscape rather than a temporary change. Fitness companies are paying attention to the market possibilities and potential of digital fitness, accelerating the development of smart fitness equipment and contents (Park, 2020).[3]

Smart health equipment is regular health equipment that is mounted with smart devices (sensor devices and a tablet PC) to turn the health equipment into an IoT device. In other words, IOT, a novel technology that embeds sensors and communication functions in various objects, exchanges data between objects through the internet, and provides analyzed information to users, has been applied to health equipment as well. Created in this way, smart health equipment collects the physical information of members through sensors, presents exercise programs accordingly, stores and analyzes data on members' exercise information and physical changes, and provides them back to members. For example, sensors on smart health equipment can detect a member's movements and manage their workouts in real time, such as providing voice counts like "one, two, three" or "three reps left" while the member is exercising, or taking care of their posture such as saying, "lift higher" or "pull all the way up." On top of that, members will be able to check their physical changes and exercise information at any time by quantifying their physical changes and exercise volume and sending it to their smart bands or smartphones. It is as if a machine has taken over the role of the trainer.

The author conducted research on the emergence of smart health equipment with interest and concern. A system that allows one to get personal training without paying for an expensive personal trainer is a captivating proposition for consumers. On the other hand, the popularization of smart healthcare equipment has led to concerns that personal trainers will eventually lose their jobs. The author conducted a study throughout 2019 and 2020 and published the paper in 2021 titled "A Study Exploring the Changes in the Fitness Scene Based on the Experience of Using Smart Health Equipment" (Lee & Kim, 2021). The result showed that smart health equipment was previously a service that could not be expected in the traditional fitness industry but now impacts members' overall exercise. Especially for those who have no knowledge of exercise or are inexperienced in using equipment, smart health equipment plays a role as an assistant to generate interest in exercise and guide them to continue exercising, which is a factor that attracts members to fitness clubs and increases their satisfaction with exercise performance. Nevertheless, it was seen that there are clear limitations to smart health equipment acting as a personal trainer. In other words, it was confirmed that machines can never invade the realm of emotional factors that only humans possess, such as emotional touch and emotional exchange.

In fact, the change in the fitness scene combined with IT technology is a product of advancing science and technology under the 4th Industrial Revolution and the lifestyle pursued by contemporary man. This is because contemporary men are increasingly seeking to improve their quality of life through various activities as their leisure time increases due to economic growth and advanced industrialization; especially, they are increasingly interested in personal healthcare and are more inclined to manage their health more effectively and systematically through digital devices (Park & Yeom, 2020). In this regard, smart health equipment, which suggests exercise programs and methods in consideration of the user's physical information, exercise purpose, and target exercise volume and monitors and gives feedback to members in real time on whether they are performing appropriate exercises accordingly, can be seen as a tool that can meet the needs of contemporary man and a result that reflects the trend of the present time.

CONCLUSION

In March 2016 in Korea, Lee Sedol of nine dan rank and the AI Alpha Go faced off in the fifth game of the DeepMind Challenge Match (Wikipedia, 2024) for a Go matchup that confirmed the potential for sports participatory agents to compete against AI robots rather than humans in the future. It also confirmed the possibility that sports participatory agents, including sports participants, competitors, leaders, and learners, do not always have to be humans.[4] In this way, the 4th Industrial Revolution has transformed many aspects of our lives, whether we realize it or not. Furthermore, the impact that individuals feel based on their level of interest and involvement in sports activities is communicated in incredibly distinct manners.

Today, we talk about the transformation of sports in the wake of the 4th Industrial Revolution, but for developing and underdeveloped countries, such a topic is akin to an unrealistic film. In other words, the 4th Industrial Revolution is creating a polarization of sports or health benefits depending on the technological growth of each country. This is a far cry from the training systems or performance enhancement programs of elite sports. It is about the right to play sports and maintain and manage one's health. In the end, the impact of how the contents of the 4th Industrial Revolution can shape the sporting conditions in each country will likely be a crucial requirement for the sporting experience and benefits of its citizens.

Meanwhile, under the influence of the 4th Industrial Revolution, the sports world is growing rapidly based on the IT industry, but unforeseen consequences are emerging. The drastic growth of VR sports is blurring the lines between sports and games, and the idea of systematic and rationalized healthcare using wearable devices has been criticized as machine-dependent body management, the illusion of figures, and dependency on tools. Like nomophobia (NO mobile-phone phobia), no-watch phobia is confusing us. In addition, the rise of smart health equipment is serving as a factor threatening the jobs of personal trainers.

The 4th Industrial Revolution has a non-meaningful boundary of disciplinaries with no exception of sports. Society and industry will be relocated with a deep consideration on the values. The traditional sport is not important, but a new form of sports can be survival only if it can create the values by utilizing technologies from the 4th Industrial Revolution.

Here, let us ask ourselves again this question: as critical theorists such as Horkheimer and Adorno have argued, why is it that human freedom and humanity are increasingly suppressed despite the rationality elevated by the technologies, bureaucracies, and political systems that have been created by human reason? From a critical point of view, wearable devices designed as a technology of the 4th industry can be seen as providing humans with health, which is a desire for happiness, and convenience for health management at the same time, so that they can have happiness and freedom from illness; however, when looking deeper, we can find an image of humans who are becoming restricted and blind by wearable devices. In other words, wearable devices designed to help people manage their health efficiently and systematically are, over time, causing people to think about their health as if they cannot manage it without these devices and to adapt their lifestyles according to these devices. Due to the illusion of figures, the dependency on tools, etc., humans are losing their independence and freedom and are more likely to degenerate into tools of machines and become completely dependent. In response, Horkheimer (2006) warned that mechanization, which underlies the capitalist economic system, seemed to bring true happiness through the pursuit of human convenience and rationality, but in fact, it further bound human beings and even their thinking became materialistic, blind, and conformist.

It is no exaggeration to say that all around us right now, the benefits of the 4th Industrial Revolution and the positive effects of its advancements are being touted. Of course, this does not mean denying the positive aspects of developing innovative and diverse content, but we need to be aware of the fact that we can unknowingly lose our human independence in the process of blindly subordinating reason.

Meanwhile, Lee (2018) claimed that when humans rely on machines to exercise, they are likely to lose their sense of identity and entrust themselves to the machine, which leads to the problem of losing themselves in sports and becoming mechanized. In other words, in sports, the 4th Industrial Revolution could bring about increased reliance and blind faith in machines, which could make humans subject to domination and surveillance, as well as mass unemployment of sports professionals. The author strongly agrees with this. Health equipment that was just a tool has transformed into smart health equipment by combining with IT technology and is assuming a function and role beyond a simple instrument. In this respect, we need to look at the phenomenon with more critical thinking rather than just accepting the rapidly changing sports scene due to the advancement of science and technology.

In fact, the Korean Baseball Organization (KBO) has announced plans to implement an automatic ball-strike system (ABS) and pitch clock starting in 2024 (KBO, 2024). The most important significance of this plan is that all pitchers and batters will be subject to the same strike zone judgment, making the game fairer. This is a very reasonable logic. But underlying this, there is widespread distrust of umpires who call strikes.

We now live in a world where humans do not trust humans. The power of machines is serving as the grounds for a lack of full trust in humans. Critical scholars urge us to reflect on whether the rationalization of society by the progress of science and technology is truly for human happiness and liberation or whether it leads to bondage and alienation. There is an urgent need for further scholarly reflection and phenomenological examination of these claims in terms of the sociology of sport.

NOTES

1. Gamification is a neologism that combines the words game and fication and refers to the technique of applying the elements of fun, reward, competition, etc., found in games to other fields. Gamification is used in a variety of fields and is particularly playing a big role in motivating participants in sports activities.
2. In Korea, the place where people enjoying entertainment, such as sing a song and playing a computer game, is called as "singing room" and "PC room." In the room, people are enjoying a group leisure activity with friends.
3. Refers to fitness equipment that provides exercise programs based on the user's physical information and real-time voice feedback on exercise posture, exercise speed, etc. Various terms exist to refer to this, such as "smart fitness equipment," "smart fitness," "health mate," "smart coach," "unmanned training," etc., but this study uses the term "smart health equipment."
4. Go is a competitive game by placing Black and White stone on checkerboard. It is one of sports where Black and White stone try to occupy more spaces with a lot of strategies. Go has a level system to see the ability of people who enjoying Go. Traditionally, "Dan rank" is used. Lower "Dan rank" indicates better ability. Amateurs have the level from 1 to 7, and pros have the level from 1 to 9. Lee Sedol has the top level of nine dan rank.

FIVE KEY READINGS

Klaus Schwab. (2016). *The fourth industrial revolution.* **Song, Gyeongjin translator. Seoul: Mega Study Co.**

In this book, Klaus Schwab said, "What is the 4th Industrial Revolution? What and how will it change? How will it affect us? What are the ways to use it for the public good?" It clarifies the answer. This book fully contains the thoughts and strategies of those who have clearly recognized the four sides of the 4th Industrial Revolution, such as intellectuals and businessmen who are pioneers in each field and have begun to think and prepare for them.

Lee, H. (2018). **Fourth industrial revolution and better sports.** *Korean Journal of Sport Studies, 57*(4), 17–28.

Lee Hak-joon tried to find out what is required for better sports in the era of the 4th industrial revolution. In this study, the issues of the 4th industrial revolution were considered to have the advantages and disadvantages of crisis and opportunity, surveillance, and freedom. He also argued that for better sports, it is necessary to be able to pursue physical excellence, happiness, and meeting.

Goo, K. (2023). **The development of sports content in the fourth industrial revolution.** *Philosophy of Movement: The Journal of the Korean Society for the Philosophy of Sport, Dance, and Martial Arts, 31*(1), 39–50.

This study was to examine the role and direction of sports in the era of the 4th Industrial Revolution by analyzing various elements of the 4th Industrial Revolution and the development of sports content expressed in various sports phenomena. If there is a lack of systematic alternatives in accordance with the development pattern of sports content, an imbalance between production and consumption will arise, and newly added value cannot be created.

Kim, C. (2018). **The change and role of sport in the age of the fourth industrial revolution.** *Korean Journal of Physical Education, 57*(3), 17–27.

As sports role in the era of the 4th Industrial Revolution, Kim insisted on establishing the value of sustainable sports, realizing social welfare in sports through social capital enhancement, discourse on ethical issues in sports sites, convergence of new media technologies to sustainable sports, and enhancing the practicality of sports studies.

Max Horkheimer. (2006). *Zur Kritik der instrumentellen Vernunft.* **Park, Guyung translator. Seoul: MOONYE PUBLISHING.**

Horkheimer tried to overcome the regression of enlightenment arising from the totalization of instrumental reason through the harmony of objective and subjective reason. In addition, Horkheimer seeks the fact that the cause of the crisis in the dehumanized modern society was reduced to 'instrumental reason' in the process of civilization through rational reason that arose from the means of enlightenment that liberated humans from natural forces. This book is evaluated as a book that marked a turning point in the development of critical theory.

REFERENCES

Ahn, J. (2023, July 27). A Sports incorporates high-tech technology. *The Chosun Ilbo.* https://www.chosun.com/economy/weeklybiz/2023/07/27/SUD5FK7OHJGC5KLRNVOKIF3CL4/

Ahn, T., Yoo, J., Sin, J., & Lee, D. (2019). *A survey on the status of elementary school supply project in the virtual reality sports.* National Sports Promotion Corporation.

Brousell, L. (2014, March 17). The misjudgment disappears?!. 8 Way to use analytics in Sports. *CIO.* https://www.ciokorea.com/news/20271

Byun, J. (2017). A study of the industrial revolution's impact on cultural industry. *Journal of Culture Industry, 17*(3), 109–118.

Cho, I. (2017, October 12). Adidas puts robots on 'AM4' shoes for runners. *Robot Newspaper*. http://www.irobotnews.com/news/articalView.html?idxno=11926

Cho, K. (2020). A convergent and combined activation plan for exercise rehabilitation in the era of the fourth industrial revolution. *Journal of Korea Entertainment Industry Association, 14*(8), 407–426.

Choi, I. (2019, March 13). Daegu, ICT Fusion Sports Content, develop. *The Kukmin Ilbo*. http://news.kmib.co.kr/article/view.asp?arcid=0924067158&code=11131419&cp=du

Goo, K. (2023). The development of sports content in the fourth industrial revolution. *Philosophy of Movement: The Journal of the Korean Society for the Philosophy of Sport, Dance, and Martial Arts, 31*(1), 39–50.

Goo, K., & Kim, S. (2018). Issues of sports circle in the era of 4th Industrial Revolution. *Philosophy of Movement, 26*(2), 7–17.

Han, J. (2022). Development of community-based digital health care. *Journal of the Korea Institute of Information and Communication Engineering, 26*(12), 1826–1831.

Han, N., Yang, D., & Chi, S. (2020). Analysis on the application of the fourth industrial revolution and the sports convergence industry. *The Korean Journal of Sport, 18*(3), 821–834.

Hong, J. (2016, October 02). The Fitness Band interferes with the exercise!? High-tech paradoxes. *SBS News*. http://news.sbs.co.kr/news/endpage.do?newsid=N1003813735&plink=ORI&cooper=NAVER

Hong, S. (2019). The future of sports science in the fourth industrial revolution. *The Korean Society of Sports Science, 28*(3), 775–784.

Horkheimer, M. (2006). *Zur Kritik der instrumentellen Vernunft*. Park, Guyung translator. MOONYE PUBLISHING.

Jang, Y. (2018). Future of taekwondo contents industry base upon the development of virtual reality system. *Taekwondo Journal of Kukkiwon, 9*(1), 177–195.

KBO. (2024, January 25). *KBO, Automatic Ball-strike System(ABS) and detailed operation regulations for Pitch Clock*. Korean Baseball Organization press release.

Kim, S. (2015, November 25). (Health & Beauty) Let's take care of our weight and health smartly. *The Dong-A Ilbo*. http://news.donga.com/3/all/20151124/74983005/1

Kim, Y. (2017). Social trend and sports(1): The fourth industrial revolution and sports. *Philosophy of Movement: Journal of Korean Philosophic Society for Sport and Dance, 25*(4), 101–115.

Kim, C. (2018). The change and role of sport in the age of the fourth industrial revolution. *Korean Journal of physical education, 57*(3), 17–27.

Kim, M. (2019a). Issues and tasks of sports science technology convergence policy on the fourth industrial revolution: Focusing on future tasks and response. *Korean Journal of Physical Education, 58*(4), 349–362.

Kim, M. (2019b). The convergence of ICT sports rehabilitation and school physical education in the era of the 4th Industrial Revolution. *The Journal of Learner-Centered Curriculum and Instruction, 19*(12), 145–156.

Kim, Y. (2021). A study on the application of AI (artificial intelligence) levels depending on leisure sports events. *Journal of leisure and recreation studies, 45*(3), 91–100.

Kim, M., Park, S., Park, C., Park, B., & Kim, S. (2021). Development of sports data distribution platform system and calculation of profit sharing weight. *The Journal of Sports and Entertainment Law, 24*(3), 259–267.

Lee, S. (2017). Social influence and Legal tasks of intelligent information technology in the era of the fourth industrial revolution. *Yonsei Journal of Public Governance & Law, 8*(1), 47–74.

Lee, H. (2018). Fourth industrial revolution and better sports. *Korean Journal of Sport Studies, 57*(4), 17–28.

Lee, D. (2020). *The growth of digital healthcare and online fitness*. Information and Communications Industry Promotion Agency.

Lee, J., & Kim, S. (2021). An exploration of changes in the fitness field according to the experience of using smart fitness equipment. *Korean Journal of Sociology of Sport, 34*(4), 21–42.

Lee, J., & Kwon, K. (2019). The critical research of healthcare focused on smartwatch users. *Korean Journal of Sociology of Sport, 32*(2), 92–109.

Lee, J., & Kwon, K. (2021). Popularity of screen golf in Korea and its sociocultural meaning. *International Journal of Environmental Research and Public Health, 18*(24), 1–13.

Park, S. (2020, July 02). The Gym trainers in the mirror. Digital fitness. *The Chosun Ilbo.* Https://www.chosun.com/site/data/html_dir/2020/07/02/2020070200309.html

Park, J. (2020, May 07). *Digital transformation example-Nike.* Magazine Digital Transformation.

Park, B., & Yeom, D. (2020). Service proposal for leisure healthcare-based motion data management system. *The Korean Journal of Sport, 18*(2), 271–276.

Schwab, K. (2016). *The fourth industrial revolution.* Song, Gyeongjin translator. Mega Study Co.

Shin, M. (2014). *A Study on the Influential of Purchase Intention and Continuance Intention of Wearable Device: Focused on Wrist Wearable Healthcare Device.* Master's Thesis. Seoul National University of Science and Technology, Seoul.

Son, Y., & Kang, Y. (2019). The advanced form of sports and enhanced human being through the fourth industrial revolution: Why enhanced robot can not be attributed to sports. *Korean Journal of physical education, 58*(5), 21–31.

Wikipedia. (2024). *Alpha Go VS Lee Sedol.* Ko.Wikipedia.org.

World Economic Forum. (2016). *New vision for education: Fostering social and emotional learning through technology.* World Economic Forum.

Yi, E. (2009). Exercise motions of the participated in screen golf-involvement, fun, and presence factors. *Journal of Lesure and Recreation Studies, 33*(2), 73–83.

Yun, J. (2023). *Meeting of physical activity and wearable devices: Social acceptance process and subjective cognitive structure.* Doctor's Thesis. Pusan National University, Pusan.

PART THREE

CHAPTER 8

DEVELOPMENT OF SPORT POLICY IN SOUTH KOREA: HISTORICAL AND INSTITUTIONAL ANALYSIS

Taehee Kang and Sun-Yong Kwon

Seoul National University, Republic of Korea

ABSTRACT

It is generally agreed that sport development in South Korea has shown a stepwise process of its policy sector formation from elite sport, sport for all, sport industry, and school sport since the 1960s. This chapter aims to examine the historical and institutional features of sport development in South Korea. The primary focus is given to developing conceptual understandings of the identified features of sport development since the governmental involvement in sport development was initiated in the early 1960s. The organizing aspects of national sport policy are strategically investigated to provide analytical resources for mapping the historical and institutional features of sport development. The notion of policy paradigm is utilized to articulate a series of stepwise formation of sport policy subfields. Finally, paradigm shifts in sport policy are discussed for their congruence with the nation's broader political and economic contexts: industrialization, democratization, and globalization.

Keywords: Sport policy; South Korean society and sport policy; sport policy change; policy change; paradigm; historical and institutional analysis

INTRODUCTION

The enactment of the National Sports Promotion Act (NSPA) in 1962 heralded the advent of the sports policy in South Korea, thus providing a rationale to the government for supporting sports. Over the course of approximately 60 years, South Korea's sports policy has mirrored the changing times with related changes in institutions and policies. Whereas, during the 1960s and 1970s the sports policy emphasized on nurturing high-level sports, in the 1980s, a shift in policy was observed which promoted the resurgence of sports for all. This resulted in a gradual broadening of the scale and extent of policy support. Subsequently, several policy adjustments were made for fostering the sports industry and recognizing sports as a universal right for all individuals (Korea Institute of Sport Science, 2022a). Thus, it is significant to examine these institutional changes to understand their impact on the changes in sports policy for gaining insights on its long-term evolution.

Existing studies on long-term policy changes focus on policies' response to the shifts in the political landscape, such as regime changes (Choi, 2015; Jung, 2013; May & Jochim, 2013; Mullard, 2006; Wilson, 2000). Linking policy change to regime change is attributed to the substantial influence of the head of government, who plays a pivotal role in the policies of the associated institutions. Several studies have examined changes in sports policy with the change in the head of government over extended periods also referred to as regime changes, to understand the evolution of institutions and policies (Choi et al., 2019; Comeau, 2013; Green, 2004; Ha et al., 2015; Houlihan & Lindsey, 2012; Lindsey, 2020; Sam & Jackson, 2004).

Regime change is a major trigger for policy change which reflects the changing demands of the times encompassing the era's core agendas, such as international, political, and economic trends, domestic political circumstances, and public sentiment. Understanding these demands leads to a better contextualization of the policy changes. Macro-level policy shifts that dramatically differ from the directions in the past need a comprehensive assessment of regime change and the policy environment.

Hall (1993) characterized abrupt shifts in policy direction using the concept of "paradigm." He classified policy change into three levels: first order change, where only the means change while the goal remains the same; second order change, where both the goal and means change; and third order change, where the goal, means, and policy environment all three change rapidly. Policy changes that occur due to the rapid change in policy goals, means, and environment are referred to as paradigm shifts (Blyth et al., 2011; Daigneault, 2014; Hall, 1993; Hodgson, 2002). When the government adopts a core agenda due to the demand of the changing times, the resulting policies exhibit alterations in goals and means distinct from previous ones.

From the 1960s to the present, South Korean sports policy has undergone multiple phases of significant social transformations due to changes in government (Kim, 2014, 2020). In tandem with the waves of industrialization, democratization, and globalization, various systems have been instituted, and the policy's scope in terms of areas covered and target groups has broadened. This chapter examines the changes in sports policy in terms of "paradigm shifts" based on the core agendas of each of the eras of 1960–1970s, 1980s, 1990s, 2000s, and beyond. First, this chapter aims to identify the core agendas and prevailing sentiments of each era. Second, this chapter analyzes how the transformation was reflected in the changes in government's policy directions. Additionally, it discusses the specific changes in sports policy in a historical context with a focus on institutions and policies.

A TIMELINE OF CHANGES IN KOREA'S SPORTS POLICY

Society and Sports Policy in the 1960s–1970s: Industrialization and Elite Sports Policy

Social Paradigm in the 1960s–1970s: State-Led Industrialization

In the early 1960s, South Korean society was marked by political complexity and turmoil, along with economic hardship characterized by increasing poverty. President Rhee Syngman's 12-year rule with the First Republic ended, when irregularities were revealed in the presidential and vice-presidential elections in March 1960 leading to the April 19 revolution (Bark, 2001; Kil, 2001; Kim, 2020; Kwak & Kang, 2018). The Democratic Party of Korea, which assumed power through the cabinet responsibility system, struggled to bring stability to the tumultuous political landscape due to internal party conflicts, and failed to earn public's trust in addressal of various societal issues facing the country at that time. Economically, the country had been grappling with persistent poverty since the conclusion of the Korean War in 1953 and South Korea's per capita gross national income was only $79, rendering it as one of the world's poorest nations (The Bank of Korea, 2020). All facets of society were in dire conditions, and a significant leap forward was necessary to tackle numerous challenges.

Park Chunghee assumed power in 1961. His administration took on the task of restoring political stability and addressing the economic development issues that prior governments had failed to resolve. The foremost priority was to alleviate the widespread poverty, which required the formulation and execution of an economic development plan. South Korea was then in a post-Korean war state where all sectors were impoverished, and the private sector lacked the capacity to drive societal development. Majority of the issues confronting South Korean society needed government-led solutions. The goal of nationalism, which focused on the state rather than individual freedom and values, was emphasized to achieve rapid economic growth (Lee, 2015; Tosa, 2015; Won & Hong, 2015). Majority of the Korean citizens at the time shared the perception that individuals exist for the country and shall sacrifice for it. The prevailing nationalistic mindset and ideology during this period can be exemplified by the first line of the 1968 National Education Charter: "We have been born into this land, charged with the historic mission of regenerating the nation" (Kwak, 2018).

Park Chunghee's government unveiled the first five-year plan for economic development in 1962 to propel Korea's economy forward. The state-led economic growth policy was to establish the groundwork for setting up of fundamental industries to address people's "livelihood" concerns. The first plan (1962–1966) and second plan (1967–1971) promoted economic growth, essentially by boosting exports, expanding critical industries and facilities for social overhead capital, and investing in heavy chemical industry (Kim, 2020; Scitovsky, 1985; Westphal, 1990).

The industrialization drive of the 1960s and 1970s commenced with these five-year economic development plans. Park Chunghee's administration executed four five-year economic development plans until 1981. This government-led, robust economic growth policy based on nationalistic sentiment was successful in achieving domestic and international goals. Thus, domestically, favorable outcomes were achieved in Korea's economic instability and poverty and internationally, Korea transformed from one of the world's poorest countries into a respected member of the global community.

Sports Institution and Policy in the 1960s–1970s: Focus on Elite Sports
The investment and support for the sports sector was the result of the strong government-led policy based on nationalism in the 1960s and 1970s. Sports were harnessed as a tool for South Korea to transform its image as one of the world's poorest nations situated on the fringes of the global community (Ha & Mangan, 2002; Hong, 2011; Won & Hong, 2015). High rankings in international competitions were considered an effective strategy for enhancing South Korea's standing in the global community and improving its national image. The government's investment and support for elite sports in the 1960s led to the establishment of sports institutions and policies.

The Supreme Council for National Reconstruction, the governing body at the time, referred to Japan's Sports Promotion Law to pass the NSPA on May 16, 1961, Korea's first law related to sports. A year later, the NSPA was enacted on September 17, 1962, with the Park Chunghee administration in power. Article 1 (Purpose) of the NSPA stipulated that the legislation's purpose was to improve the physical and mental health of the Korean people, which was the responsibility of the state and local governments. However, unlike what was stipulated, the NSPA was primarily geared toward supporting, using and investing in elite sports as a means to an end. The legislation stipulated support for elite athletes for winning medals at international competitions and grounds were established. (Son & Shin, 2008).

Subsequent to the establishment of the government's support through the NSPA, a separate system or policy for promotion of elite sports was implemented later. First, the Tae Neung National Training Center was established in 1966, where national athletes could train. This facility allowed national athletes to undergo systematic training and live together and primarily focused on winning medals at international competitions. This support for national training led to a system for rewarding elite athletes. Institutional mechanisms were established to offer pension benefits and exemptions from military service for Olympic and Asian Games medalists, and education laws were amended for athletes' university admissions (Han, 2019; Han & Tak, 2017; Hong, 2012). The investment in elite sports by supporting national athletes produced remarkable results in international competitions, such as the women's team victory at the 1973 World Table Tennis Championships and South Korea's first gold medal at the 1976 Montreal Olympics.

The use of sports as a means to gain international recognition was evident in the tumultuous relationship between North and South Korea during the 1960s and 1970s. North Korea surprised the world by reaching the quarterfinals of the 1966 World Cup in England which came as a shock for South Korea, the political rival of North Korea. Thereafter, the South Korean government established the "Yangji" soccer team under the Korean Central Intelligence Agency in hopes of outperforming North Korea in soccer (Korea Football Association, 2003). This exemplifies how sports was utilized as a tool to defeat communism in its battle with liberal democracy. During industrialization, when economic development, social stability, and regime maintenance were crucial, South Korean society actively advanced its sports policy through substantial investments in elite sports (Bridges, 2012, p. 38).

Society and Sports Policy in the 1980s: Emergence of Democratization and Sports for All

Social Paradigm in the 1980s: Political Democratization and the Role of Civil Society

For most of the 1960s to the 1980s, South Korea's leadership was held by military veterans as Presidents. President Chun Doohwan, who took office in 1981 after President Park Chunghee, was also from the military. Their strong and charismatic leadership was effective in achieving the goals of economic development, which was Korea's top priority since the 1960s, and garnered massive public support (Kim, 2014).

South Korea's economic growth achieved within a short period, also called the "Miracle of the Han River," awed the global community and garnered much attention. However, beneath the impressive economic achievements lurked a series of disasters resulting from an unwavering pursuit of performance at any cost. During the Chun Doohwan administration, reports emerged on "political and economic patronage," the close nexus between influential politicians and corporate leaders, as well as nepotism (Bark, 2001; Kil, 2001). The government tainted by various instances of authoritative corruption could not gather people's support and found maintaining strong leadership based solely on economic achievements as challenging.

With economic development many people who had struggled with poverty earlier escaped from their former "livelihood" concerns. The undoubted nationalistic ideals, of making personal sacrifices for state-led policies or for the nation's good, of the 1960s and 1970s lost their resonance in the 1980s. The private activist groups which were excluded from politics earlier as well as university students strongly stood up against the government's authoritarian behaviors. Civil society, stifled by the powerful ruling leadership, expressed its discontent with the government's wrongdoings through acts of resistance and protests (Kim, 2006, 2010). Nationalism, which had guided state operations in the 1960s and 1970s, failed to produce the same impact as it did in the 1980s.

The civil society's long-standing discontent exploded in 1987. On June 29, the leader of the ruling Democratic Justice Party, Roh Taewoo, announced reforms in the direct election system. This was a significant milestone in the South Korean society's journey toward political democratization led by the public. However, the results of the presidential elections held in December of the same year resulted in the victory of Roh Taewoo as president with a military background, contrary to public expectations. The inherent limitation of the 1987 democratization was that it was not an arbitrary decision made by the government but rather made in the face of resistance from civil society (Howe, 2018; Kang, 2012, pp. 101–102).

The election of Roh Taewoo as president made it challenging for the government to meet the expectations for reform and change as a result of the democratization and it relinquished its authority to distance itself from the authoritarian system, which in turn led to a lackluster performance and ineffective policies, that not many citizens had witnessed previously. The opposition party in the majority in the National Assembly also gave a severe blow to the president's authority. The Roh administration, elected through the democratization process driven by civil society, exhibited characteristics of a government transitioning from an authoritarian regime to a democratic society (Kang, 2012, p. 16). The key policies of the Roh government can be summarized as "Northern diplomacy," "Three-party joint party," and "price stabilization." The people-elected Roh administration's inability to formulate policies that emphasize the role of civil society is attributed to its inherent limitations (Hahm & Rhyu, 1999; Kang, 2012, p. 164).

Sports Institution and Policy in the 1980s: Vitalization of Sports for All
Roh administration's reforms and policies were unsuccessful in satisfying the civil society's expectations and desires for democratization. Public sentiment and society's expectations remained unmet primarily due to the aforementioned inherent limitations. In sports, the successful hosting of the 1988 Olympics marked a pivotal moment with a shift in the policy focus from elite sports to public health and participation in sports. The outstanding performance of the Korean national team and the emergence of star athletes at the 1988 Olympics motivated the general public to participate in sports. Furthermore, people's involvement in sports increased as they had more leisure time due to improved economic conditions (Korea Institute of Sport Science, 2022a; Kwak & Kang, 2018).

To encourage Korean people's participation in sports from across the nation, the government amended the NSPA in March 1989. The amendment mandated that local governments create conducive conditions for physical activity, including provision of facilities for promoting physical education, and provisioning schools to open their physical training facilities to the public. Although, the previous NSPA had proposed promoting healthy living and participation in physical education activities but lacked specific provisions for increasing physical education participation. It is noteworthy that the local governments' role in promoting sports for all and the accessibility of school physical training facilities emerged prominent in 1989. Additionally, in the same year, the government designated the "National Sport Participation Survey" as a nationally authorized statistic to be conducted biennially. This survey examines various aspects, including people's participation in physical activities and the sports they engage in. The results are incorporated into government policies to promote sports for all (Choi et al., 2019; Ewha W. University, 1991).

The successful hosting of the 1988 Seoul Olympics resulted in public's increased enthusiasm for sports participation which prompted the government to establish a comprehensive plan for promoting sports for all. The government's Comprehensive Plan for the Improvement of National Sports for All, also known as the "Hodori Plan," unveiled in 1989, shortly after the Olympics, revolved around three core components. This plan included specifics on expanding the number of facilities for sports for all, disseminating sports-for-all programs, and cultivating and deploying sports-for-all instructors for the participation of Korean people. The Hodori Plan laid the foundation for the creation of community-based facilities established today, such as swimming pools, tennis courts, and local gyms, as well as sports-for-all programs such as sports-for-all dissemination and sports class development (Korea Institute of Sport Science, 2022a; Park, 2018).

The successful hosting of the 1988 Olympic Games, along with improvements in system through relevant legislative actions promoting sports for all and the government's comprehensive plan necessitated an administrative body capable of execution when required. Post conclusion of the 1989 Seoul Olympics, the National Sports Promotion Corporation was established using the surplus funds generated from the Olympics and the organization resources and manpower of the organizing committee. Its primary objective was to raise and oversee financial resources through a "fund" to manage initiatives commemorating the successful completion of South Korea's hosting of its first Olympics. Further, to support sporadic groups of enthusiasts of sports for all, a private organization for sports for all, The Korea Council of Sport for All was established in 1991 as a nonprofit, and served as both the central authority and a grassroots organization for promoting the government's policies for sports for all (Korea Institute of Sport Science, 2022a).

South Korea's rapid economic development and increased income levels led to a demand for political reforms including democratization. These demands, coupled with the growth of civil society aiming to enhance the general population's quality of life, were reflected in the sports sector's structures and policies. The 1988 Seoul Olympics occurred concurrently with the declaration of the amendment of the direct election system in 1987, and a structure was provided for the field of sports for all along with the establishment of a dedicated organization for its planning and execution which had previously received little government attention. Considering that many of the foundational policies related to sports for all established at this time remain in place today, it can be concluded that the impact of the societal paradigm shift centered on democratization in the late 1980s had a profound significance on South Korea's sports sector, particularly in terms of promoting sports for all (Bridges, 2012, p. 83).

Society and Sports Policy in the 1990s: Globalization and Advancement of the Sports Sector

Social Paradigm Shift in the 1990s: Globalization and Transitioning to a Developed Country

The late 1980s and early 1990s witnessed a significant transformation in the global landscape. The fierce rivalry between the liberal and communist blocs characterized by the long-standing Cold War came to an end. China, declared its commitment to openness in 1978, with the subsequent opening of Shanghai in 1990, and actively embraced market-oriented policies. The reunification of Germany, earlier divided into West and East Germany, was achieved with the fall of the Berlin Wall. The reforms initiated in Soviet Union in 1989, resulted in its ultimate collapse in 1991. Led by the United States, the international environment now emphasized the value of freedom, and a hegemonic order in a market economy was established (Gray, 2018).

Korea, following the successful hosting of the 1988 Seoul Olympics aspired to achieve a higher level of development in line with the global shifts. While the Roh administration was characterized by a transitional phase that did not fully address the transition to a democratic society in the new era distinct from the previous one, Kim Youngsam's administration elected in 1992 took on the challenge of consolidating democracy, for meeting the demands for transitioning to a new era, and positioning South Korea among the developed nations (Kil, 2001; Kim, 2020, p. 168). The prevailing sentiment and public opinion favored Korea to achieve a developed country status. This was rooted in its remarkable economic growth experienced since the 1960s and its strong bonds and alliances with the United States, whose influence as the hegemonic power in the international arena was unparalleled. (Jung, 2005).

President Kim Youngsam outlined "globalization"(*segyehwa*) as the government's policy direction in harmony with the changing global landscape and domestic public sentiment. The globalization concept in the Kim administration's policy was different from the academic perspective of globalization. In academics, globalization is a significant government policy discussed much before the establishment of the Kim administration. The Kim administration's concept of globalization(*segyehwa*) was a political slogan aimed at overcoming the negative effects of the previous era and enhancing the nation's competitiveness across various domains, including politics, the economy, society, culture, and sports (Kim, 2014).

A symbolic decision that reflected the globalization strategy of the Kim administration was South Korea's accession to the Organization for Economic Co-operation and Development (OECD) in December 1996. Korea had emerged as a major economic power of a considerable size since the late 1970s; thus, many OECD leader member states of the international capitalist economic order began to press for Korea gaining a member country status. Membership of the OECD signified an embrace of the economic system and order promoted by the OECD, which resulted in economic reforms and increased openness within the Korean society (Jung, 2005; Moon & Mo, 1999). Korea was no longer a poor country on the outskirts of the global community, but rather a part of the international community standing shoulder-to-shoulder with leading economic powers as it became an OECD member.

On the domestic front, in harmony with its globalization strategy, the government championed key policies such as "History Correction," "Financial Real Name System," and "Local Self-Governance" to address the previous era's deficiencies. The implementation of these policies underscored the government's direction and determination to reshape the country's overall structure to meet the standards of developed countries (Jung, 2005; Kim, 2014). Thus, under the Kim administration, Korea adopted the framework of the global economic order, in line with the policy of globalization. Domestically, Korea pursued reforms similar to the principles of globalization (*segyehwa*) to join the league of developed countries.

Sports Institution and Policy in the 1990s: Reforms for Sports Sector Advancement
The government rallied to propel Korea to the status of a developed country in all fields, including politics, economy, society, and culture even before the announcement of the "globalization declaration" by President Kim Youngsam in 1995. The first and foremost goal was to become a developed country which was reflected in the promotion of Korea's sports institutions and policies (Korea Institute of Sport Science, 2022a). In the early to mid-1990s, South Korea's sports policy centered on excelling in international competitions against strong countries and increasing participation rates in sports for all. The Kim Youngsam administration launched The First National Sports Promotion Plan (1993–1997) in 1993 and introduced a comprehensive five-year strategy that outlined specific measures for advancing the sports sector during its tenure. The Kim administration's sports policy aimed to raise both elite sports and sports for all to Seyha gain recognition in the international community (Choi et al., 2019).

The 1980s led to promotion of various sports-related policies due to the growing interest in sports for all. However, the primary focus was on enhancing the nation's stature through elite sports, resulting in a higher allocation of resources to elite sports initiatives. Notably, South Korea showed an impressive performance in the 1988 Olympics, where it secured 12 gold medals; however, to maintain such high performance on the international stage, the government continued its support for Korea to remain in the top 10. In the sports for all, the goal was to boost participation rates among the general population. During the 1990s, countries considered advanced in the field of sports for all boasted participation rates exceeding 50%, including Finland with 80%, the Netherlands with 63%, and the United Kingdom with 47% (Gratton et al., 2011; Houlihan & Lindsey, 2012). Meanwhile, the sports participation rate in South Korea was 27.2% and 37.6% in 1989 and 1994, respectively, which was significantly lower compared to the rates of the developed countries (Korea Institute of Sport Science, 2022b). Thus, the government persisted in its promotion policies aimed at expanding facilities, developing programs, and nurturing instructors with the goal of achieving a 50% participation rate, similar to the developed countries (Korea Institute of Sport Science, 2022a).

The Kim administration adhered to a "lean government" policy to streamline the government's administrative structure. Accordingly, the Ministry of Sports underwent a transformation, merging into the Ministry of Culture, Sports, and Tourism, while the oversight of school sports was allocated to the Ministry of Education. Despite the reduced roles of the government departments in sports, the budget allocated to sports and the proportion of sports funding within the national budget increased. This surge in government support for the sports sector can be attributed to funding initiatives (such as Cycle race, Sports betting business, and Boat race) carried out through the Korea Sports Promotion Foundation and the stable funding opportunities.

During the 1990s, South Korea sought to attain the status of a developed nation by hosting major sporting events. The successful organization of the 1988 Seoul Olympics instilled confidence in South Korea's effective management of international events. In 1990, the government expressed its intent to host the 2002 World Cup and the bidding process resulted in its securing a co-hosting arrangement with Japan in 1995. The bid for the 2002 World Cup aligned with the Kim administration's commitment to elevate the country's global standing as part of its campaign pledge upon taking charge in 1993 (Seoul Metropolitan Government, 2003). In 1995, Seoul won the bid to host the 2002 Busan Asian Games, and in 1999, Gangwon Province announced its candidacy for the 2010 Winter Olympics. The government's active bidding for these major sporting events can be viewed as the government's policy objective for further advancement of its sports sector.

Society and Sports Policy in the 2000s: Informatization and Paradigm Shift in Sports Policy

Social Paradigm Shift in the 2000s: Embracing Advanced Science and Technology and the Western Economic Order (Informatization and Globalization)

In the 2000s, the development of science and technology resulted in the rapid development of information and communication. The world's focus shifted on the first country likely to achieve stability and international competitiveness in informatization. Following the two oil shocks of the 1970s, the international community recognized the need for addressing the constraints due to limited resources and their global impact. Thus, it was foreseen that the world would transition into an information society, shifting from an industry centered on manufacturing and industrial production to one grounded in knowledge and information (Babenko et al., 2019; Jang, 2004). Korean society made efforts to align with this trend. Domestically, Korea faced an economic crisis in the late 1990s and experienced a new wave of social change that emphasized democratic consolidation, the growth of civil society, and individual human rights.

The Korean government's preparation for the information age commenced in the mid-1990s. In 1994, the Ministry of Communication, which was mainly responsible for postal service was restructured and renamed as the Ministry of Information and Communication (MICT), and its expanded responsibilities included the development of the info-communications industry. In 1995, the Framework Act on Information Promotion was enacted, providing an institutional foundation to promote informatization. An alternative system needed to be established as the existing legislation lacked provisions to support emerging information technologies. In 1996, the Basic Plan for the Promotion of Information was established, which included specifics on rapidly expanding high-speed internet network infrastructure across the country (Chung, 2020, pp. 108–111).

Through government restructuring, institutionalization, and planning in the mid-1990s, Korea became one of the first countries to secure the fastest high-speed internet networks in the world. Numerous venture IT companies emerged, providing the groundwork for IT industry development. In the mid- to late 2000s, the informatization wave underwent another significant transformation. The development and widespread adoption of smartphone technology resulted in the widespread use of smart mobile devices by majority of individuals (Chung, 2020, pp. 108–111) which presented an opportunity for informatization and the evolution of the IT industry into a knowledge-based convergence industry, transcending mere information access and exchange (Korea Institute of Public Administration, 2014).

Domestically, Korea experienced a severe economic crisis triggered by the 1997 global financial meltdown, necessitating the adherence to economic institutions for receiving assistance from the IMF (Kil, 2001). The social transformation that began in the late 1990s following the globalization paradigm was different from the Kim's administration globalization (*segyehwa*) strategy of the early 1990s. The globalization of the early 1990s was a voluntary aspiration to position the country as an active member of the international community, while the globalization of the late 1990s and early 2000s was imposed by external forces (Kim, 2020, p. 230).

From a different aspect, in the 2000s, Korean society witnessed civil society's increased role and influence bolstered by the establishment of democracy following democratization in 1987. South Korean society gradually shifted away from its long-standing country-centered nationalist outlook to placing greater importance on individual values and human rights. The Korean government enacted the National Human Rights Commission of Korea Act and established the National Human Rights Commission of the Republic of Korea, dedicated to safeguarding the fundamental human rights of individuals (Korea Institute of Public Administration, 2014).

Sports Institution and Policy in the 2000s: Developing the Sports Industry and Enacting the Three Sports-Related Laws
A major characteristic of the sports industry in the 2000s was the growing prominence of professional baseball and soccer, which were introduced in the 1980s, as an integral leisure activity of the Korean people. As professional sports garnered the attention of many Koreans, professional basketball and professional volleyball were launched in 1997 and 2005, respectively. The highly popular sports evolved into professional sports, and the high value generated in the sports sector prompted the government to support the sports industry as a deserving

target (Korea Institute of Sport Science, 2022c). The informatization process in the mid- to late 2000s, fostered knowledge-based convergence industries in various sectors, such as products, facilities, and services. The government started taking interest in the sports sector which was popular among the public. The wave of informatization and the government's decision to promote the sports industry, recognized globally as a convergence industry, aligned with the prevailing trends of the era.

Throughout the 1990s, the government's support to the sports industry was primarily through loans for sports equipment and facilities. In the 1990s, Korean athletes' achievements in international competitions and the growth of the professional sports industry increased nationwide awareness on the importance of the sports sector. The Korean government established the Sports Leisure Industry Division under the Ministry of Culture, Sports and Tourism in 2004 as a central government-level body exclusively tasked with nurturing and supporting the sports industry. Also, a mid- to long-term plan for the sports industry was established in 2001 to promote and cultivate the sports industry. In 2007, the Sports Industry Promotion Act was enacted, as establishing support policies for the promotion of the sports industry under existing laws was difficult. After the enactment, the sports industry sector was allocated a separate budget in 2007, and the volume of support increased from 2.4 billion won in 2007 to 95.7 billion won in 2019 (Korea Institute of Sport Science, 2022a).

The continued investments in elite sports that began in the 1960s led to substantial achievements in sports by winning of medals in international competitions, and producing numerous world-class athletes, thus raising the country's status. However, this performance-centric approach of elite sports policy resulted in several issues. As the nationalistic mindset of the people gradually shifted toward placing greater importance on the value and rights of individuals, numerous preexisting unaddressed issues resurfaced. This led to discussion on multiple areas in the Korean elite sports that needed improvement in the 2000s. Elite sports in South Korea were heavily rooted in academic sports, which led to various government initiatives (Hong, 2021).

The discourse on human rights in the sports sector, which initially centered on elite athletes, expanded in the 2010s to encompass the rights of all citizens. Enjoyment of sports was recognized as a right of all citizens, and a system to understand and support sports policies as part of welfare was needed (Jung, 2022). Consequently, the Framework Act on Sports was enacted in 2021, along with the Athlete Welfare Act, for the welfare of elite sports athletes, and the Sports Club Act, which expanded citizens' opportunities to enjoy sports. The issue of human rights in the sports sector, discussed since the 2000s, eventually saw the establishment of new institutions in the 2020s.

CONCLUSION

Korea's sports policy, which initially centered exclusively on elite sports, underwent substantial transformation following pivotal shifts in each era, expanding its purview to encompass sports for all and the sports industry, and introducing novel concepts such as sports welfare. Applying Hall's (1993) concept of "policy paradigm shift," it cannot be ascertained that Korea's sports programs and policies of approximately seven decades and over evolved through a third order change which is a simultaneous change in goals, means, and policy environment. However, this chapter classified the change in Korea's sports system and policies into four distinct periods to understand how each period's paradigm acted as a catalyst in governmental change and policy orientation with the passage of time and its reflection in the sports system and policies. Each era's principal agendas aligned with the prevailing governmental basis, and the sports policy exhibited a trend of setting different goals and expanding its target groups in each era.

Korea's sports institution and policies did not undergo abrupt directional changes but rather adapted incrementally to accommodate evolving circumstances, thereby extending the policy's scope. It is fitting to assert that policy adjustments were driven by the identification of the core agenda of the times and the subsequent modification and supplementation of policies to address public expectations, without necessitating a complete overhaul of the existing framework. In the long run, it will be intriguing to observe how the Korean sports system and policies will respond to the changing dynamics of the new eras.

This study centers on the influence of prevailing societal agendas on sports institution and policies. Government data and various literature sources show a significant correlation between sports policy and the dominant paradigms of each era. By focusing on the interplay between society and sports, this study seeks to illuminate the evolution of sports as a social component, intricately intertwined with societal dynamics. Several studies have highlighted the value and significance of sports within this societal context (Hay & Macdonald, 2010; Kim, 2018; Malcolm, 2014; Park & Han, 2018; Pujadas, 2012). In this chapter, we aim to reaffirm the indispensable role of sports as a vital social component with a comprehensive analysis of the evolution of sports policy over time.

Numerous studies on the evolution of sports policy often attribute changes to regime transitions. This observation underscores the significant impact of political transitions on the formulation and alteration of sports-related regulations and directives. Specifically, we seek to shed light on the intricate relationship between society and sports by examining how societal transformations are reflected in sports policy. It is evident that sports policy has undergone significant transformations, with sports no longer perceived as passive entities solely influenced by societal forces. Through studies analyzing the societal impact of major sporting events like the 1988 Seoul Olympics (Lim, 1994; Park, 2018) and research addressing sports as a crucial medium for social capital formation (Putnam, 2000), it becomes imperative to consider the inherent meaning and role of sports. While ongoing efforts persist in identifying the social significance and role of sports, we believe it is essential to delve deeper into this relationship from various perspectives. By doing so, we can elucidate the influence and significance of sports themselves, an aspect often overlooked in previous analyses.

FIVE KEY READINGS

Hall, P. A. (1993). Policy paradigms, social learning, and the state: The case of economic policymaking in Britain. *Comparative Politics, 25*(3), 275–296.

Hall's thesis considers policy changes as a dynamic process involving three key variables: goals, tools, and the environment. He conceptualizes policy changes in a manner where goals and tools can undergo rapid transformation, resembling paradigm shifts. These paradigm shifts are characterized by changes that occur gradually over an extended period, often unfolding sequentially. The analysis of policy changes is conducted in relation to the evolving context of the policy environment.

Daigneault, P. M. (2014). Reassessing the concept of policy paradigm: Aligning ontology and methodology in policy studies. *Journal of European Public Policy, 21*(3), 453–469.

Daigneault conducted a review of several studies that were built upon Hall's 1993 concept of a policy paradigm. These research endeavors, which relied on the established policy paradigm, emphasized the importance of focusing on the policy ideas.

Kwak, D., & Kang, J. (2018). Modern sport in Korea: A historical perspective. In *Sport in Korea* **(pp. 15–30). Routledge.**

This chapter delves into the historical progression of Korean sports. It begins with the introduction of Western sports in the late 19th century and the subsequent phase of industrialization in the 1960s. The chapter then traces the evolution of government-led sports policies in South Korea, examining how government interventions have contributed to the nation's journey toward becoming a sports powerhouse.

Choi, Y., Jo, S., & Ok, G. (2019). Evolution of the sports for all policy in National Sports Promotion Plan in South Korea, 1962–2017. *The International Journal of the History of Sport, 36*(9–10), 876–891.

This thesis investigates the evolution of South Korea's sports-for-all policy, with a particular emphasis on the relevant laws, institutions, and government initiatives. It scrutinizes the enactment of the National Sports Promotion Act in 1962 and examines the government's sports-for-all policy, which has been in place since the 1988 Seoul Olympics.

Ha, J., Lee, K., & Ok, G. (2015). From development of sport to development through sport: A paradigm shift for sport development in South Korea. *The International Journal of the History of Sport, 32*(10), 1262–1278.

This thesis explores the transformation of Korean sports, which shifted its paradigm from being "the development of sports" primarily centered on elite sports during the 1960s and 1980s to "development through sports" after the 1980s. Within the context of South Korea's societal changes, the paper conducts an analysis of how this shift in the sports paradigm came about.

REFERENCES

Babenko, V., Perevozova, I., Mandych, O., Kvyatko, T., Maliy, O., & Mykolenko, I. (2019). World informatization in conditions of international globalization: Factors of influence. *Global Journal of Environmental Science and Management*, 5(Special Issue), 172–179. https://doi.org/10.22034/gjesm.2019.05.SI.19

Bark, D. S. (2001). The administrative process in Korea. In Kil & Moon (Ed.), *Understanding Korean politics: An introduction* (pp. 175–199). State University of New York Press.

Blyth, M., Hodgson, G. M., Lewis, O., & Steinmo, S. (2011). Introduction to the special issue on the evolution of institutions. *Journal of Institutional Economics*, 7(3), 299–315. https://doi.org/10.1017/S1744137411000270

Bridges, B. (2012). Sport, nationalism and international relations. In *The two Koreas and the politics of global sport* (pp. 7–21). Global Oriental.

Choi, Y. (2015). Social changes, welfare politics, and the change of the welfare state. *Korean Journal of Sociology*, 38(1), 161–184.

Choi, Y., Jo, S., & Ok, G. (2019). Evolution of the sports for all policy in National Sports Promotion Plan in South Korea, 1962–2017. *International Journal of the History of Sport*, 36(9–10), 876–891. https://doi.org/10.1080/09523367.2019.1675643

Chung, C. S. (2020). *Developing digital governance: South Korea as a global digital government leader*. Routledge.

Comeau, G. S. (2013). The evolution of Canadian sport policy. *International Journal of Sport Policy and Politics*, 5(1), 73–93. https://doi.org/10.1080/19406940.2012.694368

Daigneault, P. M. (2014). Reassessing the concept of policy paradigm: Aligning ontology and methodology in policy studies. *Journal of European Public Policy*, 21(3), 453–469. https://doi.org/10.1080/13501763.2013.834071

Ewha W. University. (1991). *1991 National Sport Participation Survey in Korea (11-1371000-000289-11)*. Ministry of Culture, Sports, and Tourism.

Gratton, C., Rowe, N., & Veal, A. J. (2011). International comparisons of sports participation in European countries: An update of the COMPASS project. *European Journal for Sport and Society*, 8(1–2), 99–116. https://doi.org/10.1080/16138171.2011.11687872

Gray, K. (2018). Plus ça change? South Korea's democratization and the politics of the Cold War. In *The quality of democracy in Korea: Three decades after democratization* (pp. 239–260). Palgrave Macmillan.

Green, M. (2004). Changing policy priorities for sport in England: The emergence of elite sport development as a key policy concern. *Leisure Studies*, 23(4), 365–385. https://doi.org/10.1080/0261436042000231646

Ha, J., Lee, K., & Ok, G. (2015). From development of sport to development through sport: A paradigm shift for sport development in South Korea. *International Journal of the History of Sport*, 32(10), 1262–1278. https://doi.org/10.1080/09523367.2015.1062756

Ha, N., & Mangan, J. A. (2002). Ideology, politics, power: Korean sport-transformation, 1945–92. *International Journal of the History of Sport*, 19(2–3), 213–242. https://doi.org/10.1080/714001746

Hahm, C., & Rhyu, S. Y. (1999). Democratic reform and consolidation in South Korea: The promise of democracy. In *Democratization and globalization in Korea: Assessments and prospects* (pp. 69–88). Yonsei University Press.

Hall, P. A. (1993). Policy paradigms, social learning, and the state: The case of economic policymaking in Britain. *Comparative Politics*, 25(3), 275–296. https://doi.org/10.2307/422246

Han, S. (2019). The military exemptions system for National Athletes: A discussion of imagined communities. *Korean Journal of Sociology of Sport*, 32(1), 47–59. http://doi.org/10.22173/ksss.2019.32.1.35

Han, S., & Tak, M. (2017). Trajectories of the Sport-specialty student system before 1972: The entrenchment of sports scouting practice within the National Entrance Examination System. *Korean Journal of Sociology of Sport*, 30(3), 19–45. http://doi.org/10.22173/jksss.2017.30.3.19

Hay, P. J., & Macdonald, D. (2010). Evidence for the social construction of ability in physical education. *Sport, Education and Society*, 15(1), 1–18.

Hodgson, G. M. (2002). The evolution of institutions: An agenda for future theoretical research. *Constitutional Political Economy*, *13*, 111–127. https://doi.org/10.1023/A:1015301101712

Hong, E. (2011). Elite sport and nation-building in South Korea: South Korea as the dark horse in global elite sport. *International Journal of the History of Sport*, *28*(7), 977–989. https://doi.org/10.1080/09523367.2011.563630

Hong, E. (2012). Applying a Western-based policy community framework to the analysis of South Korean elite sport policy: The role of businesses and armed forces. *International Journal of Sport Policy and Politics*, *4*(1), 23–37. https://doi.org/10.1080/19406940.2011.630012

Hong, D. (2021). An analysis of human rights policy in sports in South Korea. *The Journal of Sports and Entertainment Law*, *24*(1), 23–52. http://doi.org/10.19051/kasel.2021.24.1.23

Houlihan, B., & Lindsey, I. (2012). *Sport policy in Britain*. Routledge.

Howe, B. (2018). Human-centered challenges to Korean democracy. In *The quality of democracy in Korea: Three decades after democratization* (pp. 51–72). https://doi.org/10.1007/978-3-319-63919-2

Jang, I. (2004). Toward solidarity and cooperation in globalizing Northeast Asia: A reflection on the international socialization and civilization in the region. *Korea and World Politics*, *20*(4), 107–136.

Jung, T. (2005). A character of the Kim Young Sam's reform politics and political mobilization. *Journal of Korean Studies*, *23*, 281–306.

Jung, Y. (2013). Understanding the relationship between changes in government and policy in the UK. *Korean Society and Public Administration*, *23*(4), 103–141.

Jung, H. (2022). The analysis of the enactment process of the basic law on sports by multiple streams framework. *Korean Journal of Convergence Science*, *11*(7), 21–39.

Kang, W. (2012). *Reconsidering the Roh Tae Woo Era: South Korea at the Crossroads*. Nanam.

Kil, S. H. (2001). Development of Korean politics: A historical profile. In *Understanding Korean politics: An introduction* (pp. 33–70). State University of New York Press.

Kim, S. (2006). Civil society and democratization in South Korea. In *Korean society* (pp. 65–84). Routledge.

Kim, T. (2010). Democratization process and civil society in Korea. *Korean Governance Review*, *17*(2), 77–95.

Kim, J. (2014). The discursive structure of developmentalism in Korea: A comparison of Geundaehwa, Segyehwa, and Seonjinhwa discourses. *Economy and Society*, *103*, 166–195. http://doi.org/10.18207/criso.2014..103.166

Kim, C. (2018). The change and role of sport in the age of the fourth industrial revolution. *Korean Journal of Physical Education*, *57*(3), 17–27.

Kim, K. (2020). *The traditional Korean political economic model*. *The Korean developmental state* (pp. 75–119). Springer.

Korea Football Association. (2003). *The history of Korean Football 100*. Korea Football Association.

Korea Institute of Public Administration. (2014). *Major government policies and state administration in Korea* (Vol. 6). Korea Institute of Public Administration.

Korea Institute of Sport Science. (2022a). *2020 Sport White paper* (11-1371000-000015-10). Ministry of Culture, Sports, and Tourism.

Korea Institute of Sport Science. (2022b). *2021 National Sport Participation Survey in Korea* (11-1371000-000289-11). Ministry of Culture, Sports, and Tourism.

Korea Institute of Sport Science. (2022c). *2021 Sport Industry White Paper* (11-1371000-000655-10). Ministry of Culture, Sports, and Tourism.

Kwak, M. (2018). A study on propagation of ideologies of the national education charter by social education from 1968 to 1972. *Critical Studies on Modern Korean History*, *40*, 375–417. http://doi.org/10.36432/CSMKH.40.201810.10

Kwak, D., & Kang, J. (2018). Modern sport in Korea: A historical perspective. In *Sport in Korea* (pp. 15–30). Routledge.

Lee, H. (2015). Revisiting statism for a policy thinking. *Korean Public Administration Quarterly*, *25*(2), 427–454.

Lim, T. (1994). The influence of Seoul Olympics on the change of the leisure and recreation culture: Laying stress on the sight-seeing recreation. *Korean Journal of Leisure and Park*, *11*, 131–147.

Lindsey, I. (2020). Analysing policy change and continuity: Physical education and school sport policy in England since 2010. *Sport, Education and Society*, *25*(1), 27–42. https://doi.org/10.1080/13573322.2018.1547274

Malcolm, D. (2014). The social construction of the sociology of sport: A professional project. *International Review for the Sociology of Sport*, *49*(1), 3–21.

May, P. J., & Jochim, A. E. (2013). Policy regime perspectives: Policies, politics, and governing. *Policy Studies Journal*, *41*(3), 426–452. https://doi.org/10.1111/psj.12024

Moon, C., & Mo, J. (1999). Introduction: Recastiong democratization and globalization under the Kim Young Sam government. In *Democratization and globalization in Korea: assessments and prospects* (pp. 11–22). Yonsei University Press.

Mullard, M. (2006). Does politics make a difference? Thatcher, Blair and the politics of public expenditure. *Public Management Review*, *8*(3), 463–482. https://doi.org/10.1080/14719030600853394

Park, H. (2018). Seoul 1988 Olympic Games and the social politics of the Gaze. *Society and History*, *110*, 353–389.

Park, B., & Han, S. (2018). Technology enhancement vs technology doping: Social construction of sporting fairness. *Korean Journal of Physical Education*, *57*(5), 93–103.

Pujadas, X. (2012). Sport, space and the social construction of the modern city: The urban impact of sports involvement in Barcelona (1870–1923). *International Journal of the History of Sport*, *29*(14), 1963–1980.

Putnam, R. D. (2000). *Bowling alone: The collapse and revival of American community*. Simon and Schuster.

Sam, M. P., & Jackson, S. J. (2004). Sport policy development in New Zealand: Paradoxes of an integrative paradigm. *International Review for the Sociology of Sport*, *39*(2), 205–222. https://doi.org/10.1177/1012690204043463

Scitovsky, T. (1985). Economic Development in Taiwan and South Korea: 1965-81. *Food Research Institute Studies*, *19*(1387-2016-115993), 215–264. https://doi.org/10.22004/ag.econ.135678

Seoul Metropolitan Government. (2003). *A Report on the 2002 FIFA World Cup Korea/Japan in Seoul*. Seoul Metropolitan Government.

Son, S., & Shin, H. (2008). A study on intention and background of enactment of National Sports Promotion Act. *The Korean Association of Sports Law*, *11*(3), 135–150. http://doi.org/10.19051/kasel.2008.11.4.253

The Bank of Korea. (2020). Korean system of national accounts: Concepts, sources and methods 2020. https://www.bok.or.kr/eng/bbs/E0000746/view.do?nttId=10062561&menuNo=400228&pageIndex=1

Tosa, M. (2015). Sport nationalism in South Korea: An ethnographic study. *Sage Open*, *5*(4), 1–13. https://doi.org/10.1177/2158244015604691

Westphal, L. E. (1990). Industrial policy in an export-propelled economy: Lessons from South Korea's experience. *The Journal of Economic Perspectives*, *4*(3), 41–59. https://doi.org/10.1257/jep.4.3.41

Wilson, C. A. (2000). Policy regimes and policy change. *Journal of Public Policy*, *20*(3), 247–274.

Won, H., & Hong, E. (2015). The development of sport policy and management in South Korea. *International Journal of Sport Policy and Politics*, *7*(1), 141–152. https://doi.org/10.1080/19406940.2014.900104

CHAPTER 9

DEVELOPMENT, SPORT DIPLOMACY, AND SOFT POWER IN SOUTH KOREA

Dongkyu Na

Kyung Hee University, Republic of Korea

ABSTRACT

This chapter presents an empirical effort for the theoretical applicability of sport diplomacy to sport for development (SFD) research by examining how sport played a role in pursuing South Korea's development at given four historical stages: (1) A prelude to Korean SFD before 1945, (2) sport for a new Korea between 1945 and 1960, (3) sport for developmental state between 1961 and 1979, and (4) sport for coming-out parties of the 1980s. This chapter supports current scholarly attempts to situate the 21st century sport for development (SFD) within the history of sport for social good, as well as approaches integrating the role of sport in the 19th century colonization and/or in the modern version of development during the post-war era. By adding an Asian case (South Korea), this chapter contributes to existing SFD literature mostly focusing on Western countries and their former colonies in Africa and South/Central America. It also contributes to the understanding of soft power's dualistic characteristics that direct domestic and international audiences with a new insight into the sport-development nexus in the history of South Korea.

Keywords: Sport for development; sport diplomacy; dual soft power; developmental state; Korea; non-western perspective

INTRODUCTION

Sport for development (SFD) studies rarely concern state-led approaches to the use of sport in development in non-Western countries, nor do they provide a comprehensive analysis of the integration of sport and development to cover the diverse fields of international relations, the regional/global politics of development cooperation, and the domestic politics of foreign aid, particularly through new donor countries in the Global North such as South Korea. In fact, most SFD organizations and programs have been led by Western countries like Canada, the United States, the United Kingdom, Australia, and Norway (Schulenkorf et al., 2016), and their goals and approaches fully represent Western values and practices entrenched in civil society-based and community development orientations and led by nongovernmental actors (Giulianotti et al., 2019). It is also important to note that the fundamental aim of the SFD movement is to obviously contribute to the achievement of new development agenda which requires a structural reformation of development in various ways. Nevertheless, it has been limited to provide a macro-level insight into SFD concerns over structural problems in development (Lindsey, 2017). David Black (2017, p. 12) also underlines that scholarly interest in SFD has been much focused on "bottom-up manifestations of SFD," reflecting donors' taste of traditional actors in international development.

SFD in the 21st century underlines its direction toward the achievement of non-sport-oriented goals (development), distinct from sport development that contributes to enhancing the world of sport (Kidd, 2008). However, Black (2017) indicates that little SFD initiatives over the past decades detach themselves from elite sport sector like the way in which the Mathare youth Sports Association (MYSA), one of the most successful SFD organizations, pursues local youth's capacity building and empowerment in slums of Kenya on one hand. On the other hand it sets up semiprofessional football teams to secure "economic security" for the maintenance of the whole MYSA programs and initiatives (Coalter, 2010, p. 306). This inevitable blending of SFD and sport development in practice makes us to critically concern Asia's approaches to sport, based on elite sport orientations and thus state-focused objectives (Levermore, 2016). This seems to associate with the criticism of Asian sport that is quite "politically" contaminated and "purposefully" oriented. Similarly, the 21st century SFD movement that aims to overtly stay away from the governmental and sport-specific orientations has little broken a deep connection with elite sporting world supported by a state and its political aspirations (Black, 2019). Therefore, ignoring the Asian approach to the use of sport in development may discourage us to unveil the dynamics and the broader phases of the blending of the SFD movement in the 21st century with the traditional model of sport development.

Lindsey (2017) points out the lack of interest in the roles played by governance from a network of different stakeholders in SFD at both domestic and global levels. It is linked to a call for the use of a "more systematic" approach to development governance to figure out challenges in the prevalence of project-based SFD which is the short-term and microlevel manifestation

(Lindsey, 2017, p. 13). It is reminiscent of Ben Sanders' (2016, p. 1) consideration of mainstream approaches to SFD that are much biased toward "microlevel" interventions to deal with individuals' capacity building, rather than an attempt to "challenge and reform the societal structures." It is also concerned that the civil society-based values of SFD today make it hard to uncover the political dynamics of the sport-development nexus stemmed in the soft power of sport and diplomatic aspects of development (Rofe, 2021).

This indicates the need for further research to extend its analysis into quite a bit untouchable field of research in SFD, which is state-led, targets a non-Western case (South Korea), questions the solid dichotomy of sport development and SFD, and draws diverse theoretical and conceptual understandings of sport diplomacy and soft power. This chapter contributes to responding to these concerns and calls in the SFD community that comes across another decade.

SOUTH KOREA'S APPROACHES TO THE USE OF SPORT IN DEVELOPMENT

SFD is dominantly understood in the ways that (1) sport as a tool is used to achieve social development goals; (2) it is essentially led by nongovernmental organizations (NGOs) or actors based on civil society values and principles; (3) bottom-up orientations are recommended; and thus (4) it should be separated from sport development that directs the enhancement of "the organizational and institutional world of sport" (Darnell, 2012, p. 5). In this definition, the latter term sport development takes a ply of engaging in "organized training and competition" (Kidd, 2008, p. 373), which is linked to the nature of elite sport. It is based on a longer history of sport combining with a social and political complexity, traced back to the practice of sport-for-good in the 19th and 20th century (Millington & Kidd, 2019), sport for the Cold War hegemony (e.g., Darnell et al., 2019), and the ways in which states use sport for their national and political interests (Giulianotti, 2011).

The problem occurs in following a rigid concept of SFD lodged in the sector of Sport for Development and Peace (SDP) which seeks to fully separate from the traditional features of sport development, particularly when it comes to the examination of the use of sport in the history of South Korea's development. In fact, South Korea's long-lasting uses of sport in domestic and international development have been historically state-driven and top-down orientations equipped with political and diplomatic considerations (Na & Dallaire, 2022a), and sport in the process of nation-building was often used to render the public mass to voluntarily engage with the state-driven national development projects fabricated by the name of a "honorable" path for "our people's today's sacrifice for the nation's tomorrow" (Park, 1964). For example, the Park Chung-hee regime (1961–1979) associated the development of physical education with its national Five-Year Economic Development Plan (FYEDP) through the propagation of physical education discourse that encouraged people to cultivate themselves as "sound Korean people" (Ha & Mangan, 2002, p. 228), embodied by physically and mentally healthy Korean people, leading to the modernization of our nation. In the run-up to the 1988 Seoul Games, the military regime of Chun Doo-hwan (1980–1988) intentionally promoted nationalistic sentiments and narratives that formulated the Games as a showcase to project "national confidence" and the nation's incomparable potential to achieve a rapid modernization to the global community (Mangan et al., 2011, p. 2345). Furthermore, South Korean use of sport in development cooperation has been consistent with the majority of state-led programs and initiatives that forthrightly pursue national interests and diplomatic aspirations (Na & Black, 2022).

Following that, the application of the mainstream SFD approach into the analysis of the South Korean case at both domestic and international development levels may not present a more comprehensive picture of the blending of sport with development particularly in the South Korean context. In other words, the predominant SFD approach of the 21st century is embodied by traditional Western donors in the Global South, and it has been mostly applied into the analysis of SFD projects operated in the soils of Africa, Latin America, and Asia that was former colonies of the Western donors (Darnell et al., 2018; Schulenkorf et al., 2016). At a global setting, this Western-led SFD approach often directs its analysis to the power relations between the former colonizers and their former colonies (Hayhurst, 2014). In addition, traditional Western donor states like the United States, Canada, and Australia have the history of colonialism between European settlers and indigenous in their countries. Unlikely, South Korea was a victim of Japanese colonization, and it has no such colonial history and conflict between members of the Korean public.

Importantly, mainstream research has neglected alternative understandings of the dynamics of the sport-development nexus, particularly concerning Asia's use of sport in development which is heavily influenced by states' political purposes and national interests (Giulianotti et al., 2019). Indeed, leading Asian donor countries like China, Japan, and South Korea use sport as a tool to participate in the Western model of development – but in process adapt it to reflect a distinctively "Asian" set of practices (Black & Peacock, 2011). Furthermore, the Asian use of sport in development has been historically deployed to support their political aspirations, in contrast to the mainstream Western SFD model which is NGO-driven and explicitly targets social development goals (Giulianotti et al., 2019). In this respect, Western-based insights can offer a distorted view of Korean SFD as a politically contaminated practice. It is also possible to reconfirm the replicated aspects of the mainstream SFD model based on the Western modalities, rather than capturing unique features and sociopolitical dynamics of a certain country's intervention in the link between sport and development. In fact, some researchers who has absorbed insights from the mainstream SFD literature consider South Korea's way of utilizing SFD as "wrong" and needing to be corrected to conform with the "right" path in accordance with the criteria of the mainstream SFD model (Ha et al., 2015, p. 1274). Existing literature has often addressed that sport development and SFD cannot be understood in a simple dichotomy, but they share many similarities and generate synergy development effects (Black, 2019; Giulianotti et al., 2019; Huish et al., 2013; Levermore, 2016;

Young & Okada, 2014). In this respect, the term SFD in this chapter refers to South Korea's all approaches to the use of sport to pursue development objectives both at domestic and international levels.

SPORT DIPLOMACY AND SOFT POWER IN SOUTH KOREA

A traditional sport diplomacy is directed toward the ways in which sport is utilized as a diplomatic tool of a state to achieve foreign policy objectives (Murray, 2018). Recently, many scholars have offered a distinct insight into the roles played by sport itself in exercising a certain level of political and diplomatic effects in international community, manifested in Murray and Pigman's (2014) term sport-as-diplomacy. Sport-as-diplomacy refers to the ways in which three forms of diplomacy – communication, representation, and dialogue –are produced by nongovernmental actors (i.e., the International Olympic Committee [IOC] and the *Fédération Internationale de Football Association* [FIFA]), and/or they occur in the effects of high-profile global sport competitions. Let us focus on the appearance of South Korea's unified women's hockey team at the 2018 PyeongChang Winter Games. It was the first time to form a unified Korean team for the Olympics, and such the monumental event happened in the Korean peninsula (Lee, 2019). Despite little demonstrating its performative excellence, the unified Korean team itself exerted its diplomatic effects likely in attracting global attention, producing peaceful mood in inter-Korean relations and the surrounded regional and international relations, and rising the non-state actor IOC as a key actor of global diplomacy. In the same vein, Rofe (2016, p. 214) prefers to use the term "sport and diplomacy" to consider each angle of the two notions as "equally valuable lenses" that offer an inclusive insight into "contemporary global society." It is a theoretical attempt to see sport not just as a tool to pursue a state's diplomatic goals, but to treat the two realms of sport and diplomacy as "separate but equal" instead of one subordinate to the other (Rofe, 2016, p. 215). This approach detects the complexity and multifacets of combining sport with diplomacy in changing international orders of the post-Cold War era (Rofe, 2016). Concerning the "politico-diplomatic nature of international sport" (p. 709), Black and Peacock (2013) illustrate that international sport plays a role in making the similar level of political and diplomatic effects with traditional club diplomacy. It is thus important to consider the two areas to be equal to analyze the mixing of sport and diplomacy in the international level.

Another indispensable concept in sport diplomacy is soft power. Soft power, coined by Joseph Nye (2008), is the ability "to establish preferences tends to be associated with intangible assets such as an attractive personality, culture, political values and institutions, and politics that are seen as legitimate or having moral authority" (p. 95). In this sense, soft power is not simply a power or authority to influence others and to affect the actions of others, but it is the ability to appeal to and attract, a so-called "attractive power" (Nye, 2008, p. 95). A state's soft power is largely generated by its culture based on the internal social and political characteristics of the state, and the domestic specificities should be accepted both at home and abroad (Nye, 2008). At this point, it can be associated with Grant Jarvie's (2021) emphasis on the operation of soft power at the juncture between "domestic and foreign policy" (p. 7) within the larger context of a country's national policy. It is reminiscent of Grix et al.'s (2019) "dual soft power" (p. 53), embodied in the manner that soft power targets domestic and international audiences, as well as its effects take place at home and abroad. Russia's strategy to the 2014 Sochi Olympics and the 2018 FIFA World Cup is a telling example of dual soft power that aims to promote Vladimir Putin's political legitimacy and Russian national identity domestically, as well as "signaling its arrival on the world stage and showcasing itself to the world" (Grix et al., 2019, p. 53), regardless of whether the result would be positive or not. In addition, China employed the 2008 Beijing Olympics for the rebranding of Chinese international image to be modernized and culturally advanced, and its targets also domestically directed the improvement of Chinese people's confidence and self-esteem (Manzenreiter, 2010). That is, the 2008 Beijing Olympics can be seen as the manifestation of China's dual soft power that integrates international prestige into Chinese nationalist identity (Grix et al., 2019).

This chapter builds on the conceptual and theoretical framework above to provide four rationales for the examination of South Korea's approaches to the use of sport in development from the combining perspectives of Korean development, sport diplomacy, and soft power. First, in its early stage of nation-building right after the end of Japanese colonial rule (1910–1945) and the end of Korean War (1950–1953), Korea sought to participate in global sporting competitions to announce its new identity as an independent sovereign state to the global community (Hong, 2011). Second, state-led national development projects in the 1960s and 1970s were associated with the practice of sport development that cultivate sound people of South Korea to engage in the path actively and voluntarily for the nation's prosperity (Ha & Mangan, 2002). Third, the state's endeavor to host sports mega-events like the 1986 Asian Games and the 1988 Seoul Olympics in the 1980s and 1990s was directed toward a national desire to showcase its rebirth to a developed and modernized nation from one of the poorest countries in the world (Collins, 2011). Lastly, South Korea's use of SFD in a global setting overtly has targeted national interest and diplomatic objectives as its involvement in international development has been long political and diplomatic orientations (Na & Dallaire, 2022b).

DYNAMICS OF THE SPORT-DEVELOPMENT NEXUS OVER THE COURSE OF KOREAN HISTORY

A Prelude to South Korean Sport for Development (SFD)

Given that sport is used for the diplomatic representation of identity (Rofe, 2016), it is noteworthy that sport under Japanese colonization played a certain role in resisting Japanese identity and projecting Korean identity that occurred in global sporting competitions. Indeed, under the Japanese rule as Korean marathon runners Sohn Kee-chung and Nam Sung-yong won gold and bronze medals respectively at the 1936 Berlin Olympics (Korean Sport & Olympic Committee, 2020a). In the same year, Kim Jeong-yeon, Lee Sung-duk, and Chang Woo-sik as Korean speed skaters competed for the Empire of Japan at the 1936 Winter Olympics in Garmisch-Partenkirchen (Korean Sport & Olympic Committee, 2020a). They were the first Koreans to appear in the international "winter" sports competition. Obviously, the Imperial Japan took a direct diplomatic benefit through the exhibition of the Korean (but wearing the Japanese flag) athletes' excellence at the high-profile global sport competitions. Nevertheless, the global presence and achievement of the athletes featuring ethnic Korean identity also allowed to promote Korean national pride and superiority. In this respect, it was meant to be a Korean sport diplomacy that domestically targeted Korean people under the Japanese colonization, and also meant to the identification of a long-lasting history of Korean sport diplomacy.

This chapter is only concerned with the context of South Korea that has unique development trajectory, history, and practice, distinct from those in North Korea since the division of Korea in August 1945. It is also important to note that the post-1945 era, after the end of the Second World War, brought about (1) an institutional approach to development (Williams, 2012); (2) its contribution to the development of newly independent nations (Pieterse, 2010); and (3) the use of sport in the process of nation-building fully started off with the Cold War proxy strategy (Black, 2019). In keeping with that, the following sections address how sport and development has been linked in the history of South Korea, and also how such linkages have worked at the juncture between sport diplomacy and soft power, particularly focusing on the period of South Korea's 20th century development between 1940s and 1980s.

Sport for a "New" Korea 1945–1960

Right after the end of Japanese colonialization, sport was used to contribute to the construction of a newly independent Korea in great social, economic, and political disorders of the early stage of nation-building. For example, the Joseon Sports Council had been first established on July 13, 1920, but forcefully dissolved on July 4, 1938. It was restored in November 1945 with an attempt to host a series of domestic sport events to promote an independent Korea and Korean identity, freed from the humiliating label of Japan and Japanese. This was evident in the hosting of "Jayuhaebang Gyeongchug Jeongug-jonghab-gyeonggi-daehoe" (National Sports Festival for Freedom and Liberation Celebration) on October 27, 1945, which originated from the hosting of the 1920 All-Korea Baseball Series (also known as the first Korean National Sports Festival). This event was held with the *Taegeukgi* (national flag of South Korea) and led by Korean peoples themselves for the first time in the post-Japanese colonization, along with the aims to "enjoy happiness to get our country back" (p. 13), to reestablish national identity as independent Koreans, and thus contributing to the development of a "new" Korea (Korean Sport & Olympic Committee, 2020a).

Meanwhile, South Korea put in effort to participate in international sporting events to raise its profile as a new sovereign country in the global community. Even before the establishment of its official government on August 15, 1948, South Korea decided to participate in the 1948 St. Moritz Winter Olympics (January 30–February 8, 1948) and 1948 London Summer Olympics (July 29–August 14, 1948) to disseminate Korean sovereignty through the representations of national anthem and national flag that could be recognized by members of the global community (Bridges, 2013). Considering the extent to which the diplomatic facet of elite sport at international events is "a relatively low-cost, low-risk but high-profile tool of foreign policy" (Keech, 2001, p. 72), participating in high-profile international sport events like the Olympics, described as a global festival, would be the most cost-effect way for the then newly independent country South Korea to project its liberation and free from Japanese colonization worldwide.

Prior to South Korea's debut at the Olympics in 1948, there was a historical event to attract global attention to the new South Korea at the 1947 Boston Marathon which is the "oldest annual marathon and the most prestigious road racing" in the world (Boston Athletic Association, n.d.). Suh Yun-bok won the gold medal with the establishment of a new world record, setting a series of consequent "new" records as "the first Korean" and "the first Asian" featured in the prestigious Boston Marathon. Dong-a Ilbo on April 22, 1947 described that Suh Yun-bok conquered the Boston Marathon with the title of "The glory of world conquest to our young person! Great! Such a national flower…" (The glory of world conquest, 1947, p. 3). As shown in the newspaper title, Suh's winning at the globally prominent sporting competition promoted South Korea as a new sovereign state in the post-war order. As such, Suh's achievement also introduced a new Korean identity to the world, erasing the former colonial subject of Imperial Japan. Likewise, newly independent countries in Central and South America pursued membership in FIFA to hold strong symbolic meaning for "nationalist independence movements" in the context of decolonization (Millington, 2019, p. 64). In fact, independent nations in the 1960s and 1970s used football to display their sovereignties by hosting regional and international football events featuring "new national teams to mark independence" and/or making the scene of newly independent nations' debut in high-profile football competitions (Fletcher, 2017, p. 424).

Historically, international marathon competitions were treated to be practice that enabled South Korea to showcase its physical prowess and athletic excellence at the global setting, thus propagating its ideological superiority over North Korea in the early stage of two Koreas competition in the larger context of the Cold War era. Focusing on the globally distinguished achievement that three South Korean athletes, Ham Ki-Yong, Song Kil-Yoon, and Choi Yun Chil, swept gold, silver, and bronze medals at the 1950 Boston Marathon, it was narrated that:

> Under difficulty in promoting international propagation, our three athletes' superiority at the international arena of the Marathon and their securing the crowns of victory would be enough to allow us to reach the attainment of international propagation. (International propaganda and marathon, 1950, p. 2)

This shows the then-perception of (1) the function of sport that was one of the most effective ways to pursue South Korea's international propagation in the phase of the fierce ideological battle with North Korea, (2) the importance of athletes that played a significant role in promoting South Korea's global diplomacy, and thus (3) diplomatic roles played by South Korean sport and athletes to contribute to showcasing not just South Korea's physical prowess but also Capitalist bloc's ideological superiority over the Communist bloc including North Korea.

Sport for Developmental State 1960–1979

During the period of the 1960s and 1970s, sport began institutionally combining with the domestic and international practices of state-led development projects and initiatives. In other words, this period was the beginning of South Korea's inclusive blending of sport with development at both domestic and international levels, particularly in three ways that (1) sport was domestically used for the success of state-led national development projects, (2) South Korea's intentional approaches to sport diplomacy started off with its first engagement in development cooperation, (3) and thus allowing for the workings of soft power at the interplay between sport and South Korean development home and abroad.

From 1945 to 1948, impending issues in development were directed to tackle extreme inflation, repair the loss of economic system, and resolve serious concerns of hunger and disease (Pirie, 2008). The restoration project of the post-Korean War was little achieved until South Korea got on the track in the first Five-Year Economic Development Plan (1962–1966) led by the military regime of Park Chung-hee (see Yoon, 2011). At the same time, state-led direction of sport development fully started in accordance with the forceful trajectory of Park's developmental state, gearing toward the modernization of South Korea (Kim & Sorensen, 2011). That is, sport development was linked to practice of the Park's developmental state in which economic development and modernization of the nation were the predominant focus of South Korean society. Under the circumstance, sport was used for cultivating South Korean people to actively and voluntarily participate in a range of state-led national development projects.

Saemaul Chejo (New Village Gymnastics) shows that Park's developmental state was directly linked to the state-led promotion of sport in the way that the state-made gymnastics was institutionally disseminated to the public. Evident in the second page of the Auxiliary Textbook for Saemaul Leaders (Korean Sport Committee, 1974), the *Saemaul Chejo* "contributed to the goal of *Saemaul Undong* that builds an affluent society and a sound social ethos, eventually leading to the achievement of *Saemaul Undong*"; it "required the public to develop their strong spirit and physical strength to root out the decadent tendency of villages"; and thus "this simple and interesting gymnastics was disseminated that it pursues physical education as part of Korean people's lives." It is noteworthy focusing on the hosting of the first *Saemaul* Football Event in October 1972. It aimed for "the guidance of sound Korean people and the enhancement of a sense of belonging to a community" (Saemaul football event, 1972, p. 8). In fact, most sport initiatives with the prefix "Saemaul" in development projects targeted South Korea's prosperity and modernization, and thus actively participating in the *Saemaul* sport initiatives was naturally considered a right path to commitment to the nation. Nye (2004) addresses that one country's soft power is formulated by its domestic policies and values in response to impending issues and hegemonic ideologies over the country. Following that, sport in Park's developmental state and its practices brought about the formation of nationalism as a resource to ignite South Korea's sport diplomacy and soft power, as well as producing an initial stage of Korean people's self-participation in state-led initiatives with an *honorable* aim for national interest.

During Park's presidency, sport was first used for South Korea's official development assistance (ODA). As a form of ODA, South Korean Taekwondo instructors were first sent to Lesotho in 1972 under the supervision of the then Ministry of Foreign Affairs (KOICA, 2001). South Korea in the 1970s institutionally utilized ODA as a diplomatic tool to improve relations with nonaligned and socialist countries in the Third World and to flaunt its superiority over North Korea in the Cold War context (KOICA, 2001). Behind the scenes, the Nixon Doctrine in 1969 caused to diminish the United States' role in Asia with the cutback of its forces in South Korea, followed by the improvement of US–China diplomatic relations (Oberdorfer & Carlin, 2014). Furthermore, North Korea became a new member of Non-Aligned Movement (NAM) in 1975, but South Korea's membership was denied. In light of the political circumstance, South Korea's concerns for its diminished role in international relations, different from North Korea's enhanced global positioning, drove it to forthrightly use development cooperation as a way of tackling diplomatic relations with socialist and nonaligned nations in the Cold War context of the 1970s (KOICA ODA Institution, 2016).

Johnson (2018) argues that the development of international Taekwondo in its initial stage was deliberately directed to introduce "Korean culture globally" (p. 1650), and it led to an overt nationalistic purpose based on the painful experience of the extermination of "Korean culture and language under Japanese rule" (p. 1650). Following that, the humiliating experience of Japanese colonialization and subsequent national devastation caused by the Korean War urged South Korea to employ Taekwondo to make it both the nation's representative martial art and national sport featuring a tool of ODA. Furthermore, based on the context of Cold War regional and global politics of the 1970s, the direction of sport ODA in Park's regime was predominantly determined by the nation's diplomatic objectives to promote South Korea and its culture globally (distinct from those in North Korea), enhance friendly relationships with nonaligned and socialist countries in the Third World, and thus to achieve superiority over North Korea.

Sport for Coming-Out Parties in the 1980s

Reinvention of a nation or changing the nation's image is common in using sport diplomacy (Murray, 2018). In fact, South Africa has readily connected global sport events to its national development projects, particularly with an attempt to display a new, post-apartheid image of the country (Millington, 2019). South Africa also sought to host the 2010 FIFA World Cup to project its rebranding of national representation as a democratic and reconciliated country in the post-Mandela era, along with the nation's aspirations for economic drive and being featured in the global community (Cornelissen, 2004). Likewise, hosting the 1986 Asian Games aimed to make up for the lost reputation of South Korea and change its "irresponsible" and "underdeveloped" image in the international community at least in Asian region. Indeed, South Korea first won the right to host the 1970 Asian Games in Seoul in 1966, but belligerent rhetorical and real threats from North Korea urged the South not to continue (Huebner, 2018). In January 1968, North Korean guerrillas penetrated South Korea with a mission to assassinate Park Chung-hee, and another raid by Northern guerrilla occurred in October of the same year. Along with the domestic unrest from a series of North's threats, as well as concerns over the financial issues, the Park regime had no choice but to call the hosting of the 1970 Asian Games off. This induced South Korea to be seen a country which was yet developed to host the global sporting event. Thus, South Korea's second try to host the Asian Games in 1986 was a chance to rinse out its previous image of the "irresponsible" and "undeveloped" country. This was also linked to the nation's attempt to promote its regional power with the reshaping of South Korea's new international image. It was evidenced by the Centennial History of Korean Sports IV (Korean Sport & Olympic Committee, 2020b) which stated South Korea's intention at a diplomatic level to "wipe out its discredit on the previous withdrawal," thereby "promoting relationships with Middle East countries, China, and Southeast Asian countries" (p. 126).

More importantly, South Korea's making up for the Asian Games can be seen as the manifestation of soft power that directed a domestic audience, Korean people. As such, hosting the Asian Games in Seoul again that served to redress South Korea's reputational damage was meant to instill national pride and confidence into the Korean public. This way can be found in Russia's use of sport, exemplified by the 2014 Winter Olympics and 2018 FIFA World Cup, to direct its soft power domestically to recapture the Soviet's glory days, detach the gloomy days of Perestroika, and "heal the psychological wounds of the 1990s" (Grix et al., 2019, p. 60). Likewise, a primary achievement from the successful hosting of the 1986 Asian Games in Seoul was to "arouse a sense of national belonging and confidence amongst the Korean public" (Korean Sport & Olympic Committee, 2020b, p. 148).

Furthermore, Taekwondo was firstly adopted as a formal sport for the 1986 Asian Games, and it was the first time for South Korean Taekwondo to appear as an official sport event in the history of the Asian Games and globally popular games recognized by the IOC. Koh (2005) argues that the Seoul Games played a significant role in transforming the Asian Games to a real (Asian) global festival through the way that non-Western (Asian) traditional sports, Taekwondo and Judo, were firstly added to global sport events. Considering that, the 1986 Asian Games was functioned to be "sport-as-diplomacy" (Murray & Pigman, 2014) in the ways in which a diplomatic effect occurred itself in sporting practice through the adoption of Taekwondo (and Judo) as an official sport to the Asian Games for the first time over the history. On top of that, it is possible to note that the 1986 Asian Games was the first global sport event held in South Korea to promote cultural exchange with other countries through a Korean *traditional* sport, Taekwondo. That is, Taekwondo as a representative cultural product of South Korea was firstly adopted into one of formal sports in the Asian Games, and thus cultural interactions between Korea and other countries took place through Taekwondo based on typical Korean culture. Notably, cultural aspects of Taekwondo has allowed South Korean soft power to make it longer and a long-term effect as Jarvie (2021) underlines the importance of cultural exchanges based on the pursuit of building "sustainable collaboration" and "long-term partnership" (p. 8).

Let us move on to the 1988 Seoul Olympic Games. The Seoul Olympics is commonly deemed to be a stepping-stone for furthering South Korea's democratic development. In fact, democratic movements and struggles in the run-up to the Seoul Olympics impelled Chun Doo-hwan to adopt a direct presidential election system and peacefully step down in the face of global attention to South Korea (Cho & Bairner, 2012). Interestingly, a soft power approach can provide a *unique* insight into the Chun regime's acceding to a demanding for South Korea's democratization that directed three aims: (1) to fully promote the Seoul Olympics as a coming-out party to join international community; (2) to reshape its regional and international identity as a mediator, contributor, and/or facilitator for the Harmony and Progress, manifested in the Seoul's motto, between the West and East; and (3) to boost the representation of a newly achieved modernity combined with long-stranding traditional Korean culture. In other words, the Chun regime's acceptance of democracy enabled South Korea to fully gain expected effects of soft power generated by the hosting of the 1988 Seoul Olympics to project its new national images of modernized, culturally abundant, and democratic developed South Korea to the world.

Correspondingly, Mohammed Al Thani (2021) argues that the 2022 Qatar FIFA World Cup was designed to achieve Qatar's soft power aspirations to enhance national pride (domestically) and "to reshape its conventional national branding" (internationally) (p. 1746). To maximize such soft power effects, there was no alternative but to resolve human rights issues of low-skilled workers in Qatar, which impaired Qatar's expected soft power outcomes from the hosting of the 2022 World Cup (Thani, 2021). Qatar thus took preemptive action with an effort to mitigate negative international images of the country and its World Cup through the promotion of the state-led SFD initiatives that represent Qatar's commitment to human rights in accordance with the global standard. Likewise, the 2022 Beijing Winter Olympics was designed to show off China's advanced and environment-friendly technology, thereby successfully signaling itself as a "rising superpower" (Lee, 2021, p. 12). At the same time, Lee (2021) addresses that China in the run-up to the Olympics sought to position itself as a "responsible world leader" (p. 11) through the promotion of the 2022 Beijing's missionary role in spreading "hope" all over the world in the state of the COVID-19 pandemic. Unfortunately, just before the opening ceremony of the 2022

Olympics, Western media continued to rebuke human rights violations in China. Serious concerns and criticism of China's human rights abuses and undemocratic approaches to civil society were constantly raised by global NGOs (Wade, 2022). Unlikely to Qatar's responses, China maintained a firm rebuttal to the allegations and considered relevant criticism and boycott movements as an old-fashioned political strategy of the United States and the West to stunt China's chance to rise a global superpower (Walker, 2021). This would lead to the extent that China's expected soft power outputs from the 2022 Beijing Olympics were not fully achieved. In this respect, regardless of its authentic intentions, the Chun regime's decision to adopt people's demanding for democracy eventually resulted in maximizing soft power effects of the 1988 Seoul Olympics to project a new national identity of South Korea to the global community.

CONCLUSION

Recently, there has been a theoretical effort to combine sport diplomacy with SFD. Rofe (2021) draws a global sport diplomacy framework to systematically explain how diplomatic effects take place in SFD through a form of communication, negotiation, and/or representation. Black and Peacock (2013) and Murray (2018) provide a theoretical insight into sport at the international level that should be treated as an independent variable to produce diplomatic effects, thereby allowing for the identification of multiple actors in SFD. Nevertheless, follow-up empirical research barely involves a case study to present an in-depth, systematic analysis of a county's particular use of sport in its development history. Using a theoretical framework of combining sport diplomacy with the broader aspect of SFD, this study identified a significant role of sport in the development history of a certain country (South Korea), and further allowed me to capture the phases beyond the understandings of sport that simply functions as a tool for national prestige. In the words, this study not only confirmed a traditional role of sport, particularly manifested in developing countries, to (1) show off one country's physical prowess at international competitions, (2) promote a new national/international identity, and thus (3) signify a rising "modernized" country in the global community. It also uncovered the ways in which sport in development was a governing technology to encourage the public to voluntarily engage in South Korea's development projects, and a typical Korean sport – Taekwondo – has practically served as a tool of ODA for South Korea's regional and international diplomatic leverage in the development history of South Korea.

Next, this study supported current scholarly attempts to situate the 21st century SFD within the history of sport for (social) good, tracing back to the roles played by the British public school to foster colonial subjects in the 19th century (e.g., Black, 2019; Darnell et al., 2019; Millington & Kidd, 2019). Given the fact that Korea's affirmative use of sport began right after the end of Japanese colonization, this study responded to the current call by focusing on the development history of South Korea, which was a newly independent country and was transformed to a developed (donor) country from the so-called underdeveloped recipient, to thus disclose sport's significant roles in pursuing South Korea's development objectives in its history. This contributes to SFD research and community by adding an Asian (South Korea) case to existing literature which mostly focuses on Western countries and their former colonies in Africa and South and Central America, as well as providing a comprehensive understanding of SFD involving different subjects of international relations, foreign aid, and the politics of development cooperation.

Lastly, this study provides follow-up research on Grix et al.'s (2019, p. 4) focus on the dualistic characteristics of soft power that direct domestic and international audiences to build a theory, the "ideal type" to access soft power strategies of states. Following the concept of dual soft power, this study revealed soft power effects of the 1986 Seoul Asian Games that not only recovered South Korea's damaged international reputation but also infused Korean people with a sense of national confidence. Furthermore, this study utilized a soft power framework to provide a *unique* understanding of Chun's decision to adopt democracy in South Korea. Such decision maximized soft power effects of the 1988 Seoul Olympics, and thus it would be useful to persuade a certain state or regime in the face of international criticism and sanctions regarding human rights and democratic values. That is, expected soft power benefits can enable the state to follow a more softened way to react international criticism in the run-up to Sports Mega-Events, rather than taking a tough line.

FIVE KEY READINGS

Darnell, S. C., Field, R., & Kidd, B. (2019). *The history and politics of sport-for-development: Activists, ideologues and reformers.* **Palgrave Macmillan.**

Extending the history of sport-for-development today back to the manifestation of sport-for-good in the period of 19th century colonialism, Darnell et al. provide the historical analysis of sport as a tool of development that has been long popular due to its apolitical, universal, and transnational features. The authors draw on a Gramscian theoretical framework to unpack hegemonic positions, knowledge, and structures of sport-for-development within the development and sport-for-good chronicle.

Grix, J., Brannagan, P. M., & Lee, D. (2019). *Entering the global arena: Emerging states, soft power strategies and sports mega-events.* **Palgrave Macmillan.**

In this book, Grix et al. build on the work of existing Olympic studies and five case studies of emerging states – Brazil, Russia, India, China, and South Africa – to build the relatively firm ideal type of soft power strategies, as well as providing a better understanding of dual soft power strategies that direct domestic and international audiences. The authors shed light on Sports Mega-Events (SMEs) as a critical driver for development at international, regional, and/or domestic levels from a soft power lens.

Millington, R., & Kidd, B. (2019). The history of SDP. In H. Collison, S.C. Darnell, R. Giulianotti, & D. Howe (Eds.), *Routledge handbook of sport for development and peace* (pp. 13–23). Routledge.

In this chapter, Millington ad Kidd argue that the 21st century's sport for development (SFD), or contemporary Sport for Development and Peace (SDP) movement, is not new, but traced back to the use of sport for social good from the late 18th or early 19th century. They advocate to understand the contemporary SFD in the broader history of development to delve into power dynamics and political implications of SFD outcomes.

Black, D. (2017). The challenges of articulating 'top down' and 'bottom up' development through sport. *Third World Thematics: A TWQ Journal*, 2(1), 7–22.

David Black addresses the importance of a more comprehensive understanding of sport for development (SFD) as a relatively new field in relation to the broader politics and praxis of global development, particularly through situating SFD in the dynamics of connections between top down and bottom up orientations throughout the post-Second World War development era. Focusing on top down and bottom up manifestations of SFD in different sectors of global sport and global development, as well as sport mega-events (SMEs), he provides an inclusive and critical insight into the maturation of SFD in relation to the politics of partnership in development. He calls upon scholars and educators within and beyond the sociology of sport and sport studies to encourage students to critically look at and think further about social, economic, and political role of sport in development.

Rofe, S. (2021). Sport diplomacy and sport for development SfD: A discourse of challenges and opportunity. *Journal of Global Sport Management*, 1–16

In this article, Simon Rofe illustrates the theoretical applicability of sport diplomacy to the broader aspects of Sport for Development (SFD) within the United Nations Sustainable Development Goals (SDGs). He believes that sport diplomacy provides a more inclusive insight into the use of sport in international development in three concerns of communication, negotiation, and representation.

REFERENCES

Black, D. (2017). The challenges of articulating 'top down' and 'bottom up' development through sport. *Third World Thematics: A TWQ Journal*, 2(1), 7–22.

Black, D. (2019). SDP and global development. In H. Collison, S. C. Darnell, R. Giulianotti, & D. Howe (Eds.), *Routledge handbook of sport for development and peace* (pp. 35–45). Routledge.

Black, D., & Peacock, B. (2011). Catching up: Understanding the pursuit of major games by rising developmental states. *The International Journal of the History of Sport*, 28(16), 2271–2289. https://doi.org/10.1080/09523367.2011.626680

Black, D., & Peacock, B. (2013). Sport and diplomacy. In A. F. Cooper, J. Heine, & R. Thakur (Eds.), *The Oxford handbook of modern diplomacy* (pp. 708–729). Oxford University Press.

Boston Athletic Association. (n.d.). *About the B.A.A and the Boston Marathon*. https://www.baa.org/about/boston-marathon. Accessed on June 15, 2023.

Bridges, B. (2013). London revisited: South Korea at the Olympics of 1948 and 2012. *International Journal of the History of Sport*, 30(15), 1823–1833.

Cho, J., & Bairner, A. (2012). The sociocultural legacy of the 1988 Seoul Olympic Games. *Leisure Studies*, *31*(3), 271–289. https://doi.org/10.1080/02614367.2011.636178

Coalter, F. (2010). The politics of sport-for-development: Limited focus programmes and broad gauge problems? *International Review for the Sociology of Sport*, *45*(3), 295–314. https://doi.org/10.1177/1012690210366791

Collins, S. (2011). East Asian Olympic desires: Identity on the global stage in the 1964 Tokyo, 1988 Seoul and 2008 Beijing games. *International Journal of the History of Sport*, *28*(16), 2240–2260. https://doi.org/10.1080/09523367.2011.626678

Cornelissen, S. (2004). 'It's Africa's turn!' The narratives and legitimations surrounding the Moroccan and South African bids for the 2006 and 2010 FIFA finals. *Third World Quarterly*, *25*(7), 1293–1309. https://doi.org/10.1080/014365904200281285

Darnell, S. C. (2012). *Sport for development and peace: A critical sociology*. Bloomsbury Academic.

Darnell, S. C., Chawansky, M., Marchesseault, D., Holmes, M., & Hayhurst, L. (2018). The state of play: Critical sociological insights into recent "Sport for Development and Peace" research. *International Review for the Sociology of Sport*, *53*(2), 133–151. https://doi.org/10.1177/1012690216646762

Darnell, S. C., Field, R., & Kidd, B. (2019). *The history and politics of sport-for-development: Activists, ideologues and reformers*. Palgrave Macmillan. https://doi.org/10.1057/978-1-137-43944-4

Fletcher, D. (2017). Confederation of African football. In J. Hughson, K. Moore, R. Spaaij, & J. Maguire (Eds.), *Routledge handbook of football studies* (pp. 423–433). Routledge.

Giulianotti, R. (2011). Sport, peacemaking and conflict resolution: A contextual analysis and modelling of the sport, development and peace sector. *Ethnic and Racial Studies*, *34*(2), 207–228. https://doi.org/10.1080/01419870.2010.522245

Giulianotti, C., Coalter, F., Collison, H., & Darnell, S. C. (2019). Rethinking sportland: A new research agenda for the sport for development and peace sector. *Journal of Sport & Social Issues*, *43*(6), 411–437. https://doi.org/10.1177/0193723519867590

Grix, J., Brannagan, P. M., & Lee, D. (2019). *Entering the Global Arena: Emerging states, soft power strategies and sports mega-events*. Palgrave Macmillan.

Ha, J., Lee, K., & Ok, G. (2015). From development of sport to development through sport: A paradigm shift for sport development in South Korea. *The International Journal of the History of Sport: Sports, Government and Governance in Asia (II)*, *32*(10), 1262–1278. https://doi.org/10.1080/09523367.2015.1062756

Ha, M., & Mangan, J. (2002). Ideology, politics, power: Korean sport – Transformation, 1945–92. *International Journal of the History of Sport*, *19*(2–3), 213–242. https://doi.org/10.1080/714001746

Hayhurst, L. M. C. (2014). Using postcolonial feminism to investigate cultural difference and neoliberalism in sport, gender and development programming in Uganda. In K. Young & C. Okada (Eds.), *Sport, social development and peace* (pp. 45–66). Emerald Group Publishing Limited.

Hong, E. (2011). Elite sport and nation-building in South Korea: South Korea as the dark horse in global elite sport. *The International Journal of the History of Sport: Asia*, *28*(7), 977–989. https://doi.org/10.1080/09523367.2011.563630

Huebner, S. (2018, March 1). *South Korea's first major sporting event and why it never took place*. Wilson Center. https://www.wilsoncenter.org/blog-post/south-koreas-first-major-sporting-event-and-why-it-never-took-place

Huish, R., Carter, T. F., & Darnell, S. C. (2013). The (soft) power of sport: The comprehensive and contradictory strategies of Cuba's sport-based internationalism. *International Journal of Cuban Studies*, *5*(1), 26–40.

International propaganda and marathon athlete. (1950, May 10). *Kyunghyang Shinmun*, 2.

Jarvie, G. (2021). Sport, soft power and cultural relations. *Journal of Global Sport Management*. https://doi.org/10.1080/24704067.2021.1952093

Johnson, J. A. (2018). Taekwondo and peace: How a killing art became a soft diplomacy vehicle for peace. *International Journal of the History of Sport*, *35*(15–16), 1637–1662. https://doi.org/10.1080/09523367.2019.1618838

Keech, M. (2001). The ties that bind: South Africa and sports diplomacy 1958–1963. *The Sports Historian*, *21*(1), 71–93. https://doi.org/10.1080/17460260109443377

Kidd, B. (2008). A new social movement: Sport for development and peace. *Sport in Society: Sport and Foreign Policy in a Globalizing World*, *11*(4), 370–380. https://doi.org/10.1080/17430430802019268

Kim, H., & Sorensen, C. W. (2011). Introduction. In H. Kim & C. W. Sorensen (Eds.), *Reassessing the Park Chung Hee Era, 1961–1979* (pp. 3–17). University of Washington Press.

Koh, E. (2005). South Korea and the Asian Games: The first step to the world. *Sport in Society*, *8*(3), 468–478. https://doi.org/10.1080/17430430500260511

KOICA ODA Institution. (2016). *Gukjegaebalhyeoblyeog ibmunpyeon* [International development cooperation: Introduction]. SIGONG media.

Korea International Cooperation Agency (KOICA). (2001). *Hanguk gukje Hyeobryeok dan 10nyeon* [10 Years of KOICA]. KOICA.

Korean Sport and Olympic Committee. (2020a). *Centennial History of Korean Sports III*. Korean Sport & Olympic Committee.

Korean Sport and Olympic Committee. (2020b). *Centennial History of Korean Sports IV*. Korean Sport & Olympic Committee.

Korean Sport Committee. (1974). Saemaul Chejo. In *Saema-eul jidoja bugyojae* (p. 2). Saemaul Leader Center. [Auxiliary Textbook for Saemual Leaders]

Lee, J. W. (2019). Olympic ceremony and diplomacy: South Korean, North Korean, and British media coverage of the 2018 Olympic Winter Games' opening and closing ceremonies. *Communication & Sport*, *9*(5), 761–784.

Lee, J. (2021). Olympic Winter Games in non-western cities: State, sport and cultural diplomacy in Sochi 2014, PyeongChang 2018 and Beijing 2022. *International Journal of the History of Sport*, *38*(13–14), 1494–1515. https://doi.org/10.1080/09523367.2021.1973441

Levermore, R. (2016). Development and peace through sport in 'Confucian Asia'. In L. Hayhurst, T. Kay, & M. Chawansky (Eds.), *Beyond sport for development and Peace: Transnational perspectives on theory, policy and practice* (pp. 53–67). Routledge.

Lindsey, I. (2017). Governance in sport-for-development: Problems and possibilities of (not) learning from international development. *International Review for the Sociology of Sport*, *52*(7), 801–818.

Mangan, J., Ok, G., & Park, K. (2011). From the destruction of image to the reconstruction of image: A sports mega-event and the resurgence of a nation – The politics of sport exemplified. *International Journal of the History of Sport*, *28*(16), 2339–2364. https://doi.org/10.1080/09523367.2011.626688

Manzenreiter, W. (2010). The Beijing games in the western imagination of China: The weak power of soft power. *Journal of Sport & Social Issues*, *34*(1), 29–48.

Millington, R. (2019). International governmental organizations in the SDP sector. In H. Collison, S. C. Darnell, R. Giulianotti, & D. Howe (Eds.), *Routledge Handbook of sport for development and peace* (pp. 59–69). Routledge.

Millington, R., & Kidd, B. (2019). The history of SDP. In H. Collison, S. C. Darnell, R. Giulianotti, & D. Howe (Eds.), *Routledge Handbook of sport for development and peace* (pp. 13–23). Routledge.

Murray, S. (2018). *Sports diplomacy: Origins, theory and practice*. Routledge.

Murray, S., & Pigman, G. (2014). Mapping the relationship between international sport and diplomacy. *Sport in Society: Sport and Diplomacy*, *17*(9), 1098–1118. https://doi.org/10.1080/17430437.2013.856616

Na, D., & Black, D. (2022). The forthright political stance of sport for development in Korean official development assistance. *International Journal of the History of Sport*, *39*(12), 1326–1349. https://doi.org/10.1080/09523367.2022.2159387

Na, D., & Dallaire, C. (2022a). An archaeology of Korean sport for international development discourse in Korea International Cooperation Agency (KOICA). *International Journal of Sport Policy and Politics*, *14*(2), 273–290. https://doi.org/10.1080/19406940.2021.1999300

Na, D., & Dallaire, C. (2022b). The diplomatic roles of Korean state-run sport for development programs. *International Review for the Sociology of Sport*, *57*(8), 1177–1196. https://doi.org/10.1177/10126902211065337

Nye, J. S. (2004). *Soft Power – The Manes to success in world politics*. Public Affairs.

Nye, J. S. (2008). Public diplomacy and soft power. *The Annals of the American Academy of Political and Social Science*, *616*(1), 94–109. https://doi.org/10.1177/0002716207311699

Oberdorfer, D., & Carlin, R. (2014). *The two Koreas: A contemporary history*. Basic Books.

Park, C. (1964, March 10). Je6hoe geunlojaui nal mesiji [Message of the 6th Workers' Day]. *Presidential Archives*. https://www.pa.go.kr/research/contents/speech/index.jsp. Accessed on June 3, 2023.

Pieterse, J. N. (2010). *Development theory deconstructions/reconstructions*. Sage.

Pirie, I. (2008). *The Korean developmental state: From dirigisme to neo-liberalism*. Routledge.

Rofe, J. (2016). Sport and diplomacy: A global diplomacy framework. *Diplomacy and Statecraft: Diplomacy and Sport*, *27*(2), 212–230. https://doi.org/10.1080/09592296.2016.1169785

Rofe, S. (2021). Sport diplomacy and sport for development SfD: A discourse of challenges and opportunity. *Journal of Global Sport Management*, 1–16.

Saemaul football event kicked off today [saemaeul chuggu oneul gaemag]. (1972, October 21). *Chosun Ilbo*, 8.

Sanders, B. (2016). An own goal in sport for development: Time to change the playing field. *Journal of Sport for Development*, *4*(6), 1–5. https://jsfd.files.wordpress.com/2020/08/sanders.an_.own_.goal_.commentary.pdf

Schulenkorf, N., Sherry, E., & Rowe, K. (2016). Sport for development: An integrated literature review. *Journal of Sport Management*, *30*(1), 22–39. https://doi.org/10.1123/jsm.2014-0263

Thani, M. A. (2021). Channelling soft power: The Qatar 2022 World Cup, migrant workers, and international image. *International Journal of the History of Sport*, *38*(17), 1729–1752. https://doi.org/10.1080/09523367.2021.1988932

The glory of world conquest to our young person again! Great, Such a national flower, Suh Yun-bok conquesting the Boston Marathon [segyejepaeui yeonggwan tto ulijeolm-eun-ie! janghada minjog-ui kkoch, dangdang seoyunbogjepae, boseuton segye malaton eseo]. (1947, April 22). *Dong-a Ilbo*, 3.

Wade, S. (2022, February 3). Another Beijing Olympics with human rights still major issue. *AP*. https://apnews.com/article/winter-olympics-china-civil-liberties-4d2cbac3487bad6f7a74b1442970610e

Walker, R. (2021, February 9). West's calls for boycotting Beijing Winter Olympics a reflection of self-serving politics. *Global Times*. https://www.globaltimes.cn/page/202102/1215412.shtml

Williams, D. (2012). *International development and global politics: history, theory and practice*. Routledge.

Yoon, S. (2011). POSCO: Building an institution. In H. Kim & C. W. Sorensen (Eds.), *Reassessing the Park Chung Hee Era, 1961–1979* (pp. 43–65). University of Washington Press.

Young, K. & Okada, C. (Eds.). (2014). *Sport, social development and peace*. Emerald Group Publishing Limited.